T0080248

ON BEING AND BECOMING

GUIDES TO THE GOOD LIFE

Stephen Grimm, series editor

Seeing Clearly: A Buddhist Guide to Life
Nicolas Bommarito

On Being and Becoming: An Existentialist Approach to Life
Jennifer Anna Gosetti-Ferencei

ON BEING AND BECOMING

An Existentialist Approach to Life

Jennifer Anna Gosetti-Ferencei

OXFORD
UNIVERSITY PRESS

OXFORD
UNIVERSITY PRESS

Oxford University Press is a department of the University of Oxford. It furthers
the University's objective of excellence in research, scholarship, and education
by publishing worldwide. Oxford is a registered trade mark of Oxford University
Press in the UK and certain other countries.

Published in the United States of America by Oxford University Press
198 Madison Avenue, New York, NY 10016, United States of America.

Library of Congress Cataloging-in-Publication Data
Names: Gosetti-Ferencei, Jennifer Anna, author.
Title: On being and becoming : an existentialist approach to life /
Jennifer Anna Gosetti-Ferencei.
Description: New York, NY, United States of America : Oxford University Press, 2021. |
Series: Guides to the good life | Includes bibliographical references and index.
Identifiers: LCCN 2020001345 (print) | LCCN 2020001346 (ebook) |
ISBN 9780190913656 (hardback) | ISBN 9780190913670 (epub) |
ISBN 9780197516867
Subjects: LCSH: Existentialism. | Life. | Ontology.
Classification: LCC B819 .G654 2020 (print) | LCC B819 (ebook) |
DDC 142/.78—dc23
LC record available at https://lccn.loc.gov/2020001345
LC ebook record available at https://lccn.loc.gov/2020001346

9 8 7 6 5 4 3 2 1

Printed by Sheridan Books, Inc., United States of America

For Arthur and Alden

CONTENTS

SERIES EDITOR'S FOREWORD

Several ancient philosophers held that the point of studying ethics was not just to learn about ethics—as one might learn about chemistry, astronomy, or history—but to become a better human being. They also recognized that this was not easy to do. In order for thinking about ethics to make a difference in our lives, they argued that our habits and inclinations needed to be educated right alongside our minds. They therefore claimed that what mattered to living well was not just what we thought but *how* we thought, and not just how we thought but how we emotionally responded to the world and to other people.

The books in this series highlight some of the transformative ideas that philosophers have had about these topics—about the good life, and the practices and ways of life that help us to pursue it. They tell us what various philosophers and traditions have taken to be most important in life, and what they have taken to be less important. They offer philosophical guidance about how to approach broad questions, such as how to structure our days, how to train our attention, and how to die with dignity. They also offer guidance about how to deal with the sort of everyday questions that are often neglected by scholars, but that make up the texture of our lives, such as how to deal with relationships gone wrong, family disruptions, unexpected success, persistent anxiety, and an environment at risk.

Because the books are written by philosophers, they draw attention to the reasons and arguments that underlie these various claims—the particular visions of the world and of human nature that are at the root of these stances. The claims made in these books can therefore be contested, argued with, and found to be more or less plausible. While some answers will clearly compete with one another, other views will likely appear complementary. Thus a Confucian might well find that a particular practice or insight of, say, Nietzsche's helps to shed light on his or her way of living in the world, and vice versa. On the whole, the idea is that these great philosophers and traditions all have something to teach us about how to be more fully human, and more fully happy.

Above all, the series is dedicated to the idea that philosophy can be more than just an academic discipline—that it can be, as it was for hundreds of years in the ancient world, a way of life. The hope is also that philosophy can enhance the ways of life we already feel pulled toward, and help us to engage with them more authentically and fully.

Stephen R. Grimm
Professor of Philosophy
Fordham University
September 2019

ACKNOWLEDGMENTS

I am not able to name here all of the many friends and colleagues who have, over the years, illuminated for me aspects of the human condition discussed in this book. I am indebted to many. I can here only thank in particular those who, during the time of the preparation and writing of this book, offered invaluable support, friendship, or inspiration: Steve Magill, Alexandra Delp, Melissa Kearns, Kim White, Mary Jo Salter, Alex von Thun, Susan von Thun, my sister Victoria, my sister Angela, and my mother, Marietta. This book is dedicated with love to my sons, Arthur and Alden, to their being and becoming.

Part I

Encountering Existentialism

| PROLOGUE

The fact that you have picked up a book like this one and have begun to read it suggests that you strive for a fulfilling life. Presumably you aim, like many people do, to live as well and as meaningfully as possible, well aware that you have only one life, and that it is finite. Each day you press forward with no clear path signposted just for you. Your existence comes with no set of instructions for how exactly to go about it. You will be well aware, perhaps with some anxiety, that only you can make some crucial decisions which will shape your existence, determine how your one life will play out. Existential philosophy begins by thinking from the standpoint of an individual concretely existing, wondering how to make sense of this existence.

This may be anything but straightforward. In a busy, overcrowded world, there will be distractions everywhere from any goal you might try to keep in mind. At times you may not know which goals to strive for. Difficulties will arise. Some demands upon you will conflict with others, and responsibilities may come to feel relentless. Perhaps they do right now. You may come to wonder what this life is all about, and sometimes even despair at the lack of an answer. A sudden loss or change can render exigent otherwise merely nagging uncertainties. All of these concerns are the stuff of existential philosophy.

If philosophy can be applied to spiritual ailments, existentialism is one of the most versatile prescriptions. Most people at some point in their lives will experience moments of suffering that have an existential cast. This is suffering that impacts your sense of self, making you wonder who you really are or ought to be, making you wonder about the purpose of your existence. The works of existentialist philosophers elaborate on such phenomena as despair, anxiety, dread, angst, forlornness, the tragic, the absurd, nothingness, being-toward-death, ennui, oppression, and inauthenticity.

While not solving such human difficulties, existentialism recognizes and studies them in philosophical terms. Indeed, when a crisis is diagnosed as "existential," it is salvaged from the indignity of mere pain and recognized as bearing what the Danish philosopher Søren Kierkegaard called a "subjective truth." The remedy of existential thinking comes in the form of relating individual struggles to a human condition understood as universal, and of illuminating the freedom and responsibility, or the creativity, with which they can be tackled.

Existentialists regard our struggles in the light of human finitude, the limits of our life span as well as of our knowledge. Kierkegaard pointed out that while a life can only be understood in hindsight, or "backward," as it were, it must be lived forward. Your most important decisions come with no reliable prediction of the ensuing results. In order to live you must constantly press beyond the limits of what you can know for certain, venturing beyond the borders of what is comfortable, taking risks. In order to find fulfillment, you might ask whether it is necessary, as Kierkegaard wrote in relation to himself, to find that idea or purpose for which you would be willing to live and die.

Then there is temporal finitude—the fact that you have only one existence, and no matter how long it is, it will be, from a cosmic perspective, very brief. The German philosopher Martin Heidegger argued that mortality singularizes in an existential sense. Since no other individual can die your own death, or live out the time you alone are allotted, your existence is singular. You are your time. The awareness that you will die someday and cannot know precisely when can provoke angst or anxiety. Yet if you do not flee from, but embrace this awareness, you may experience a moment of reckoning, perhaps one of heightened clarity, about your very being. Existentialism helps us to place such experiences in a philosophical framework. It sheds new light on them, and on the human-wide relevance of our otherwise private predicaments.

Yet for all its focus on suffering, existentialism is also a deeply affirmative philosophy, as I shall emphasize in this book. Existentialist thinkers consider as the most important philosophical topic the marvel that we are here at all. Gabriel Marcel, for example, describes existence as both a mystery and a cause for wonder. He defends this mystery and wonder against any philosophy or science that would reduce existence to a logical formula, a quantitative calculation, an object of manipulation. Existentialism rebels against any way of understanding in which you would be merely an abstraction or a bearer of general traits of the species.

Existentialists notice that at every moment of our self-awareness, there is also a world here for each of us. You are, as Heidegger described, "being-in-the-world"—never isolated but existing in and through the world of which you are a part. Why do these fragmentary bits of the world you experience—just a fraction of all that is—appear to you as part of a complete world, even though you will never experience or even be able to imagine this whole in its totality? What makes you as a human being concerned about your particular place in such a world?

Existentialists argue that while this world has no intrinsic meaning, you give it meaning by your actions and interactions with it, by your ways of seeing and understanding it, through your actions and choices. Through your various projects, you lend the world your feeling, your interpretation, your own existential significance. You contribute to the structure and sense it takes on. Like all of us, and yet in ways specific to you alone, you transform the world through your participation in it, and transform yourself in the process.

For the world which withholds any ready-made meaning is also the world of your possibilities. You did not choose the conditions into which you've been "thrown," as existentialists put it—you did not choose the laws that govern the physical world, the time and place of your birth, the already established meanings, language, culture, laws, and institutions that shape the social world around you, the position from which you start out in life. Within this given context, much about how your existence will unfold is up to you. This freedom of course comes with responsibility. Even if the way forward seems narrow, there is not a single path, but choices along the way. You may venture this way or that way, and you may change the trajectory, too. You recognize various possibilities of what you might do and you may become anxious or enthralled in light of what is possible.

Existentialism offers a means to reflect on the world in this way and on shaping yourself as to take up your own place in it. It allows you to think about your being here, your existence, as an active, creative becoming. For existentialism argues that each of us is not to be regarded as a finished being with a predetermined purpose, or as merely a member of a species, or as a statistic. You are a unique individual, shot through with possibility. You can take up what you are given and transform it. You do not arrive in the world a finished self, but must, as Friedrich Nietzsche insisted, "become who you are."

Liberating us from the idea that our essence is fixed, that our path is set by our given circumstance or inherited identity, existentialism recognizes our freedom to shape our own existence. It does not ignore differences in circumstance among us, but views subjectivity—our free, self-reflective consciousness—as the starting point. It tells us that as subjects we are always "transcending"— going beyond what we have been or already are—toward new actualizations. But it is always from this first-person perspective— from the point of view of "I" as a transcending subject, as a unique individual—that, for existentialists, any philosophical truth is truly relevant.

In the present moment we may find ourselves in the midst of so many assaults to public truth and meaning that existentialists' advocacy of the individual self, of the first-person perspective, may seem particularly appealing to some readers. Yet others may be wary of existentialism's focus on the self for the same reason, associating the philosophy with the selfish individualism or narcissism or even rampant subjectivity that seems to plague our culture. One critic recently claimed to be cured from the existentialist focus on subjective life by turning to the more analytic philosophy of Ludwig Wittgenstein. An Austrian philosopher who rejected the idea of a private language, Wittgenstein argued that we have no privileged access to our own minds, if that means thought that would be unmediated by language or the presence of others. Wittgenstein thus presumably held any talk of the inner life to be nonsense.

But so, too, did one of the most famous existential philosophers, Jean-Paul Sartre. He held in suspicion the idea that the self was some interior realm of a soul or an "ego" or some essential core of who we are. Like other phenomenological philosophers before him, who studied how the world appears to us as phenomena, Sartre viewed consciousness as always "outside" itself, out there in the world, directed toward the objects of perception and action. We can reflect on our own consciousness, of course, but never in isolation from the world—for consciousness is always conscious *of* something besides itself.

Even Kierkegaard, who proposed "inwardness" as a philosophical category, did not think that brooding over the self was the goal of contemplation—though some of the pseudonymous "authors" of his books spilled an awful lot of ink in the agonies of self-reflection. Kierkegaard responded to the acute consciousness human beings can have of themselves as the site of our experience. But for Kierkegaard, authentic inwardness requires individual passion, commitment, and decision—all of these directed toward something outside and higher than the self. Only by recognizing that the self is grounded in something higher than itself can one avoid despair. Wittgenstein, by the way, thought Kierkegaard the most profound thinker of his century.

Existential philosophy does not only indulge the self but reveals the world from the point of view of the individual. It dignifies our vulnerabilities by relating them to those shared by all other human subjects. It is true that the themes of existentialism can feel stunningly personal, but they relate the individual experience to universal structures of human existence. Many existentialist thinkers—Sartre, Marcel, Simone Beauvoir, Albert Camus, and Kierkegaard, too—insisted that recognizing the conditions of your own "subjectivity" ought to imply recognizing that of others. Consideration of your own suffering in existential terms involves recognizing others' potential for suffering. Awareness of your own becoming, your capacity to evolve in the light of possibilities, entails recognizing the potentiality of other existential subjects. Recognition of your own freedom entails recognizing the freedom of others. Existentialism is personal, but it does not promote selfishness, for it attends to what is personal for all human beings capable of reflecting on their existence.

In a time of cultural fragmentation and often fraught identity politics, it may be salutary to consider what from an existentialist perspective we all share in common. Focusing on commonalities does not preclude recognition of difference or of inequality, for existentialism recognizes above all the particularity of each individual and of what they call "facticity" or the "factical" situation into which they've been thrown. In fact, existentialist thinkers—particularly Sartre, Beauvoir, and Camus, along with African American thinkers related to existentialism such as W. E. B. Du Bois, Ralph Ellison, and Richard Wright, and the critic of colonial oppression Frantz Fanon—analyzed oppression as an existential problem. Existentialist philosophers regarded the fight against oppression as the ultimate task of any existentially oriented ethics. There is a great deal we share in common from an existentialist perspective, and it is understanding this that underlies any defense, against oppression, of our common humanity.

What are these existentially relevant traits shared in common? We are all mortal and live life once and in one direction. None of us can foretell the future or retrace time to undo our mistakes. While existentialist thinkers are diverse in their approaches to human life—a fact that will be emphasized in this book—they all, in one way or another, advocate human freedom and recognize the responsibility this entails. Above all, they describe the human being as having no predetermined path, but one which, if it is to be freely chosen, must be creatively and courageously forged. We are beings who are ever becoming, transcending our present moment in light of possibility. While existentialism regards as philosophically significant the uncertainty and even despair that all of us at one time or other can experience, they also affirm action, creativity, self-determination—or, in a word, becoming.

EXISTENTIALISM IN STYLE AND SUBSTANCE

Existentialism is often taken to be more a style of life than a philosophy, and, having gone out of fashion like all styles do, is now best recalled in nostalgia, like film noir. Popular accounts depict existentialism as essentially a French, more particularly, a Parisian invention. Existentialism may be presented as a philosophy primarily for late adolescents first discovering themselves or for bohemian critics of conformity rather than for proper grown-ups—unless they happen to be living in Paris smoking cigarettes, cocktail in hand. Existentialism may be taken for a gloomy, agonized outlook on the world or an indulgence of modernist nihilism. These persistent clichés in the popular reception of existentialism need correcting if we are to appreciate its substance and its relevance today.

Like most clichés, these have some element of truth to them, but they sell existentialism short. It is revealing to find out where they break down.

It is true that existentialism swept the world of popular culture in the post-war period like no other philosophy in modern memory, and it became associated with a distinctive look as well as outlook. Affinities emerged between fashion and a philosophy oriented by freedom and self-realization. We find this expressed in the 1940s portraits of Albert Camus by Cecil Beaton in *Vogue* magazine, and even more so in those by Henri Cartier-Bresson in which Camus dangles a cigarette in movie-star fashion, appearing mysterious and contemplative behind an upturned collar. Jean-Paul Sartre and Simone de Beauvoir exhibited a studied indifference to conventional appearances, while the scruffy suit, the black shirts of Sartre, the turban worn by Beauvoir became iconic, a kind of anti-fashion. Their lifestyle as public intellectuals in an open relationship, writing in cafés and frequenting jazz clubs, became the trademark of existentialist living. Some of the followers of existentialism, like Juliet Greco who introduced Sartre to her lover Miles Davis, wore the stereotypical black turtlenecks and trousers, a look that was mimicked by students across university campuses in the 1950s and beyond. Audrey Hepburn donned the outfit playing an amateur philosopher-turned-fashion model in the film *Funny Face* (1957). It was inherited by the next generation of French public intellectuals such as Giles Deleuze and Michel Foucault, despite their qualms with existentialist philosophy itself.

Yet as we will see in this book, existentialism's core ideas—among them freedom, authenticity, and responsibility for our actions and values—are entirely contrary to being merely fashionable, to sacrificing substance for style or even for lifestyle. Existential freedom to define ourselves can be lived authentically only with individual commitment. Its ideas may be inwardly embraced. Its outward manifestation may be unrecognizable as such to anyone else, and it can be lived in as many ways as there are individuals.

Is it fair to think of existentialism as a Parisian invention? Well, existentialism's most famous advocates were based in Paris. Yet as a modern philosophy it originated elsewhere—in the nineteenth-century philosophy and literature of Denmark, Germany, and Russia. Some of its core ideas are anticipated in ancient Greece and Zen Buddhism. The French existentialists themselves were not insular Parisians but enthusiastically welcomed a variety of influences from abroad, including black American writing and music and Afro-Caribbean critiques of colonialism. Camus hailed from French-occupied Algeria, a landscape and cultural context that profoundly shaped his thinking. Not Paris, but Algerian cities, set the backdrops for his greatest novels, *The Stranger* (1942) and *The Plague* (1947). Camus described his own thought as "impulses born of the desert."

Existentialism naturally appeals to those who newly confront life-defining choices, who may be inclined to reject the expectations of previous generations, and critically aware young people often fall into this category. Existentialism's ideas are both aspirational and revolutionary, and thus may be harder to approach by those settled into long-established habits or comfortable with the status quo. But its central concerns—the meaning or meaninglessness of life, the inescapability of death, freedom and responsibility, the demand to define ourselves through our choices and the anxiety and responsibility this generates—pertain to every stage of human life. Existentialist ideas are relevant at every moment in which we are self-aware and capable of freely chosen action.

But isn't existentialism fueled by nihilism? Is it not graffitied all across the existentialist rebellion that nothing matters after all? It may seem fair to denounce as pessimistic a philosophy for which ideas such as angst, absurdity, and being-toward-death serve as central concepts. It is true that existentialists question the meaning of existence, both of the cosmos and of human life in particular. Existentialist thinkers disqualify traditional values and reassurances, detailing the anxieties attending this loss of sources of meaning. Yet all of them promote creative responses to this situation, issuing, in Camus's words, a "lucid invitation to live and to create." They affirm the freedom of our yet to be determined possibilities. And they credit each existing individual an intrinsic dignity, grounded in the liberty to establish new values by which to live and to create.

As we shall see, existentialism has many dimensions. To appreciate all that existentialist ways of thinking have to offer, we must work through the prevailing clichés and discover why existentialist philosophies deserve a more nuanced consideration as a philosophical approach to living.

The associations of existentialism with Parisian post-war style and youth-led cultural change, of course, arose from its role in European intellectual life between and after two world wars in Europe. Debates about existentialist philosophy raged in Paris, and enthusiasm for its ideas soon spread around the globe. The devastations of war and an uncertain new political and social order in its aftermath invited new ways of regarding the world and the place of the individual within it. For readers in the midst of this cultural crisis, existentialism's probing of human existence was breathtaking. Its emphasis on individual freedom was both liberating and daunting. Existentialist thinkers recognized that old views of reality inherited from traditional philosophy, religion, and even science no longer sufficed once we wish to explain human experience, or the meaning of our being here at all. What existentialists replaced these traditions with was freedom. "You are free, therefore, to choose," wrote Sartre in "Existentialism," a famous lecture defending the philosophy, "that is to say—invent."

Like every radical new way of thinking, existentialism ignited controversy. Its break with convention angered religious authorities, political parties, and more traditional philosophers. This philosophy was highly personal. It rendered a matter of urgent consideration the freedom of every individual—not merely to act as we will, but to become what we aim to be—and the anxieties we face in recognizing this freedom. Existentialists held out the possibility of living an authentic life as the very basis of truth. Concrete, lived experience of the single individual emerged from the shadow of abstract systems, class struggles, bureaucratic institutions, and long-defended traditions, and became the primary subject-matter for philosophy.

The French existentialists—especially Sartre, Beauvoir, and Camus—appeared with this message at a crucial moment. Their mantra of freedom, authenticity, and responsibility and their acknowledgment of anxiety especially appealed to the French public freshly liberated from German occupation. That these philosophers were heroes of the Resistance lent credibility to their emerging ethics. When the war ended, they became famous overnight, in part through public debates about the responsibility of intellectuals and the launching in 1945 of *Les Temps Modernes*—a journal named after Charlie Chaplin's most celebrated film, *Modern Times*.

Sartre and Beauvoir dominated the Parisian intellectual scene, becoming philosophy's first international celebrities. Along with

Camus and Maurice Merleau-Ponty, they lectured to overflowing auditoriums. Yet it was Gabriel Marcel who, at a colloquium in 1945, first described these thinkers as "existentialists," and it is a term he could have used decades earlier to describe his own philosophy, such as expressed in his essay "Existence and Objectivity" (1925). Apart from Marcel, only Sartre and Beauvoir came to fully embrace the term, but all of them—and some philosophers who rejected the label—benefited from its currency. Interviews with existentialists were broadcast on television and radio, their photos appeared in newspapers and magazines. Existentialists were featured in the post-war 1940s press not only in major European publications but also, in addition to *Vogue*, in *Time, Newsweek, Mademoiselle, New York Times Magazine, Life*, and *Harper's Bazaar.* Their writings were reviewed in periodicals from Argentina to Japan. In 1949, Merleau-Ponty's arrival in Mexico City was front-page news.

The popularity of these new philosophers of existence was in no small measure due to their literary talents: the creativity of their philosophizing was infectious. They wrote for and reached a broad audience, with public lectures, novels, stories, plays, reviews, occasion essays, magazine articles, and heavy philosophical tomes. Both Camus and Sartre were offered the Nobel Prize for Literature, the former accepting in 1957, the latter refusing in 1964, while Beauvoir captured prestigious national honors at a time few women writers were celebrated. A recent discovery suggests that even Merleau-Ponty, the most academically lauded of them (he was the youngest person to have been given a chair at the elite Collège du France), published a novel in 1928 under a pen name, Jacques Heller. But even his philosophical writings presented existentialist ideas in the language of life, with strikingly imaginable examples, and vividly captured the imaginations of readers.

The emergence of French existentialism, however, is unthinkable without its sources in other traditions. French existentialists drew, first of all, on recent German philosophy, introduced through others from still farther reaches of the globe. It was through Emmanuel Levinas, a Jewish émigré from Lithuania, that the Parisians discovered the phenomenology of the German-speaking philosopher Edmund Husserl, born in what is now the Czech Republic. Husserl's philosophy would provide their method and their breakthrough, a new way to describe human consciousness and its experience of the world. Camus wrote that with phenomenology "the universe becomes incalculably enriched." For Husserl, whose seminars in Freiburg Levinas attended in the late 1920s, had turned philosophy toward "the things themselves," to the way they actually appear to us in experience, or to phenomena. Merleau-Ponty, who was present at two lectures Husserl gave in Paris and later consulted the Husserl archives in Leuven, would develop phenomenology by analyzing how our embodiment contributes to the way the world looks to us, and constitutes the situation in which we can exercise freedom.

Sartre embraced the methods offered by Husserl in the early 1930s, when, upon reading Levinas's dissertation on Husserl, Sartre went on to Berlin to study phenomenology. In Freiburg, both Levinas and Sartre met Martin Heidegger, Husserl's former student. Heidegger had adapted the phenomenological method to the question of human existence in *Being and Time* (1927) and this work became a partial template for Sartre's own magnum opus,

Being and Nothingness (1943). For his meeting with Heidegger, Sartre carried a letter of introduction from a mutual acquaintance from Japan, the scholar Kuki Shuzo. While studying with Heidegger, Shuzo had taught the German philosopher important principles of Japanese aesthetics that would influence the latter's theory of language and art.

It was again Levinas, along with Jean Wahl, in essays each published in 1932, who introduced Heidegger's ideas to the French intellectual public. In the same year, another German philosopher, Karl Jaspers, published a three-volume *Existenzphilosophie*, with "Existenz" designating the individual's lived, actual consciousness as a subjective dimension of the wider encompassing horizon of being. Meanwhile, the influence of Heidegger spread further through the Russian émigré Alexandre Koyève, whose Parisian lectures were attended by the rising stars of French philosophy.

The attraction of German sources for existentialist thought waned after Germany's defeat in the war. Germany was resented for so much destruction in Europe, and the international appetite for German ideas among the global public diminished for some decades as Germany was held accountable for the Holocaust. Germany itself was of course for a time occupied, with Berlin and indeed the country itself divided for the next forty years, and much of it would long be in ruins. But there was also much damage to German intellectual life brought about by the Nazis leading up to the war.

For example, as a Jewish-born convert to Christianity, Husserl was stripped of his university affiliation in Germany in 1935. Abandoned by all but his most dedicated followers, Husserl died three years later, his philosophy having never directly reached a general audience. Around the same time, despite early fame, Heidegger would fall into disrepute for his affiliation with National Socialism. Heidegger's political and moral failures tainted the reception of German philosophy for decades, and his fall from grace helped to ensure that existentialist thought would, for the next half century, be promoted as a predominantly French phenomenon. Jaspers, himself having been dismissed from his professorship and forbidden to publish by the Nazis, became alienated from his former colleague. Jaspers lived for a time in exile with his Jewish wife in Switzerland and turned his attention after the war to the problem of democratic political renewal.

Upon learning of Heidegger's Nazi involvement, Levinas too abandoned all reference to Heidegger's thought, breaking off a book project already under way. Levinas would not mention Heidegger explicitly in print for almost two decades, yet devoted much of his philosophy to shaping an ethics that inverted Heideggerian categories and undermined the primacy of "being" as the object of philosophical thought. After his father and brothers were killed by the German Schutzstaffel (SS) in Lithuania, and his mother-in-law perished in a concentration camp, Levinas broke away from existentialism to develop a radical ethics based on the individual's absolute responsibility for the other. Not the self, but the other, was the foundation for all ethical thought for Levinas. Yet existentialist preoccupations—concepts of being, the *il y a* or the "there is," the status of subjective consciousness and its relations to the other—continued to shape his philosophy.

In contrast to these German complications, French existentialism was palatable to a public hungry for new ways to think about the modern, post-war world. French existentialists were free to speak to universal themes and international politics and traveled widely to celebratory reception. In New York City, for example, Sartre, Camus, and Beauvoir presented existentialism with what Americans savored as Parisian glamor. And Paris itself, largely intact after the war, drew intellectuals and artists from abroad, including black American writers and musicians fed up with segregation and the many manifestations of racism at home.

This makes it understandable that recent popular introductions to existentialism—some of them fine ones—look back nostalgically on the Left Bank in Paris in the 1930s and '40s as its epicenter, with the spotlight fixed on Sartre and Beauvoir and their café culture. As a philosophical couple of unprecedented and compatible genius, with an unconventional open relationship, they became existentialism's icons, and consciously cultivated their celebrity for the cause. Sartre himself was the most vocal popularizer of existentialism, defending the movement against its many critics, and he was the most prolific of its advocates. Beauvoir voiced almost unwavering support of Sartre's philosophy. Yet Beauvoir made a singular, revolutionary contribution of her own, arguably a more consequential one, in lived terms, than that of any other philosopher of the century. For her book *The Second Sex* (1949) inaugurated a "second wave" feminist movement (the first devoted to women's suffrage) by challenging essentialist assumptions about femininity. That philosophical study supported dramatic changes in the politics and practice of gender in Western culture for the rest of the century, effects of which are still unfolding today.

The existentialism of the Left Bank—particularly that of Sartre—offered a highly individualist vision. Sartre's was an atheist existentialism. In the absence of God, the human subject alone, bereft of any traditional assurances of life's meaning, was considered the sole source of values. Even Sartre's contribution to projects of communal liberation, such as those of Marxism, were grounded on the philosophy of the free individual subject fighting against an objectifying or oppressive world. The fact that the ideology of communism flatly rejected individualism of the kind espoused by existentialism was a contradiction against which Sartre would have to struggle politically.

Yet the wider tradition of existentialist thinking is far more nuanced and varied than Sartre's model alone would suggest, and, as we shall see, the wider picture of existentialism challenges some of Sartre's presumptions. Where Sartre laid out stark oppositions—self versus other, subject versus object, being as opposed to (and by) nothingness—Beauvoir wrote of "ambiguity." Merleau-Ponty's late thinking of the "flesh of being" admits a far more ambiguous intertwining of self and world than Sartre's oppositions. For Merleau-Ponty, self and world are each folded into the other and the division is never absolute. Marcel promotes the mystery of being and of self and others, invoking reverence, availability, and commitment of the subject toward the world, rather than struggle or opposition. Jaspers's thought, neglected for a time along with the general post-war dismissal of German philosophy, presented human existence as but a dimension of encompassing being. His recognition of the boundaries of knowledge—that knowledge of world, being, or the self is never exhaustive—was designed to resist their objectification.

Apart from German sources, French existentialists drew on nineteenth-century Russian and Danish thought, in which almost all of existentialism's main themes—the focus on concrete human existence, the singular individual, anxiety, authenticity, the death (or inaccessibility) of God, despair, absurdity—were brought to the forefront of philosophical analysis. The Russian writer Fyodor Dostoevsky's *Notes from Underground* illustrated the agony of a soul at odds with a world he found inauthentic, while his *Crime and Punishment* explored the depths of individual human conscience struggling with the problem of freedom. Dostoevsky's *The Brothers Karamazov* contemplated the possibility of the death of God and what may be permissible in God's absence. Leo Tolstoy's story "The Death of Ivan Ilyich" provided Heidegger with insight into our awareness of death and a model for inauthenticity.

The earliest history of existentialism, by Wahl in 1946, recognized the nineteenth-century Danish philosopher Søren Kierkegaard as the first "philosopher of existence." Sartre, Beauvoir, Heidegger, Marcel, and the German writer Franz Kafka were all directly and deeply influenced by Kierkegaard. The Dane had analyzed the anxiety we feel when faced with possibilities, and he based his expansive philosophy on the irreducible singularity of the individual. Kierkegaard's impact on philosophy was widespread and profound. Even as an analytic philosopher, as we have noted, Wittgenstein recognized Kierkegaard as a profound thinker. While writing his own *Notes on Logic*, Wittgenstein learned Danish to read Kierkegaard in the original.

Kierkegaard's influence made its way across the Atlantic, too. In the 1930s Walter Lowrie published English translations and a biography of Kierkegaard, and the Danish philosopher's ideas became something of a vogue among American intellectuals. By the 1940s, with worldwide conflict and the Allied fight against fascism, Kierkegaard's ideas were ripe for the picking. Kierkegaard's philosophy defended the individual as irreducible to systematic philosophy and it wholly resisted the idea of historical destiny. Kierkegaard recognized faith not as a matter of deference to authority, tradition, or common truth, but of individual courage. It demanded a leap taken in "fear and trembling," and most often alone. Kierkegaard, moreover, described inauthenticity as a failure of inwardness, with the self's own vision refracted through the opinions of the crowd, a view that President Roosevelt claimed help him to understand how human beings such as many living in Nazi Germany could be vulnerable to the falsities of extreme nationalism. Kierkegaard's works would come to influence such diverse artists as the painter Mark Rothko and the writers James Baldwin, Walker Percy, W. H. Auden, and Thornton Wilder. Kierkegaard, along with Friedrich Nietzsche, offered Dr. Martin Luther King Jr.'s first contact with existentialist thinking. Later King went on to read Heidegger, Jaspers, Sartre, and Paul Tillich and came to regard existentialism, with its understanding of the "finite freedom" of humanity, as grasping "the true state of man's existence."

Wahl's history of existentialism also paid tribute to the nineteenth-century philosopher Nietzsche. Long before Nietzsche's ideas about the "overman" had been appropriated by National Socialists—they ignored Nietzsche's scathing criticisms of the German temperament and his desperate rejections of anti-Semitism—his works were widely read by the artists and writers of modernism. Franz Kafka, Rainer Maria Rilke, Thomas Mann, James Joyce, and D. H. Lawrence were among those influenced by Nietzsche, who was also revered by early Expressionist painters and by Surrealist and Dadaist artists.

Nietzsche considered the human being not as a quintessentially rational being, or as cast in God's image, but as shot through with the forces of nature, viewed from a cosmic perspective. In *The Birth of Tragedy* (1872) and other works, Nietzsche revealed what he took to be the irrational nature of reality, a world of chaotic change with a vitality unacknowledged in abstract thinking and expressible only fully in art. Nietzsche's account of reality as a churning chaos obscured by the conceptual order we impose upon it anticipates the experiences of Sartre's character Antoine Roquentin in the novel *Nausea* (1938). The affliction of the novel's title occurs when the ordinary look and meaning of things around Roquentin fall away, and what Sartre calls the radical "contingency" of existence is exposed.

It is well known that some of the central works of black American culture were influenced by French existentialism but less often acknowledged that the relationship was reciprocal. In 1903, in *The Souls of Black Folk*, W. E. B. Du Bois formulated his idea of a "double consciousness." This was meant to indicate something like the impossibility of having a singular, unified identity or awareness of self under conditions of oppression. Du Bois's work was published more than three decades before Sartre described a split consciousness in *Transcendence of the Ego* and the instability of identity and the objectification of self by others in *Being and Nothingness*. Richard Wright's novel *Native Son* (1940) absorbs the concept of double consciousness for describing the experience of oppressed alterity or otherness. Along with *Black Boy*, Wright's autobiography, the novel provided Beauvoir with a literary model for describing the effects of inequality on the self, as she explores in *The Second Sex*. Wright's writings were published in Sartre's journal

Les Temps Modernes, as Sartre held up Wright as exemplary of the notion of "engaged" literature that profoundly reveals reality. Existentialist themes—dread, anguish, death, freedom—appear not only in *Native Son* but in Wright's Dostoevsky-inspired short story "The Man Who Lived Underground" (1942). As for order of influence, Wright himself had been acquainted with the works of Dostoevsky, Kierkegaard, and Heidegger long before he encountered those of Sartre, and before meeting Sartre and Beauvoir in post-war Paris.

Ralph Ellison, another great African American writer, brought together existential thought and the inspiration of jazz music in his novel *Invisible Man*. Ellison's narrator, listening to jazz in an underground hideaway and contemplating the problem of freedom in a racist society, argued that responsibility requires social recognition denied to those rendered "invisible" by racism. Both the metaphor of containment and the idea that one's own moral agency, like one's freedom, demands recognition by others, are major themes in Sartre's play *No Exit*.

Jazz music equally influenced Sartre, who frequented jazz clubs in Paris, where he met Charlie Parker and Miles Davis. Jazz makes an appearance in *Nausea* when a recorded jazz tune repeatedly offers the solution to the vertiginous meaninglessness suffered by Roquentin. More fundamentally, the aesthetic adopted from jazz—its spontaneity and improvisation—underlies Sartre's existential ethics. Just as jazz improvisation dispenses with written composition and with conventional musical structure, favoring invention of the moment, Sartre argued that the existential moral agent cannot rely upon rules in advance or predetermined values. It is, Sartre says, up to us to "invent," the only condition being that our actions promote, rather than repress, freedom. Miles Davis recognized the indebtedness of existentialism to jazz in no uncertain terms. Recalling Sartre and the role of jazz in the existentialist scenes he witnessed in Paris, Davis insisted (laughingly, but perhaps also seriously) that he should receive some of the credit for existentialism. Upon reading *Nausea*, his compatriot Ellison had concluded that African American blues music offered "better statements of the existentialist position than Sartre's novel ever could."

Yet French expressions of existentialism enjoyed both elite academic pedigree and a broad audience. Sartre and Beauvoir were at liberty to intertwine their ideas with public life. In the spotlight, they frequented Parisian nightclubs, promoted sexual freedom, had affairs and protégés, led political demonstrations, took up many causes of social justice. The aesthetic sophistication now attributed to them is partly a retrospective gloss—their habit of writing in cafés originated with the fact that their modest wartime lodgings were poorly heated.

The fact that in reality these philosophers spent an awful lot of time reading, teaching, and writing—in short, using words to describe and analyze life—did nothing to diminish their affiliation with action. When the highest abstractions of thinking are applied to the most concrete everyday experiences, even writing can be understood as a form of active participation in life. They philosophized about everything from the perception of ordinary objects like beer glasses, suspenders, and chairs, to sex, seduction, love, friendship, the feel of walking in a city, travel, eating and drinking and smoking, jazz, painting and literature, boredom and insomnia, and sports, including soccer and swimming (Camus), skiing and boxing (Sartre). Their literary writings, too, generated new ways of reflecting on reality. In *What Is Literature?* Sartre argued that literary language offered a unique way of revealing reality. In this view he was following the views of Heidegger, who argued from the late 1920s onward (first in reference to a passage in the only novel by the poet Rainer Maria Rilke) that literary writing, poetry, and art were means of revealing being, indeed forms of truth.

French existentialism's attraction as a fashion faded away with the death of its most prominent thinkers. In 1960, at forty-six years old, Camus died in a car accident returning from holiday in the sportscar of his publisher Michel Gallimard, an unused train ticket in Camus's pocket. A year later, while sitting at his desk, Merleau-Ponty died of a heart attack, age fifty-three. By 1980, when there were, famously, 50,000 people gathered for Sartre's funeral procession, and 5,000 for Beauvoir's six years later, the backdrops of the existentialist scene had already become tourist attractions. Nowadays there seem to be no cafés left in Paris, or New York for that matter, filled with smoke, much less where famous writers and artists debate in public the phenomenology of cocktails, the meaning of freedom or the authentic life. In French academic philosophy, existentialism was overtaken by subsequent movements—first structuralism, then post-structuralism and deconstruction, movements which have themselves since passed out of currency or waned in influence. The contemporary relevance of existentialism is due to the fact that it draws both deeply and widely from the past, that its dominant tense is the present, and that, by calling upon possibility, it persistently appeals to the future.

This book is designed to explain existentialism as a philosophy for living and to show how existentialism gives voice to our most significant experiences—those almost all human beings may have faced throughout time, and their particular and specific manifestations today. Against the background of existentialism's historical roots and its modern emergence, the aim here is to examine existentialism as a way of life—or more precisely, as ways of life.

For it should already be apparent that existentialism is not a unified movement. Its themes are diverse and its thinkers were often opposed. For Kierkegaard, Heidegger, and Sartre, anxiety is central to existentialism, while Camus (for all his talk of absurdity) and Marcel emphasize possibilities for happiness and hope. Kierkegaard, Martin Buber, Marcel, and Jaspers can be counted among religious existentialists, while Sartre and Camus express atheistic views and Nietzsche is critical of Judeo-Christian religious faith. Merleau-Ponty and Marcel insist on the centrality of embodiment in human existence. Beauvoir exposes the challenges to freedom in a culture of gender inequality. In their contributions to existentialist thinking Du Bois, Ellison, and Fanon conceive the possibilities for black consciousness under conditions of racial and colonial oppression, while simultaneously revealing aspects of the human condition as such.

The term "existentialism," too, must be qualified. Only a few thinkers discussed in this book accepted the label or are likely to have done so, had it been already coined when they were writing. Others, like Heidegger, explicitly distanced their philosophies from it. Among the motivations for laboring over new ideas is the assumption that they have not been expressed before, and philosophers may focus on what is distinctive or novel in their own thought. It is not surprising that those interested in authenticity and individuality might reject any label that would lump their thinking together with diverging positions, or even with similar ones.

This however should not disqualify readers, particularly with the benefit of historical hindsight, from discerning, in patterns of influence and common threads of argument, the shape of an emerging, if heterogeneous, movement. An inclusive and multi-faceted definition of existentialism can still differentiate thinking that is existentialist in orientation from thinking that is not, as we will see shortly.

A number of commentators have coped with the problem of terms by distinguishing between "philosophies of existence"— usually including Kierkegaard, Nietzsche, Jaspers, and Heidegger, perhaps also Dostoevsky and, when they are recognized, African American or post-colonialist writers—from the "existentialism proper" of Sartre, Beauvoir, Marcel, and Camus. While there are merits to that approach—particularly overcoming the objection that many of the former thinkers did or could not embrace the existentialist label—it seems to assume that the "real" existentialism emerged on the Left Bank among a core group of French philosophers. This would overlook the deep thematic and methodological dependence of those Paris-generated ways of thinking on existentialist expression and philosophy from elsewhere. Such a distinction also tends to obscure differences even among the self-described "existentialists."

Sartre and Marcel, for example, differed not only on the subject of religion, as Marcel made clear in his essay "Existence and Human Freedom" (1946). Sartre viewed human subjectivity from a Cartesian starting point—that is, from the standpoint Descartes described in his *Meditations*, a mind thinking of itself as alone in the world—and thus in terms of a self as essentially opposed to the non-self. In contrast, for Marcel the human self is interconnected with others from the outset. Sartre conceived the experience of existential reckoning as provoking nausea, prompting a breakdown of the presumed order of reality. In contrast, for Marcel the existential awakening is characterized by wonder, astonishment, and love of being. These two self-described existentialists are more divergent in their thinking than either may be to others who rejected the label.

The difficulties become more manageable once we acknowledge the heterogeneity and diversity of existentialist thought. There is not, strictly speaking, one existentialist philosophy but a number of existentialist philosophies, or as Paul Ricoeur put it, there is not one existentialism but a number of existentialisms. The differences among existentialist thinkers—not to mention the evolving and shifting positions within their own thinking—speak to the richness of existential concerns, and the inexhaustible and sometimes conflicting possibilities for being human.

Representing this diversity involves a complex narrative, and it cannot lead us to one, coherent, unified philosophy of life whose mantra we could follow, unlike some other schools of philosophy or the work of a particular philosopher. But this complexity is also key to a richer and truer account of existentialist thought. Embracing rather than avoiding this complexity has the advantage of promoting multiple and diverging options for living, thinking, and being in the light of philosophy. Such is the vision of existentialism offered in this book. The singular term "existentialism" is used for convenience, and sometimes to differentiate all existentialisms from aspects of the tradition against which they can be united.

Despite many differences and a broad variety of themes in their works, we can find three related concerns among all of the philosophers associated with existentialism. First, they all validate concrete, individual experience over abstract systems. Second, they all expose the inadequacy of traditional interpretations of the meaning of life and the consequences that obtain from it. Third, they promote free action on the part of the human subject toward the creation of new meaning. Even Nietzsche, who directly challenges the idea of free will as philosophers had traditionally conceived it, holds that human beings have no determined and fixed essence and must become what they are through what they do and what they create. Only thus can Nietzsche recommend that we regard our life as a work of art and promote human existing as a creative process.

Existentialisms would be thus united against any assignment of human life to a predetermined place in the order of things. This is so even of the existentialists who accept religion. For Kierkegaard, for example, God is not an objective but a subjective truth, to be validated by the individual only in the highest objective uncertainty. Obtaining meaning in one's life must be achieved in a "qualitative transition" Kierkegaard likened to taking a leap, the results of which cannot be determined in advance. Existentialist philosophies tend to illuminate the question of meaning as the source both of our deepest anxieties and our highest possibilities. Existentialism does not prescribe the purpose or meaning of life categorically, but instructs that this must be worked out concretely in each individual case, and by none other than the one whose existence it is.

Acknowledging the diversity within existentialism also neutralizes some of the clichés surrounding existentialism. Existentialist concerns are relevant whether or not we have the leisure or inclination to sit around in coffee shops or jazz clubs. Existentialist philosophy examines themes just as relevant to those working hard to feed their families they hardly have time to see as they are for the student considering whether to finish a program toward a secure job or to take a road less traveled. While contemplation of existence may seem a luxury, it is relevant for anyone who, though facing restricted choices, may be awakened to some possibility nevertheless. It is for the person of wealth who may choose not to wallow in the seeming endlessness of material consumption but instead rise at the crack of dawn just to work on some worthwhile legacy. Existentialism is for the middle-aged who wonder to what extent they should sacrifice for their lonely parents or nurture their children's advantages at the expense of their own still unfulfilled dreams. Existentialism is for the old who face the prospect of death at closer range than most younger people and who may be reminded every day of their finitude. At no point, as long as we can reflect on our lives and have choices to make, are the concerns of existentialism irrelevant.

We are, as Sartre says, "condemned to be free." But we are also, as Heidegger puts it, "thrown" into the world, a world of other people, specific material conditions, factical limitations, and already established meanings. Beauvoir adds that this thrownness is also gendered, while Ellison, Wright, and Fanon illuminate its racialized dimensions. Taken in its diversity, existentialism does not absorb the differences among human situations into some overarching formula—except to identify as a universal fact both our freedom for possibilities and the limits prescribed by our finitude. Even as the power of social identity is recognized, existentialism makes of individuality and the concrete situation the starting point of every inquiry.

Once we grant its heterogeneity, multiple visions of a worthwhile or authentic life can be supported within the scope of existentialist philosophy. This multiplicity is well represented here and will not please readers looking for straightforward instructions on, or a linear prescription for, how to live. While many human beings may be searching for what is often called "the good life," existentialism reveals the extent to which our ideas of the good are generated by our affirmations and choices. If the good life means primarily popularity, pleasant distraction, identification with ostensibly lasting material things, and a contentment untroubled by nagging questions, existentialism will provide no advice whatsoever on how to achieve it.

Instead, existentialism is a difficult philosophy. For it exposes and encourages us to face our individuality, the scope of our choices, the responsibility we bear for our actions and ways of being. It illuminates the anxiety that comes with questioning external sources of meaning. It prompts thoughts about death and makes us face our finitude. Existentialism also recognizes the possibility of failure to live as individuals, or the possibility of inauthenticity. We may live inauthentically if we fail to recognize our individual involvement, our responsibility for what we are, and the possibilities we may have for being otherwise.

Yet existentialism also offers ways to consider, and validate philosophically, the concrete experience of living. Existentialism encourages us to maximize our reflective involvement in what we are and become. For existentialism affirms individuality, authenticity, and freedom, revealing the multiplicity of ways to shape a life. It starts with the individual, each of whom is unique.

Having seen the diversity of existentialism and the depths of its sources, and overcome some assumptions and clichés in popular reception of the philosophy, we will now turn to the rise of existentialism, examining its historical roots, its resonances with Romanticism, and the transition to its modern context.

Part II

The Rise of Existentialism

ANTIQUITY TO MODERNITY

2 | A PHILOSOPHY FOR HUMAN EXISTENCE

That you are here—that life exists and identity,
That the powerful play goes on, and you may contribute
a verse.

—WALT WHITMAN, *Leaves of Grass*

"You are here." We can find these words by a little red arrow on any public map. Of course, as evoked by Walt Whitman, they point to a meaning beyond one's location in space. Along with the "here," Whitman invokes time and individuality. Here and now, he reminds us, you are the brief existence that you are allotted. The identity to which Whitman refers indicates the irreducibly personal nature of this "you," who after all may "contribute a verse" to the powerful play of existence. Neither this knot of space and time, nor the individual entangled with it, is interchangeable with any other.

We may take this as simply self-evident. Yet Kierkegaard dedicated thousands of pages of intricate analysis to the theme of human individuality, among the most prominent themes in his philosophy. Born only six years before Whitman, in 1813,

Kierkegaard would come to write that "truth is subjectivity." While not denying objective truth, Kierkegaard meant that the highest truth must feel individual to us, and lived from our own perspective. Kierkegaard died in 1855, the year Whitman first published *Leaves of Grass*.

Toward the end of the same century, Nietzsche offered a similar affirmation of human uniqueness. He wrote:

> At bottom every human being knows well enough that he is a unique being, only once on this earth; and by no extraordinary chance will such a marvelously picturesque piece of diversity in unity ever be put together a second time.

Like Kierkegaard and Whitman, Nietzsche understood the very fact of our existence as cause for wonder—if not also at times provoking terror when we reflect on it. All of these nineteenth-century thinkers recognized that individual existence could elicit the deepest and most important questions. Recognizing the individual as worthy of philosophical understanding in and through the lived here and now is how existentialist thinking begins.

What does it mean, after all, for an individual to exist? To begin to answer this question, we might imagine our lives from cosmic, generally human, and personal perspectives. From a cosmic perspective, the existence of each one of us could be described as brief and unlikely to have happened at all. We inhabit a living planet that in hosting life is unlike any other planet we know, despite the reaches of science into the vastness of our surrounding universe. If we ever do find evidence of current life elsewhere, it will likely be so far away that we may never be able to reach its habitat in a human lifetime. As individuals or even as a species we are hardly measurable on the cosmic scale, yet our origins go back to the explosions of stars. Billions of years after the big bang brought our universe into being, we who exist now on this spinning blue globe are each made up of the residue of stardust. Each of us has a conscious mind, the workings of which even our most sophisticated scientists do not fully understand. Nietzsche liked to remind his readers that from a cosmic perspective we are all equally insignificant, a mere speck of dust. Yet our very awareness of this cosmic insignificance gives us an existential importance shared by nothing else in the universe.

From a human perspective, we inhabit a moment of a human world. We each exist, for example, on this train platform or park bench, here under the reading lamp, in this library or bookstore, or wherever one happens to be reading these words. Our moment in place and time belongs of course to a particular culture. While contemporary theorists like to insist on the differences among us—in our languages, customs, religions, ethical values, or ways of life—existentialists constantly refer to what all human beings share in common. For our human condition is such that all of us must be born (in some way or other) in order to arrive in the world. We all must die within a limited life span, at a point of which none of us can be certain. We all have both a beginning which we did not choose and an end which we cannot know. None of us can travel back in time to amend our mistakes, nor can we foresee the future. For an existentialist, these shared facts of the human condition vastly override our differences.

Yet we also each inhabit a unique perspective as individuals. We each have a personal history which shapes our circumstances. Each of us faces choices in living our lives that only each of us alone can make. We face questions only we alone can seek to answer. Existentialism finds the subject-matter for philosophy in considering the very individuals thinking about their existence in the first place.

In thinking about our existence as individuals, existentialism marks a radical departure from the central concerns of philosophy throughout most of the Western tradition. Since its birth in ancient Greece around two and a half thousand years ago, philosophers have for the most part sought eternal truths, principles of unchanging permanence. Plato sought universal knowledge of essences. In the seventeenth century Descartes, aiming to provide a foundation for early modern science, devised a systematic, rational account of reality, in the shadow of which the particular and the subjective were dismissed. Contemporary mainstream philosophers have often valued exclusively logical forms of argument, sweeping aside the inherently unclear or indistinct aspects of meaning or experience along with the deepest metaphysical questions. Such philosophy may dismiss altogether the paradoxical or absurd.

Yet in actually existing, we may confront questions with no clear answers. Possibilities we take up foreclose countless others, most of which have yet to be revealed. Our ethical choices can rarely be undertaken by deferring to logic alone, and any rule given in advance may find us in crucial conflict with another. We may need to make our lives meaningful apart from any systematic truth, despite the fact that no such meaning can be secured with certainty. Wholly rationalist, systematic philosophies, and the objective sciences they have traditionally supported, are of little help in coping with such questions, choices, and needs.

This is why Kierkegaard took a critical position against the intellectual tradition he inherited. Kierkegaard wanted philosophy to turn to the questions that crucially matter to us as individuals, the contemplation of which might help us to best live out our lives. This was not only an intellectual endeavor for Kierkegaard, but a personal quest also, as he wrote in his journal on August 1, 1835:

> What I really need is to get clear about what I must do, not what I must know, except insofar as knowledge must precede every act. . . . [T]he crucial thing is to find a truth which is truth for me, to find the idea for which I am willing to live and die.

What Kierkegaard needed was not just a philosophical problem to ponder, but a truth to believe in, an idea specific to his own life and soul by which he could guide his actions. Of course, in supporting a concept of subjective truth, Kierkegaard did not advocate ignorance about the objective world. He simply pointed out that even total objective knowledge of the universe, were that achievable, would never answer the question of what I ought to do, or of how I ought to live. All the existentialists in Kierkegaard's wake shared these same concerns.

Science gives us a deeper understanding of many aspects of human existence—and increasingly of human consciousness itself. Neuroscience, evolutionary anthropology, and empirical psychology, for example, study human beings respectively as physical organisms governed by brains, as members of an evolved species, or in terms of how minds work in general. These fields, the contemporary contributions of which most of the existentialist thinkers could scarcely have imagined, help us understand human beings in their physiological, cognitive, and social workings. Yet none of these fields is meant to study existence from the standpoint of a single human individual. None reflects directly one's own personal here and now. No science worthy of its name—for its truths must be objective and repeatedly demonstrable—can directly address what to live for, and how, or the challenges we face in making such choices.

One early twentieth-century existentialist, Karl Jaspers, insisted on the importance of scientific thinking, regarding reason as our only tool in studying existence. Science is necessary for philosophy, Jaspers argued, for it marks out the boundaries of knowledge and helps philosophy to avoid speculating in error. Yet Jaspers argued that in addition to science we also need philosophy, particularly existential philosophy, if we are to ask questions about the meaning of our existence, of our lives. For Jaspers argued that "truth is infinitely *more* than scientific correctness."

Jaspers argued that philosophical thinking had its own form of reason. It should not merely mimic the procedures and values of science but engage its own form of exploratory and boundary-seeking thought. Science offers knowledge of the physical universe, yet philosophy is to situate such knowledge within more encompassing questions about being as such. Philosophy considers such questions in light of the concrete actuality that pertains to our individual existence.

Existentialist philosophers, of course, are not primarily concerned with explaining the mechanics of the empirical world or the physical operations of life, but with their meaning for us as existing individuals, and with our own meaning. "It is legitimate and necessary to wonder whether life has a meaning," wrote Camus. Existentialist philosophers do not tell us what, for any individual, this is to be. Although they all refer to, or imply, the importance of freedom, along with authenticity, creativity, or responsibility, they also outline a task that is inherently individual. They aim to illuminate the question of life's meaning and legitimate our challenges and uncertainties in exploring it.

This may sound very far from the concerns of much of the Western philosophical tradition, in its task of seeking universal truth. Yet while emerging as a distinctive set of philosophies over the last two centuries, existentialism engages some of the core concepts that first emerged with ancient philosophy. Some of existentialism's crucial working concepts—including being and non-being, existence and essence—go back to the earliest Western thinkers. Existentialist thinkers reframe and revalue concepts that can be traced to an ancient debate between pre-Socratic philosophers about permanence and change.

One of the oldest known written philosophical works, a poem by Parmenides (born 515 BCE), favors but one of these terms, being, at the expense of the other, non-being, and validates nothing in between. Parmenides argued that despite all appearances to the contrary, what is, or "being," is a unity. Parmenides claimed that either being is, in the fullest sense of the word—"now together entire, single, continuous"—or it is "not at all." Being is timeless and unchanging, and all change is impossible. Being is thus conceived as something like an unchanging essence that encompasses all of what is.

In such a philosophy, reality as we perceive it—shifting, moving, and ephemeral—is therefore relegated to illusion or mere appearance. While this position is counterintuitive or even nonsensical to many modern thinkers, Parmenides was able to deliver a prescientific system by which the human mind could fix in concepts an otherwise unstable reality. Yet with this same achievement, Parmenides dismissed in one metaphysical sweep any philosophical interest in human existence as it is actually lived. Western philosophy takes off from this kind of abstraction, to which existentialism will respond in millennia to come.

It may seem that the concepts of being and non-being could describe human beings as well as other phenomena. Human beings have "being" as long as they are alive. When they die, they are no longer. Whether or not one believes that a soul lives on, human individuals, as their bodies die, are no longer the living recognizable persons they once were. As such persons, they disappear into "non-being."

Yet in life we are constantly growing or otherwise changing, and thus it is questionable whether we are ever at any given point wholly what we are. To what extent has an infant human achieved its being? When we are very old, is some of our being lost along with the experiences left behind? What continuity do we maintain between ourselves now and as we once were in the distant past? From our human and personal point of view, it is evident that things constantly shift and change, as we arrive from a particular beginning in life and pass away out of it at another point in time. It would seem we cannot relegate all of our worldly experience of change to mere appearance or illusion, as Parmenides does, without disqualifying our own reality in the process.

For from the perspective of human experience, change is everywhere. This remains so even if to some extent we tend to fix in Parmenidean fashion the world we see, clinging to a vision of reality more stable than it really is. We conceive of the world as full of stable entities, despite our knowledge from modern physics that all matter is constantly in motion. Our own bodies are ever changing with the processes of movement, growth, repair, and decay. Our consciousness, however persistent or intermittent our sense of personal identity, is an ever-moving flow of thoughts and feelings. We ourselves and people we love are born, grow, change, and age, and eventually die. We make commitments that can last the duration of our lives, but in reality, even these last only by being renewed over and over again with new actions and choices. None of this can be significant or even true in a philosophy categorically privileging being and dispensing with non-being. Life as it is lived is hardly touched by the idea of being as pure presence.

If Parmenides's philosophy seems extremely abstract, it countered the equally radical view of his predecessor Heraclitus (535–475 BCE), who sowed the seeds for a more existential confrontation with reality. Heraclitus argued that all that is, is not one but many, and is constantly in flux. The primary category for Heraclitus is becoming, a transitional state whereby things at once come into being and pass away into non-being. Heraclitus famously argued that "into the same river you could not step twice, for other waters are flowing." All things are in constant flux, according to Heraclitus, a position that will be echoed in the writings of Nietzsche. Inspired by Heraclitus, Nietzsche demanded that philosophy treat human existence not as a mere abstraction but as a living reality. He thus attacked the Platonic tradition for suppressing flux in favor of a more stable, Parmenidean vision of the universe.

For inheriting this debate from these pre-Socratic predecessors, Plato had aimed to account for both permanence and change, yet in so doing he made philosophical truth remote from actual human experience. Plato identified the realm of eternal being with the essences of things, and, echoing Parmenides, explained all change or becoming as mere appearance. Things as they appear to our senses—the changing phenomena we see—participate in but are lesser than those eternal essences we can know only with reason, with the eye of the mind. The philosopher is to take interest not, for example, in this particular tree in its particular change and growth, but in what can be known of any and all trees at any time—the form, essence, or idea of them. The same can be said of beauty, or justice—not that this beautiful object or that just arrangement of human affairs is of the highest interest; rather, the philosopher seeks the form in which all beautiful objects or manifestations of justice partake, the individual instance being just an index to that higher truth. The highest purpose of a human life for Plato is to see this world in the light of eternal ideas or forms, and of the all-encompassing idea which Plato called the good and regarded as divine.

Yet the Platonic orientation toward the eternal requires raising one's thought toward being above actual existence and fixing the eye of the mind above the life of the senses. In direct opposition to the essentialism and rationalism of Plato, both Kierkegaard and Nietzsche articulated some of the impulses for the philosophy to become known as "existentialism." For these philosophers, conceiving of being as permanent essence obscures the reality of becoming and of existence. Existence is not a pure unchanging unity but finite. It involves unwieldy multiplicity. It is messy and vital and, for us, involves difficult change. Because we may also consciously shape what we are to become, human existence, and not some higher abstract ideal, should be the central concern of philosophy. As Heidegger would later put it, the human being "is primarily being possible" as it engages with and creates in the world. This being possible is both a universal condition of humanity and, in its particular realization, unique to each one of us.

Existentialism delivered a shock to a tradition long influenced by the rationalism espoused by Plato. One of existentialism's targets was René Descartes, for whom the existence of the human mind as a "thinking thing" (he used the Latin phrase *res cogitans*) provides the foundation for early modern thought. Descartes's highly intellectual concept does not capture the human being as a finite individual living bodily in the extended world of the senses, but only as a rational mind with innate knowledge of abstract ideas which are eternally true.

With Descartes, however, an important shift occurs that provokes some existentialist insight. Descartes sought the basis for certain knowledge neither in the world nor in ideas existing in some transcendent super-worldly realm, but in the existence of the mind itself. With Descartes's notion that "I think, therefore I am," he grounded "clear and distinct" knowledge in the indubitable fact of the mind's existence. For as Descartes famously reasoned, I must exist in order even to doubt whether or not I exist—thus making my existence indubitable. This certain knowledge of the mind's existence is for Descartes a starting point for the acceptance of all rational ideas such as those of mathematics and pure physics, which, since Descartes regards them as innate, needed only to be discovered and understood in the clarity of rational reflection.

Yet both Kierkegaard and Nietzsche rejected Descartes's characterization of the self or mind in wholly rational terms. Descartes considered the mind from an epistemic standpoint— or in terms of what the mind can know. Accordingly, Descartes's method of doubt was a merely intellectual exercise, as Kierkegaard complained in his work *Johannes Climacus, or De omnibus dubitandum est* (the subtitle meaning, "everything is to be doubted"). Descartes's so-called first principle of philosophy, "I think, therefore I am," is but a tautology, since it already assumes that the mind's thinking equates to its being. Moreover, this equation, along with Descartes's doubt itself, ignores entirely the problem of ethics, the question of how one is to conduct oneself. According to Kierkegaard's pseudonym Climacus, Cartesian philosophy "has never seriously done what it said. Its doubt is mere child's play." For Descartes left the whole of established morality standing and never once considered the self in terms of freedom for action in the world. Rather than "I think, therefore I am," Descartes would have been better to proclaim, "I choose to act, therefore I am." Kierkegaard suggests here that philosophical doubt ought to lead not to epistemic certainty for the abstract mind, but to a long night of soul-searching, and potential spiritual renewal, for the existing individual.

It was from another angle entirely that Nietzsche attacked the first principle Descartes claimed to have established. Nietzsche challenged the idea that even in considering my own existence, I could know what exactly within me is doing the thinking. Who or what is it that says "I"? Is it reason, or merely instinct? How could such thinking, as Descartes characterized it, be separate from the body and its drives?

Most people can look back in hindsight on a conclusion reached or a decision made at one time or another and recognize it as driven by some desire or anxiety obscure to them at the time. Long before psychoanalysis popularized the idea of an unconscious, Nietzsche suggested that our thinking may always be subject to such motives of which we are scarcely aware—that this is part of what it means to be, as he put it, "human, all too human." Even what we consider our most rational thinking, our well-ordered view of the world, may originate in the fear of a more chaotic reality. Nietzsche wondered whether all the abstract thinking of philosophers was but a flight from the difficulties of existence, a flight motivated by an unacknowledged fear of uncertainty, of an inherently chaotic world.

While many existentialists criticized Cartesian philosophy, Descartes's turn to the mind itself nevertheless initiated a method for later existentialism, that of introspective reflection. This method formally arrived in the early twentieth-century phenomenology of Edmund Husserl, who recognized his predecessor in a work called *Cartesian Meditations*. As the study of what appears to consciousness, phenomenology delivers a method of describing human existence as it is lived in the first person, as "I" experience it. The phenomenologists turn directly to their own experience as the object of investigation, bracketing, in the "phenomenological reduction," questions about the being of the world apart from its appearance as phenomena. How the world appears to consciousness can be then captured through phenomenological analysis.

Phenomenology radically refreshed philosophy's outlook on life and reality. With phenomenology, Camus wrote, "Thinking is learning all over again to see, to be attentive, to focus consciousness; it is turning every idea and every image, in the manner of Proust, into a privileged moment." In *The Ethics of Ambiguity*, Beauvoir described existentialism's debt to phenomenology:

> Existentialist conversion should rather be compared to Husserlian reduction: let man put his will to be "in parentheses" and he will thereby be brought to the consciousness of his true condition. And just as phenomenological reduction prevents the errors of dogmatism by suspending all affirmation concerning the mode of reality of the external world, whose flesh and bone presence the reduction does not, however, contest, so existentialist conversion does not suppress my instincts, desires, plans, and passions. It merely prevents any possibility of failure by refusing to set up as absolutes the ends toward which my transcendence thrusts itself, and by considering them in their connection with the freedom which projects them.

Existentialists will appropriate this residually Cartesian, then phenomenological, method of reflecting on consciousness to consider the actual experience of living, and of what Husserl called the human "lifeworld," from the inside. One of phenomenology's advances is to show that the phenomena we take to be simply there—trees, chairs, a cocktail glass before us—are also in important ways, as phenomena, shaped by our experience of them. Husserl remained committed to what he called the "eidetic" aspect of traditional philosophy, or its search for essences. Yet he argued that such essences must be sought not above but in and through this constitutive experience of an existing subject, in and through how the world appears to one. The mode of existence of the human being, too, is to be studied in and through such experience.

Existentialists used the phenomenological method to inquire into human existence as we actually live it. They rejected the idea that human beings themselves have any predetermined essence, acknowledging only what comes to be constituted through their actions, projects, and commitments. Rather than simply having an essence—the way we could describe the essence of a tree, or of a teapot—the human subject first of all exists. Heidegger defines the human being as "Dasein," which in German literally means "being here" or "being there" ("da" can mean either) in this sense of existing. The human being is that being to whom its being here at all intrinsically matters. While other things in the world can be described as having "objectivity," to use Marcel's distinction, human beings also have "existence" in this sense.

For we are not wholly definable by objective observation but are also subjects who must define our own essence for ourselves through our own perspective and our self-initiated interactions with the world. Because we project our actions toward the future, we are (as long as we exist) never finished, always related to possibilities. Beauvoir's comparison of existentialism to phenomenology highlights the exposure of freedom as the origin of our projects. "Existence precedes essence" is how Sartre famously summed up existentialism. How existence is enacted, lived out, and fulfilled will come to define the essence of the human being— ever a work in progress.

Given the specificity of human existence, the concept of being had to be reformulated by existentialist philosophers. Heidegger distinguished the being of Dasein from that of all other beings. The human being is not just one being among others, but in a special sense "exists." This existence is not exhausted by the immediate present alone. For the "here" or "there" of Dasein's being is also, Heidegger says, not just a location in space, but a temporal dimension, one that is radically open to the future. We are, to put it another way, the place and temporally open moment for which Being (in the broadest sense) can be illuminated as a matter of concern.

In the wake of Heidegger, Sartre will shift the terminology of existential thinking somewhat. Like his German predecessor, Sartre argues that the being of the human being is absolutely distinct in kind from that of everything else. We have seen that Sartre characterizes human consciousness as "being-for-itself"—in that consciousness involves a kind of self-awareness in every experience, and can also in reflection refer back to itself—whereas all other beings are merely "being-in-itself." (Human beings insofar as they are both embodied and consciousness of course combine both, and in this context are called "being-in-and-for-itself.") Importantly, though, Sartre says that consciousness as being-for-itself is really a form of non-being or "nothingness," in several senses. For human consciousness itself has no materiality and, in that sense, exists as "nothing." Further, consciousness in being aware of other objects knows that it is *not* those objects. Additionally, consciousness makes distinctions between and among other beings, noticing that one thing is *not* the other. Consciousness can also be conscious of things that do *not* exist at all, like griffins or unicorns or a not-yet invented machine, but are merely possible. On this point, Sartre writes:

When the existentialists say that human being is different from the being of things, they are saying simply that it is human beings who set up the contrast between things—what is—and what is not but could possibly come to be, i.e., non-being.

Consciousness is thus defined in a number of ways by its relation to non-being.

In a still further sense, consciousness or a human subject is not ever equivalent to any representation of it. I can describe you physically, recount details from your life, or characterize your personality, but as conscious life you are not reducible to any of these representations. As Sartre would say, your being-for-itself always evades such representations and cannot be fixed in a positive or "essentializing" description. In that context Sartre wants to say that consciousness does not have "being" so much as it has "existence." Defining human consciousness or being-for-itself, as existence, and as nothingness, allows Sartre to identify it with absolute freedom from any given essence.

Despite their diverging terminology, the conceptual task for both Sartre and Heidegger is to distinguish the existence or form of being which characterizes human beings from that of everything else. For we are ever transcending whatever we are at the moment, and transcending the given state of other things by projecting possibilities toward and through them. We are in an important sense endowed with possibility, and thus we differ from all other beings which have any fixed essence. Existentialism recognizes human existence as being-possible, ever transcending what already is. "Existence" in this sense evades any essence by which we may define it. "Existence" in this sense is not merely positive presence but a play of becoming. It cannot be accounted for in a philosophy defined by the concept of being as presence. Heidegger's notion of existential authenticity entails recognizing the utter singularity of our existence. Sartre's conception of authenticity entails avoiding "bad faith" in any essence we want to ascribe to ourselves as beings, to affirm the freedom of our becoming.

We have seen that the traditional philosophical concepts of being, non-being, and becoming, existence and essence, remain central categories for existentialist philosophy. But with existentialism these traditional philosophical concepts are engaged in a radically new way. They are poised to describe not ideas independent of us, or human life in only objective terms, but the conditions of each individual concretely existing in and experiencing the world.

These core concepts of existential thinking may of course seem remote from everyday life. Among the occupations and preoccupations of living—in what Heidegger called our "average everydayness"—we may only rarely reflect on the nature of our own existence, on our relation to being, on our becoming, or indeed on our relation to nothingness. If we do so reflect, the very awareness of these themes may provoke anxiety. When anxiety encroaches, we may seek distractions, or sink back into long-established, comforting habits of thinking. Should we feel some tug of conscience, we may turn up the music, drive or run faster, keep ourselves busy with mundane tasks. Existentialism does not sweep these human concerns—or even these habits and distractions—under a metaphysical carpet, but awakens our awareness of them. It makes of them the central problems of philosophy and describes how we might authentically confront them.

"That you are here"—to return to the words of Whitman with which this chapter began—is existentialism's starting point. The task for the existential philosopher is to explore how we may contribute to the powerful drama of existence. Yet the stakes for existentialist philosophers may be even higher than Whitman's metaphor suggests. We contribute not only a verse for the play that is our existence. We are ourselves the characters we create. Both the performance and interpretation of this great drama of existing are up to us.

3 | HISTORICAL ROOTS OF EXISTENTIALISM

The subject-matter of the art of living is each person's own life.
—EPICTETUS, *The Discourses of Epictetus*

For all its investment in the essential and the eternal, in the systematic and certain, traditional philosophy did not entirely overlook the existing individual. Existentialist philosophers found moments of inspiration within an otherwise abstract and, they thought, overly rationalist tradition. Old philosophical ideas were critically transformed in the construction of a novel and distinctively modern account of the human predicament. Considering some of these sources can provide a richer picture of the themes of existentialism and of their enduring sustenance.

Socrates and the Stoics he inspired practiced philosophy not as mere theory but as an authentic way of life born of self-examination or self-command. Augustine, Shakespeare, and Montaigne explored inner reflection and the nature of subjectivity or the self. The Enlightenment generated a philosophy of human freedom, defending the rational autonomy of the individual. Critical engagement of these ideas shaped existentialist conceptions of authenticity, subjectivity, inwardness, freedom, and responsibility.

Inspiration for existentialist thinking can be traced all the way back to Plato's teacher Socrates, born in the fifth century BCE. Socrates was praised by Kierkegaard as a philosopher who did not abstract from the concrete existence of the one philosophizing. "The great merit of the Socratic," Kierkegaard wrote, "was precisely to emphasize that the knower is an existing person and that to exist is the essential." Kierkegaard thought that modern humanity, for all its achievements, had advanced little since the time of Socrates in its insight into human existence. He wrote in *The Sickness unto Death* that what "the world now needs as confused as it is by much knowing is a Socrates." In a similar tribute, Marcel, the philosopher who gave existentialism its name, called his own philosophy "neo-Socratic."

From an existentialist point of view, it is to Socrates's credit that he did not set about to accumulate a body of knowledge or espouse a systematic theory, but rather practiced philosophy through live dialogue. Socrates wrote nothing down, distrusting ideas that could not be vouched for or cross-examined in person. He famously claimed to "know nothing," an admission that Kierkegaard, in *The Concept of Irony*, equates to a freedom from mental capture by phenomena, an ironic understanding of the "nothingness of the determinate content of the world as it is." Socrates's mode of philosophical practice was enshrined in the writings of Plato, who represented Socrates in debate with teachers, orators, poets, and politicians of the day. Eschewing wealth and civic honors, Socrates explored through such dialogue the nature of justice, love, knowledge, and courage, matters he regarded as crucial to a virtuous life.

He famously proclaimed that the "unexamined life was not worth living."

Why did Socrates insist on the examination of life? Socrates agreed with the Sophist orators of his time that human beings strive for "the good," or for what we see as advantageous, what we think should bring us happiness. But it must be explained why then human beings, even in the best of circumstances, often go wrong. Socrates found the problem to lie in our tendency to be misled by appearances, mistaking mere opinion for knowledge. We often confuse the object of our strivings—what we take to be the good—for what is good in itself. Socrates thought that our view of the good, influenced by received opinion and habit, must be subjected to critical reflection.

Only by critically reflecting on our own beliefs, desires, values, and actions, and thus on our own lives, can we discover the difference between apparent goods and the true good. Socrates thus famously issued the directive to "know thyself." Plato would assign a higher ontology to the good, as the highest form or idea, knowable by a reason that sets its sights exclusively on the universal. But for Socrates virtue must be arrived at in examining one's own life. To "know thyself," Kierkegaard argued, meant to extricate one's attentions from external phenomena in order to exercise self-scrutiny. Further supporting the turn inward was what Socrates referred to as his *daimon*, a kind of inner voice that he claimed warned him in ethical matters. The call to live in the light of self-reflection and conscience anticipates an existentialist account of authenticity.

Not only Socrates's life but his attitude toward his own death has been held as a model of authentic choice. As we know from

Plato's *Apology* among other historical sources, in 399 BCE Socrates famously accepted the punishment of the fatal poison hemlock dealt by the Athenian authorities, though he might have proposed a lesser sentence or given up the practice of philosophy instead. In the *Crito* Plato shows Socrates refusing to accept assistance to flee before the sentence could be carried out. Kierkegaard interpreted Socrates's attitude toward death as staking everything on the unknowable possibility of the immortality of the soul, a leap beyond what finite human reason can know. This of course anticipates Kierkegaard's understanding of the paradox of faith, requiring as it does both radical uncertainty and passionate commitment.

A century after Socrates's death, Zeno of Citium founded the Stoic school, undertaking to teach at the entrance to the marketplace in Athens. Virtue, the Stoics argued, was the sole good in itself and sufficient for happiness, or perfection of the soul. The Stoics accepted relative goods, like health, wealth, and education, as rationally preferable to their opposites—so long as they aid rather than distract from a life of virtue. But Stoics believed that the individual could overcome the need for bodily pleasure, the distress of pain, and the influence of emotion, all through rational detachment. This owes something to Socrates's counsel to turn to oneself—and away from ephemeral phenomena. Epictetus, a later Stoic, argued that a person should face any fate with dispassionate acceptance.

This Stoic philosophy will be echoed in existentialist accounts of freedom, particularly that of Sartre. Stoicism defends the sovereignty of the soul, just as Sartre affirms the absolute freedom of consciousness. We have seen that for Sartre the human being as a whole person is both "being-in-and-for-itself," or existing as a physical thing in the world subject to physical conditions, and a consciousness that is self-aware and intrinsically free of all such conditions. One might think we have no control over our emotions, if these are merely inner bodily states, part of our being-in-itself. Yet Sartre conceived of emotions as modes of our being-for-itself, for they are ways of relating to objects. Consciousness for Sartre is given in both a pre-reflective mode—aware of itself through its awareness of other things—and as reflective—when it makes an object of its own activity. While emotions belong to the pre-reflective level of consciousness, they involve a kind of stance taken toward something, a stance for which we are responsible even if we have not consciously decided to feel as we do. As Epictetus argued, in reflection we can control our opinion of something, and thus our emotive stance toward it.

Like the Stoics, Sartre suggests that we can divorce our minds from the immediate pressures of emotion, by taking a reflective view of the objects of these feelings. Moreover, in what Sartre called "pure reflection," we can grasp our being and its overall project as a whole. Assuming the capacity for such independence allows Sartre to claim, in *Being and Nothingness*, that we are always free in an "ontological" sense, even if our "facticity"—or our particular conditions in the world—limits the actual exercise of our freedom. The Stoic perspective may be compatible with Sartre's claim that even under torture we have the capacity to choose, for example, whether or not to give up the names of comrades to interrogators.

Other existentialist thinkers critically engaged the Stoic view of life. Nietzsche appreciated the Stoic promotion of commanding oneself, the view that one can choose what sort of attitude to take toward things. Yet Nietzsche also challenged the idea that rational thought should suppress the emotions. Nietzsche suggested in *The Birth of Tragedy* that only one who can suffer intensely can also experience the heights of joy. Nietzsche describes, for example, the ancient Greek reveler in ecstatic worship to the god Dionysus:

> The strange mixture and ambiguity in the emotions of the Dionysian celebrant remind him, as healing potions remind him of deadly poison, of that sense that pain awakens joy, that the jubilation in his chest rips out cries of agony. From the most sublime joy echoes the cry of horror or the longingly plaintive lament over an irreparable loss.

For Nietzsche, tragedy is necessary for the full affirmation of life, just as affirming life comes with recognition of its inevitable loss. To live in avoidance of suffering, as the Stoic would do, would preclude too the highest joy, and ultimately lead to spiritual weakness. Stoic equanimity could, moreover, belie the chaos at the heart of reality embraced by a Dionysian spirit.

While Beauvoir, like Sartre, appreciated Stoic self-reflection, she directly criticized the Stoics for advocating disinterestedness rather than action. Both Sartre and Beauvoir argue that it is through our projects that we define ourselves. Sartre worried that the Stoics ignored the situation, while Beauvoir explicitly warned that the Stoic attitude can yield resignation, and thus a merely negative expression of freedom. Annulling a project because it cannot be accomplished, or limiting the range of our concerns to that which we can control, would stifle human liberation in any meaningful sense. In *The Ethics of Ambiguity*, she writes of Stoic indifference:

If a door refuses to open, let us accept not opening it and there we are free. But by doing that, one manages only to save an abstract notion of freedom. It is emptied of all content and all truth.

Beauvoir demands a more positive notion of freedom which enables action. We must be free, as she puts it, for the self-directed disclosure of being. Freedom must be fulfilled by "giving itself a content" in our projects. Camus similarly advocated existential "revolt" as a rejection of resignation, even in the face of what he considered the absurdity of life. In critical dialogue with Stoicism, existentialists worked out their concepts of authenticity.

Existentialists draw from the historical tradition a turn to the self, even if the nature of this experience, like many other themes, is understood very differently by various existentialist thinkers. According to Kierkegaard, Socrates initiated our understanding of being a self. Prior to the inward examination advocated by Socrates, Kierkegaard writes, "The self did not exist." It was left for a later age "to go deeply into this self-knowledge." The first sustained elaboration of the inner life in Western thought occurs about eight centuries after the death of Socrates, with Augustine. "Do not look outside; return within yourself. In our interior the truth resides," Augustine wrote in the *Confessions* (397–400 CE).

Augustine's work is a powerful philosophical meditation, the first autobiography in Western literature, and details the author's own religious conversion. For Augustine, truth is to be achieved not primarily by worldly inquiries but by scrutinizing inner thoughts, passions, and experiences, and receiving in this intensely focused interior the address of God. Despite their staunch atheism, Sartre and Beauvoir both wrote of existential authenticity as a form of conversion—not to faith in God, as for Augustine, but to freedom as a highest value. Beauvoir confessed in her *Memoirs of a Dutiful Daughter* that although she broke with religion, "the idea of salvation had survived the disappearance of God, and my strongest conviction was that each person must see to his own salvation." While for Augustine conversion meant abandoning worldly or material attachments to turn the whole soul toward God, for Sartre and Beauvoir existential conversion would mean giving up "bad faith"—or the idea one has any fixed essence or fate given from without—in favor of authenticity, or the "good faith" that recognizes freedom as the source of values.

Augustine's introspective study of time in the *Confessions* also influenced existentialism. Since time can be recognized only by marking change, comparing the present with the remembered past and awaiting the future, Augustine concluded that it is subjective: "It is with you, my soul, that I measure time." Husserl adapted Augustine's contemplation of time for a phenomenology of internal time consciousness, while Heidegger oriented this phenomenology in an existential direction. Heidegger identified not just consciousness, but human existence itself, with lived temporality. Not the time of the seasons, or time as measured by clocks, or as calculated by physicists, but the time of human existence, is the key to our understanding of being. In Heidegger's rendering, the anticipation of the future—particularly the most extreme end of our future, namely, our moment of death—and the retrieval of the past are crucial to Dasein's authentic seizing of the present. Augustine's influence is made explicit by Heidegger in a lecture to a theological society, *The Concept of Time*, which introduced the main ideas for his magnum opus, *Being and Time*.

Heidegger was also influenced by Augustine's concern for the self in its dealings with the world, as he makes clear in his lecture course *Phenomenology of Religious Life*. While he did not accept the idea of mental life as an interior realm to which we must turn, Heidegger understood that some kind of turn to self was necessary to recover from our tendency to lose ourselves in a world of everyday distractions. In his *Confessions* Augustine had warned against preoccupation with material objects and comforts, with the opinions and activities of others, with gossip and novel entertainments—all of which distracted one from concern for the fate of the soul. This view is echoed in Heidegger's critical assessment of the "fallen" character of average everyday life. For Heidegger the self's authenticity depends upon pulling away from this average everydayness in critical self-reflection, echoing both Socrates's call for the examination of one's own life, and Augustine's conviction that salvation must be found in retreat from the inauthentic world. In Heidegger's rendering, the self must be awakened to consider its own singular existence in light of mortality. Heidegger likened such an awakening to a "call of conscience," again echoing Augustinian conversion.

For all existentialists, the capacity for self-reflection is crucial to our awareness of freedom and of our singularity, and to the possibility of an authentic life. But the Augustinian turn inward stands in considerable tension with the views of a number of existentialist thinkers about the precise nature of the self. Kierkegaard was more comfortable than some later existentialists with the metaphor of the self's interiority. His work *Sickness unto Death*, for example, presents its pseudonymous author brooding extensively about the self and possible forms of despair. Only in authentic "inwardness" can one resolve such despair.

For Kierkegaard, the achievement of inwardness is not, however, a retreat from the world, but a recognition of the singularity and subjective truth of one's own existence as it is lived. Inwardness is advanced not to encourage refuge in interior speculation, but to forge critical self-reflection and recognition of the highest possibility. Only in recognizing dependence upon something radically outside itself can the self evade despair. If inwardness requires a turn away from the world, Kierkegaard thinks that we gain the world back in the achievement of authenticity.

Later existentialists reject the tendency to view consciousness as some kind of interior realm, while at the same time relying upon a method of introspection that recalls Socratic self-examination, Stoic reflective equilibrium, and Augustinian confession. Twentieth-century existentialists rely on the phenomenological method, the reflective examination of appearances as they appear to the first-person point of view, which requires too the "bracketing" of all presumptions about the ontological status of any object as it is in itself. Phenomenology describes consciousness as intentional, as always directed beyond its own acts. Intentionality, as Husserl defined it, means that consciousness exists only as consciousness *of* something. Heidegger adopts this notion of intentionality to describe the self, or Dasein, as being-in-the-world, where our very being and the world are interconnected. The self, Heidegger says, is ecstatic, in the literal sense of being outside itself, always moving beyond or "transcending" itself by interacting with the world, reaching toward possibilities to be actualized. Sartre in turn adapts phenomenology to conceive of self-realization as beyond the self: it is "not by turning inward, but by constantly seeking a goal outside of himself in the form of liberation, or of some special achievement, that man will realize himself as truly human."

Existentialism comes to describe the self, even in its self-reflection, not as brooding inwardly, but as transcending its own origins and its situation. While his theory echoes Augustinian conversion, Sartre is adamant that there is no interior into which the self can retreat—an error he associates with an "illusion of immanence." In reflection, consciousness turns back upon itself as an activity, in distinction from all other objects of consciousness, but we are not to think of this happening in some inner world. Interiority is but a metaphor to allow us to think about the nature of our mental lives which are, after all, invisible to others. It is a metaphor, however, which can lead us into "bad faith," according to Sartre, if we think of such an interior as having an essence, or characteristics that determine how we feel, think, or act.

Ambiguity surrounding the question of an inner life haunts the tradition inherited by existentialist thinkers and is dramatically conceived in Shakespeare's works. The self—and the difficulty of knowing, finding, and governing oneself—appears in *Hamlet* as a conflict between inner and outer realities. In *Hamlet*, Polonius's famous counsel to Laertes "to thine own self be true" could be read as an existential call to authenticity, if it did not assume simply that honest self-reckoning will make one harmonious with the world, achieving equanimity between interior thought and exterior action. For in being honest with oneself, Polonius declares, "thou canst not be false to any man." But in contrast to the inner harmony prescribed for Laertes, Hamlet's struggle reveals that complex inner lives may be lived in acute discord. How can one be true to one's own conflicting thoughts or impulses? What exactly is the status and character of such a self to which one could be true? Kierkegaard's interest in Hamlet in an appendix to *Stages on Life's Way* (1845) concerns the fact that his struggle is primarily within himself rather than against the world.

Shakespeare, like the later French existentialists, is likely to have known Montaigne's *Essays*, a series of meditative reflections in which truth is sought in intense self-examination. Montaigne's view that "every human bears the whole form of the human condition" is echoed in existentialist thought. So too is Montaigne's depiction of the self as ever changing, given only precarious unity by reflection upon it. Montaigne sees the self which is observed in reflection, in fact, to be fashioned by the very process of observation: "I have no more made my book than my book has made me," he wrote. Hamlet is similarly composed, for he seems to carve out his inwardness through introspection, constructing a self through agonized soliloquies of indecision. Facing his predicament, Hamlet debates whether or not to take arms against his troubles. Hamlet's obsessively inward brooding comes to dominate what he refers to simply as "that within," and this brooding puts him into fatal conflict with the world.

The troubles preoccupying Hamlet are of course not resolved but only exacerbated by self-reflection. Thus, Hamlet famously considers whether "to be or not to be." Paralyzed by introspection, Hamlet raises the prospect of suicide, a predicament Camus will later call the "one really serious philosophical question." While concluding that suicide cannot be philosophically sanctioned,

Camus thinks that such questioning of our own existence is an inevitable response to the modern age. If Hamlet's world has been radically disrupted by his uncle's act of regicide, in the modern world science has disrupted any religious framework for understanding our lives. Yet as Camus argues, science with its atomistic picture of reality can neither offer an alternative meaning, nor erase our need for such a meaning. Camus describes as "absurd" the conflict between our need for the meaning of existence and the silence of the world to such a need. In the absence of a God to whom we would owe our existence, there is no absolute demand to continue it.

Yet despite his interest in the question of suicide, Camus does not endorse a squalid view of the human condition. The fact that we are capable of ending, and like Hamlet may even consider ending, our existence, exposes the fact of our continued living as a free choice and therefore as an affirmation of life. Camus thinks that because we are, through autonomous self-reflection, enabled with a choice in the matter, our every breath expresses the value of living. Facing the absurd, we may reject the paralysis that assails Hamlet, and affirm life without reassurances. Even in the face of inexplicable suffering, Camus thinks, we can achieve a lucid recognition of the "grandeur" of existence as it is. We can live creatively, even though any newly created meaning will be valid only in light of the absurd.

Introspection and self-reflection are crucial ingredients for existential thought, but so too is the self's autonomy or freedom. In order to realize themselves existentially, committed individuals prone to self-reflection must also be free subjects. We must be free not only from the influence of our own emotions, as the Stoics argued, or from the distractions of the world, as Augustine argued, or free to consider whether or not to exist, as Camus emphasized, but free for the determination of our lives and for moral choice. Here existentialist thinking appropriates the core project of the Enlightenment.

Immanuel Kant's formulation of human autonomy, for example, is most consequential for existentialism. In his essay "What Is Enlightenment?" (1784), Kant answers the titular question—prompted in a query to its readers by a Berlin magazine—with reference to the courage to use one's own reason without the need for another's guidance. As an enlightened self, one must emerge from a state of being a "minor" under the guardianship of religious or political authorities, and think through questions about reality and morality through the light of one's own reason. Freedom in this context means not the absence of restrictions but the ability to rule oneself, finding the source of right and wrong in what Kant called the rational "moral law" within. In Kant's view this use of moral reason can be formulated as a categorical moral imperative, as he outlines it for example in *Groundwork for a Metaphysics of Morals*, that we must never reduce other rational beings to a mere means to our own ends. To start from one's own freedom as a rational being implies the duty to respect the freedom of all other rational beings, a principle which provides the philosophical basis for ethics.

A number of existentialists will embrace Kant's principle of autonomy, if not what they regard as an overly rationalist conception of the human being and the abstract formulation of his ethical imperative. In *Notebooks for an Ethics*, Sartre argued against Kant's abstract moral maxim in order to insist that ethics "is an individual, subjective, and historical enterprise," and suggested that we must take into account the particular concrete conditions in which individuals find themselves, thus offering a more realistic prospect for an existential ethics than the more absolute position presented in other works. Sartre further dismisses any morality based on "duty" as an "impersonal" and "alienated" form of freedom. Nevertheless, Sartre repeatedly cited and relied upon Kant's promotion of individual freedom, and its universal ascription to all subjects, in his own endeavor to introduce an existential ethics.

While Sartre rejects a Kantian ethics of duty, he nevertheless embraces an ethics of responsibility. In his "Existentialism" lecture Sartre argues that in acting I am responsible not only for my choice, but also, since my choice grounds values, for all of humanity. The embrace of universal freedom will not only comprise the central political claim of existentialism but also the basis for any existentialist values at all. Beauvoir too writes, in *The Ethics of Ambiguity*, that "The source of all values resides in the freedom of man."

We have seen that the roots of existentialist thought run deep in the Western intellectual tradition. Philosophy as authentic practice, interior reflection or subjectivity, and freedom of the individual are crucial themes for the existentialist philosophy to come. Socrates and those he inspired embodied philosophy as a living commitment that later thinkers would conceive as authenticity, and they introduced forms of reflection crucial to existential self-determination. Augustine, Shakespeare, and Montaigne explored the subjective point of view and set the stage for a philosophy critically engaging the self and its ambiguities. Kant among other Enlightenment thinkers defended individual autonomy and freedom, upon which existentialist ethics will rely. While existentialist philosophies inherit these ideas from traditional sources, they come to fruition in existentialism through a distinctively modern vision of the human predicament.

4 | ROMANTIC UPHEAVALS, MODERN MOVEMENTS

Life must not be a novel that is given to us, but one that is made by us.

—NOVALIS, *Logological Fragments I*

From the late eighteenth through the nineteenth centuries, many philosophers and writers devoted their efforts to subjective aspects of existence, embracing Enlightenment philosophy's focus on individual freedom while rejecting its rationalist constraints. Romantic thinkers rebelled against the modern cult of reason and what they considered its disenchanted vision of a world seen through the prism of mathematics and wholly determined by material forces. Often in conflict with the dominant philosophical positions of their time, these thinkers privileged individual subjectivity and freedom, feeling and imagination, along with an aesthetic program for philosophy. The creative philosophies of Kierkegaard, Nietzsche, and Dostoevsky emerged in critical contest with Romanticism and would in turn feed the existentialist impulse of modernist literature in the following century.

Against the background of revolution fomenting in America and France, writers explored the intensities of emotional life in ways that broke with social convention. In Johann Wolfgang von Goethe's epistolary novel *The Sorrows of Young Werther* (1774)—paradigmatic of the *Sturm und Drang* (Storm and Stress) movement—a young artist relates in letters to his friend Wilhelm a hopeless passion for the betrothed Charlotte that contributes to his ultimate suicide. While Werther's anguish is provoked by the impossible love relation, it is also existential in nature. Werther bemoans the prospect of laboring "for the satisfaction of needs that have no other purpose than to extend our poor existence." Werther describes human beings living as if imprisoned behind walls, afraid of any "bit of freedom" they may have. He questions the status of being itself: "Can you say that anything is, when in fact it is all transient? and all passes by as fast as any storm, seldom enduring in the full force of existence?"

Goethe's novel, banned by the Vatican and many local authorities, shook the cultural life of Europe. While Goethe himself came to reject Werther's "absurd" vision of the world and its tragic conclusion, the novel anticipated existentialist attention to individual subjectivity, especially Kierkegaard's treatment of despair and Camus's reckoning with suicide as the central philosophical question. Yet Kierkegaard will see Werther as languishing in melancholy at a lower, aesthetic stage of life, and will reject suicide as an affront against God. Accepting suicide as the central philosophical question, Camus will come up with a very different solution than Werther does. We can affirm our freedom not through suicidal action but through creative living in the face of the absurd.

Werther's suffering was appreciated by the early German Romantics, including Friedrich Hölderlin and Novalis (Friedrich von Hardenberg), who expressed their own metaphysical longing for the wholeness or unity of life. The dominant philosophical problems of the time had emerged in dialogue with Kant's metaphysics, which described a division between the human mind and the world as it is in itself (which Kant called noumenal), firmly placing the latter out of our grasp. For Kant argued that the world as we experience it (the phenomenal world) is shaped by our minds, and that we cannot know it apart from these cognitive conditions. We are, moreover, divided within ourselves as beings who know the world as determined by physical causes, and as free beings capable of moral autonomy. Recognition of these divisions between self and world and within the human subject triggered an intense philosophical longing for unity on the part of Romantic thinkers and writers. On his deathbed Goethe would famously plead for "more light." But the Romantics understood that, as de Unamuno would later put it, "we die of cold and not of darkness." What Romanticism longed for was not rational illumination of being but a retrieval of lost intimacy with it.

They found some promise of recovery in aesthetic experience, for Kant also argued that through the appreciation of beautiful nature or art we could at least indirectly glimpse, within the phenomenal world, our own noumenal freedom. Reunification of the self with the whole of being becomes for the Romantic thinkers a poetic task, as we can find in Hölderlin's epistolary novel *Hyperion*, composed in the thrall of Kantian aesthetics. Like Werther's alteration between ecstatic love and despair at its impossible consummation, Hyperion experiences a cycle of blissful belonging and agonized alienation from nature. Hölderlin's novel had a profound effect on Nietzsche, whose protagonist in *Thus Spoke Zarathustra* implores his followers to be faithful to the earth. Nietzsche would condemn Romanticism as decadent, as ultimately repudiating rather than vitally affirming the world. Yet Nietzsche's own critique of modernity, his experimental and poetic writing, his skepticism about rationality and objective truth all bear Romanticism's influence. Heidegger, too, would adapt Hölderlin's thinking in identifying in poetry the founding of truth, and would read Hölderlin's as a poetic revelation of Being.

Novalis emphasized the education of the soul or "the path of inner contemplation," as he illustrates in his novel *Heinrich von Ofterdingen*. Understanding was to be achieved not primarily through worldly education but in the inner depths, as Heinrich discovers interpreting his own dreams. Such inner contemplation will be echoed in Kierkegaard's calibrations of inwardness, even though Kierkegaard, like Nietzsche, positioned himself as a critic of Romanticism. For Kierkegaard the subjectivity expressed by Novalis exuded an intoxicating aesthetic "soulfulness" rather than a motivation for the leap toward a higher stage of existence. Romantic mystification of life distracted from a grasp of the "actual." Yet as in the case of Nietzsche, Kierkegaard's own experimental, literary mode of doing philosophy, his concern for subjective experience, and his critique of exclusively rational definitions of truth bear a distinctly Romantic heritage.

Along with exploring the intensity of the self, Romantic writers and artists aimed to "romanticize the world." Against modern disenchantment, Novalis sought through poetry "to make us aware of the magic, mystery and wonder of the world . . . to educate the senses to see the ordinary as extraordinary, the familiar as strange, the mundane as sacred, the finite as infinite." Hölderlin too thought of the poet's task as one of recollecting the lost traces of the sacred. Such re-enchantment is echoed in Marcel's philosophy of the mystery of being, and in Jasper's articulation of the "encompassing" that lies beyond the boundaries of objective thought. Re-enchantment pertains to the project of Rilke's poetry, too. Critical of modern alienation, Rilke's *Sonnets to Orpheus* opens with a description of a tree as "pure transcendence," and encourages a contemplative and even ecstatic relationship to nature.

The philosophical position of the Romantics was overshadowed throughout the early nineteenth century by the rational idealism of Hegel. In his youth Hegel too had been inspired by *Werther* and by Kant's aesthetic philosophy. Along with his classmates Hölderlin and the philosopher Friedrich Schelling, Hegel declared in an early "program" for German idealism that "the philosopher must possess just as much aesthetic power as the poet." Yet just as the stormy subjectivity of *Werther* gave way to a more classically oriented wisdom in Goethe's later writings, poetry would be eclipsed in Hegel's thinking by a wholly rational system. Hegel's systematic idealism would provide the provocation and foil for Kierkegaard's philosophy of existence.

The problems of division described by Kant's philosophy were to be resolved by a dialectical synthesis that, according to Hegel, expressed not only the power of rational cognition but the rational nature of reality itself. In contrast to his early praise for the poetic, the mature Hegel would come to assert that "what is rational is real, and what is real is rational." Hegel, moreover, rendered the rational grasp of the universal as the historical development of a total system. For Hegel, "The true is the whole. But the whole is nothing other than the essence consummating itself through its development." Art along with religion would be left behind by philosophy in the progressive expression of such all-encompassing *Geist*, meaning "spirit" or "mind."

Kierkegaard launched his philosophy in direct dialogue with Hegel's philosophy. According to Kierkegaard, such systematic, rational idealism leaves behind any real consideration of individual existence, and any prospect of thinking the problem of faith. What is individual and particular, the human subject or self, cannot be grasped merely as "a paragraph in a system." Existence had to be grasped in and through individual living, through personal experience and subjective commitment, such as Kierkegaard saw manifest in the life and death of Socrates. Kierkegaard proposed that philosophical thinking should be grounded in the existence of the individual, the person's confrontation with the idea of the infinite, and the difficult experience of singularity this entails.

Despite his criticisms of the movement, Kierkegaard also shared with Romanticism a critique of abstract rationality and social convention. In "The Present Age" (1846), part of a larger literary review, Kierkegaard regarded the modern world as having lost the revolutionary inspiration that had contributed to the early Romantic moment. Kierkegaard's essay would appear just two years before revolutions would once again erupt in Europe, yet his concern was not with political freedom but with the forms of subjectivity and the relations among individuals in society promoted by modern culture.

Kierkegaard argued that while a previous age generated individuals who acted heroically and lived passionately committed to ideals, in his own century such action and commitment had been displaced by what he calls "reflection." By this is meant not the meditative wisdom of Socrates or the Stoics but calculative thinking and a pragmatic seeking of advantage. In such a context, action, even toward the highest goals, is considered foolish wherever it does not gain worldly results, and selfless generosity is easily confused for weakness. Kierkegaard illustrates this with the analogy of a treasure sought by all at the center of a frozen lake, where the ice is thin. The spectacle of skaters coming close to the treasure is enjoyed, but the skater who risks falling through the ice is ridiculed by others, who cannot fathom the merit of risk or self-sacrifice.

Reflection, by which options are considered, measured in their advantages and disadvantages, is necessary for making any considered choice. But in a dispassionate age, reflection fails to be oriented by a higher value, and is unchecked by commitment, decision, or action. Reflection is also related to envy, which Kierkegaard calls the "negative unifying principle" of the modern age. In envy one sees oneself, one's opinions, as reflected in the eyes of others, while at the same time others are measured only in contrast to oneself. Envy binds people together in mutual selfishness. Superficiality, or the arrogant display of one's advantages, is but its inverse manifestation. Rather than inward reflection on our lives, there is endless externalization.

Kierkegaard admits that even apart from the specific situation of modern life, being or becoming a self is difficult. As he writes in *Sickness unto Death*, we escape from ourselves because it is "far easier and safer to be like the others, to become an imitation, a number, a cipher in the crowd" than to be and feel ourselves alone in our singularity. Our tendency to flee from ourselves into the crowd has source in fear of individuation, for, as he writes in *The Concept of Anxiety*, "deep within every human being there still lives the anxiety over the possibility of being alone in the world, forgotten by God, overlooked among the millions and millions in this enormous household. A person keeps this anxiety at a distance by looking at the many round about." While Romantics looked for an aesthetic solution to our metaphysical isolation, Kierkegaard held up the possibility of religious faith, yet in a form exceptionally demanding for the believer.

Later existentialists, including Nietzsche, Sartre, Beauvoir, and Camus, will identify the absence of God as an existential challenge, but Kierkegaard found the prospect of faith in God just as demanding. Kierkegaard argues that the infinite God exceeds the finite human understanding. True faith can be expressed neither in logic nor in deference to religious authority, but only through individual commitment. For Kierkegaard, faith is not rational but rather expresses "the highest passion of subjectivity." While Kierkegaard never used the expression "leap of faith" in his writings, he wrote of "the qualitative transition of the leap from unbeliever to believer." Such a leap, needless to say, lies outside the bounds of rational calculation.

There are no instructions for taking a religious leap, and it singles out the individual absolutely, as Kierkegaard shows in his meditation, in *Fear and Trembling,* on the biblical story of Abraham and Isaac. Contravening his own universal commandment "thou shalt not kill," God is said to have ordered Abraham to kill his long-awaited son Isaac. What could expose more starkly the absurdity of existence than a divine command both self-contradictory and devastating to its recipient? Only in fear and trembling, Kierkegaard argues, could Abraham choose how to respond to this command. Abraham could respond only as a "knight of faith," believing somehow that he may get Isaac back "by virtue of the absurd."

Abraham's situation is, Kierkegaard says, a paradox. Should he accept God's command, Abraham's act would make him both pious and murderous, and in this paradoxical situation he would have to overstep any universal imperative. As Kierkegaard puts it, to achieve the religious the individual must accept a "teleological suspension of the ethical." This means both accepting the universality of an ethical law and canceling it out for a still higher singularity anchored in nothing but faith. The vertiginous anxiety attending Abraham's choice characterizes the ultimate test of existence. The extremity of this kind of test defines the religious for Kierkegaard, who criticized the church of his time for offering only comforting reassurances. In such a context, faith may require personal rebellion, albeit one that for a modern knight of faith may be wholly inward.

Despite their radically different stances on the question of God, Nietzsche shares with the philosophy of Kierkegaard a concern for passionate human experience that exceeds the boundaries of rational knowledge. Nietzsche challenged the categorical oppositions by which we distinguish between truth and falsity, reality and illusion. He asked whether our drive for truth, our means of achieving certainty about the nature of reality, themselves contain a certain element of fiction.

Nietzsche was not the only philosopher to assert that "God is dead." Hegel, in a different context, wrote it first, and Dostoevsky, in "The Grand Inquisitor" chapter of *The Brothers Karamazov*, explored the ethical implications of the prospect. Yet with his proclamation Nietzsche did not simply reject religion, but identified a source of cultural hypocrisy. For modern Europe as a culture no longer believed in its old religious certainties, since science, including that of evolution, had eclipsed religious explanations for human life and its place in reality. Yet society continued to demand subordination to the idea of God, to religious norms of conduct and to the institutional powers upheld by religion, capitalizing on the moralization of fear and guilt.

At the same time, Nietzsche recognized that the rupture brought about by the "death" of God offered an opportunity for humankind. This would be not to subscribe to a different absolute truth but to overcome the need for absolutes. We could, he thought, transform ourselves into a more creative and more courageous species. As individuals we may become capable of accepting the ambiguities and complexities of a reality in flux, of the transient storm that provoked Werther's angst.

Nietzsche recognized the threat of nihilism—for if God is dead, and all values and truths can be challenged, there is no stable meaning or purpose on which we can rely. As Dostoevsky wrote, "anything is permitted" in God's absence. In his *Genealogy of Morals*, Nietzsche exposed the social conditions underlying the norms of different cultures. Nietzsche thought the human spirit had, in Europe, withered under a moral and intellectual regime at once fixated on a world beyond and castigating earthly life as sordid or ignoble. Nietzsche called for a "revaluation of all values" by exposing what he regarded as unconscious and powerful instincts underlying the human drive for knowledge, truth, and morality.

Yet Nietzsche himself rejected nihilism, holding out hope for the invention of new, life-affirming ways of being. Although he criticized a rationalist conception of autonomy and mocked the idea of a pure free will securely anchoring all rational decision, Nietzsche affirmed freedom in two ways. Freedom was to be gained through liberation from metaphysical prejudices and prudish fears, and it could be promoted through the transformations of human creativity. If not through the ideas of religion or even science, then as a work of art, life may be justified.

Nietzsche's philosophy has been criticized for praising the strong over the weak, for distinguishing the monumental acts of human exertion from the everyday habits of the masses. This unmistakably elitist tendency in Nietzsche's thinking is however countered to some extent by his liberating belief in human possibility. Nietzsche argued that whatever we have been or are, we can become something new. Our limitations as individuals are malleable, not grounded in some fixed ontology or in the authority of the status quo.

Nietzsche criticized the presumption attending some popular understandings of evolution that a more recently evolved species is necessarily superior to one that came before it, or that human life and rationality are the pinnacle of evolution. We are in some respects weaker than other species, and far more foolish. The cognition of which we are arrogantly proud has also led us to doubt the very value of our existence and to develop historic prejudices against earth-bound life. Yet as a species, Nietzsche believed, we are still a work in progress. Rather than only mute recipients of evolutionary forces, we can take part in them, and creatively contribute to what we will become.

Nietzsche's interest in creativity was expressed in an early work, *The Birth of Tragedy*, in which Nietzsche developed the idea of the Apollonian and Dionysian instincts, or impulses of nature expressed through human activity. These impulses are named after the Greek gods Apollo and Dionysus. Apollo represents an orderly view of life, the individuation and order of beings as they can be grasped by reason. Apollo is the sun god, and we recall that Plato used the sun in *The Republic* as a metaphor for the eternal forms and the light of reason that could discern them. Apollo is also the god of dreams, and Nietzsche understood how imagery can be employed in Apollonian fashion in deference to measure and boundary. The Apollonian art of Greek sculpture, for example, yields works that are idealized, static, and fixed in their boundaries. Nietzsche thinks that the vision of a world wholly ordered by fixed principles and formally knowable by reason is a beautiful illusion, one that, like Parmenides's philosophy, hides the chaos of underlying reality.

In contrast, the chaotic aspects of reality are expressed through the impulse named for Dionysus, the god of music, intoxication, and sexuality. A Dionysian insight into nature grasps the fusion of beings, the chaos of constant change as emphasized in the thought of Heraclitus (and in ancient cult worship to the god). Nietzsche's study of the origins of ancient Greek tragedy aims to demonstrate how the tension between the Apollonian and the Dionysian impulses gives rise to great art.

Yet Nietzsche's study of ancient tragedy was also intended as a critique of modern culture. While Plato had suppressed the Dionysian insight in favor of a philosophy of eternal forms, the modern age, Nietzsche thinks, suppresses the Dionysian impulse by its reductive rationalism and through a moralistic disregard for sensuous experience. Moreover, Nietzsche argues—against his one-time idol Arthur Schopenhauer—that the ancient Greeks excelled at the art of tragedy not because they were pessimistic people, but because they were overfull with life, a vitality that allowed for serene enjoyment of the tragic spectacle. If the modern human could cultivate a new spirit of tragedy—Nietzsche hoped for a time that this might be inspired in then contemporary music—this could enable the courage to embrace life in all its finitude without otherworldly reassurances.

In the final decade of Nietzsche's life, mental and physical illness made him vulnerable to exploitation by his sister and nationalist brother-in-law, who created a Nietzsche cult and archive in Weimar. Nietzsche himself was responsible for the anti-democratic bent of some of his ideas, including the idea of a superior type of human being of the future who would overstep weaker forms, and racially charged criticism of various peoples (though it should be pointed out that this included many scathing criticisms of the Germans, and that Nietzsche loathed anti-Semitism). These ideas, however, were taken out of context and distorted in their use by German nationalists, and understandably this marred the reception of Nietzsche's thought for decades after the Second World War. More recent scholars have recognized the cosmopolitan, as well as ecological, dimensions of Nietzsche's philosophy, while many of his ideas still circulate in postmodern thought.

Kierkegaard was devoted to the subjective truth of Christianity, and Nietzsche heralded the death of God, and yet their philosophies share important existential themes. Both Kierkegaard and Nietzsche critically develop Romanticism's investment in concrete individual experience, in the aspects of subjectivity overshadowed by Enlightenment rationalism, and promote creative thinking in response. For diverging reasons, both criticized institutional religion—Kierkegaard to promote the inwardness of individual faith, Nietzsche to urge the invention of new values that validate earthly life. Their philosophies each profoundly affirm human possibility and call out to the human individual not to exist passively, but to choose and to become what they might be.

Echoing the Romantic thinkers' engagement of philosophy in poetic form, Kierkegaard and Nietzsche also exercised creative modes of philosophical writing and expression. Long before the Parisian existentialists came to dominate the literary scene, Kierkegaard and Nietzsche used fiction, aphorism, and experimental writing to experiment with philosophical ideas. A number of Kierkegaard's works such as *Fear and Trembling, Either/Or*, and *Repetition* are novelistic, featuring imagined characters and scenes, and most of his works bear pseudonymous, fictional authors. Nietzsche's idea of the eternal return—the directive to live as if one's existence were to be repeated over and over again—is delivered in an allegorical novel, *Thus Spoke Zarathustra*. In Nietzsche's writings metaphor, imagery, allegory, and other literary devices are central to a form of thinking that courts productive paradox and repels systematic summation.

If Kierkegaard and Nietzsche creatively elaborated the existential philosophy of the nineteenth century, the latter emerged in fictional form with the works of the Russian author Fyodor Dostoevsky. His most famous novel, *Crime and Punishment* (1866), presented the human struggle between good and evil as impenetrable by logic. In this work Dostoevsky evoked themes of guilt, anxiety, and the limits of rationality, all of which would become important subjects for existential thinkers to come.

Dostoevsky's novella *Notes from Underground* (1864), with its revolutionary exposure of the difficulties of human freedom and the experience of dread in a world experienced as godless, left recognizable traces in existentialist literature, as we will see in the next chapter. The "underground man" describes himself as a "sick" man suffering from an excess of consciousness, echoing the analysis of despair in Kierkegaard's *The Sickness unto Death* and signaling the same critical debt to the Romantics. The underground man is also alienated from a society felt to be superficial, hypocritical, materialist, and abstract, criticisms wholly in tune with those of his Danish and German counterparts. Nietzsche, who wrote of his "extraordinary joy" in discovering *Notes from Underground* by chance in a bookshop, felt an immediate "instinct of kinship" with the Russian author.

Dostoevsky's anti-hero is the picture of alienation in a secular world. The underground man lacks the consolations of religion, yet despises fashionable philosophies according to which reason should wholly determine human action. Rationalist programs in ethics, of which a fair number were proposed in Dostoevsky's time, would have human activity orchestrated by design, as if human beings were ants building an anthill, as the underground man puts it. Even if such a plan could yield maximum harmony and contentment, it would cost us freedom, individuality, and human diversity. The underground man insists that even irrationality is preferable to a dogmatically programmed existence, or a life of efficient calculation. He goes so far as to proclaim that while to deny that "2 + 2 = 4" is obviously folly, to do so would at least preserve an aspect of our humanity, insofar as it resists conformity. For freedom, not a narrowly defined, calculative reason, is what gives the human being dignity.

But the underground man's alienation is overwhelming. This becomes crucial in the novella when he is unable to accept the love that is offered to him by a young prostitute he meant to save from a terrible fate. After failing Liza, the underground man withdraws in spiteful despair. While the underground man fails to overcome his despair, other than by retreating from society to write about it, in *Crime and Punishment* the convicted murderer Raskolnikov ultimately accepts redemption through Christian love. While they will not accept Dostoevsky's spiritual solution, twentieth-century existentialist writers will explore his motif of the despairing outsider.

In the wake of the literary philosophies of Kierkegaard, Nietzsche, and Dostoevsky, existentialism finds its own literary footing with modernism, as we will see in the next chapter. Modernity designates an era in which a culture has radically shifted from its past, while modern*ism* designates more narrowly art and literature that respond both formally and thematically to developments of modernity. The challenge to rationality and the intensification of subjective perspective that preoccupied existentialist thinkers in the nineteenth century will become adapted by modernist writers and artists as they break away from realism and invent new ways of reflecting on the modern world.

5 | EXISTENTIALISM AS LITERATURE

THE TWENTIETH CENTURY

Do I dare disturb the universe?
 —T. S. ELIOT, "The Love Song of J. Alfred Prufrock"

While scientific and industrial advances in the nineteenth century left traditional views of the world profoundly challenged, the twentieth century would see two world wars wreak unprecedented destruction and suffering, profoundly shaking confidence in historical progress. Rainer Maria Rilke's *Duino Elegies*, begun in 1912 and composed over the following decade, opens with a striking image of abandonment: "Who, if I would cry out, would hear me from the angelic orders?" Around the same time, T. S. Eliot had his J. Alfred Prufrock, an old man who had seen the moment of his greatness flicker, question whether he may "dare disturb the universe." If Prufrock demurs, existentialists will respond in the affirmative, while describing the absurdity and anxiety of a world bereft of any stable meaning.

In the aftermath of the First World War, the search for new values and literary forms to express them yielded an ambivalent sense of possibility. In 1922, the speaker of Eliot's *The Waste Land* laments "these fragments I have shored against my ruins," describing a crisis as acute for the individual as it is for war-torn Europe. Though mostly registering devastation, the poem also describes lilacs emerging, as if in a cruel paradox, from the "dead land," and persists in asking what else might grow out of "this stony rubbish." The poem's rhythms, however ironical and fractured, hint at the enthusiasms of the jazz age. Alongside bewilderment, suffering, and loss, there is exhilaration, too. Finishing the *Elegies* in the same year as Eliot's greatest poem, Rilke's speaker gives up wooing the angels, advocating instead an image of earth-bound happiness. The catastrophe of a second world war will render yet more urgent any such revaluation of modern life.

Existentialism's approaches to human existence naturally align with creative forms of expression, and throughout modernist literature we find recurring existential themes. Literature is adept at exploring individual points of view, and modernist literature tends to explore the "stream of consciousness" of its protagonists. Literature can consider ideas within concretely imagined scenarios, while modernist writers tend to swing free of conventional descriptions of reality. Such features make modern literature suited for the exploration of existentialist ideas.

Rilke's only novel, *The Notebooks of Malte Laurids Brigge* (1910), presents the fictional journals of a young impoverished nobleman who arrives in Paris at the turn of the twentieth century. Malte's alienation from the world around him echoes the agonies of Dostoevsky's underground man and would profoundly influence Sartre's fictional writings. Adrift from his ancestral roots, Malte finds urban life hostile and all-too-intense, with its crowds, noise, electric lights, and traffic. The hospital across from his lodgings symbolizes the threat of an anonymous "factory-like" death. Painfully aware of his poverty and his downtrodden appearance, Malte feels hounded by the vagrants he is afraid of resembling.

Suffering a breakdown and submitting to electric shock treatment, Malte finds solace in writing about his childhood, and in modern poetry and Impressionist art. Yet even the sense of his own precariousness also intensifies Malte's perceptions. Sounds, smells, and images are vivified, and defamiliarized: a woman holding her face in her hands is said to leave it there when she looks up, leading Malte to muse on the way faces, like masks, can be well- or ill-fitting for their wearers. Rilke's painstaking account of Malte's examination of the walls of a partly torn-down house is particularly prescient. Its intimate description of the details of perception and the variable associations of the appearance of the walls will be praised by Heidegger as "pure phenomenology."

Both Malte's perception of things in their bare presence, and the Dostoevsky-inspired alienation that prepares for such revelation, are adapted by Sartre for his own philosophical fiction. Antoine Roquentin, protagonist of Sartre's novel *Nausea*, suffers revulsion when the ordinary look of the world falls away and the essential contingency of things is exposed—beginning with a stone he cannot bring himself to throw in the sea, a scrap of newspaper on the ground he cannot bring himself to pick up. Gradually this leads to a kind of hallucinatory breakdown, with Roquentin confronted by objects such as a trolley car seat and the root of a chestnut tree, the ordinarily fixed meanings of which seem to dissolve. Roquentin gradually understands that meaning is neither necessary nor inherent in things. The sense the world has for us is dependent upon the meanings we habitually attribute to them.

While Dostoevsky's depiction of alienation is primarily moral and Rilke's is aesthetic, Sartre's is entirely phenomenological. Sartre's aim in the novel is to show that how the world ordinarily appears to us is contingent upon the constitutive contributions of the mind. The world as we ordinarily see it—as meaningful, orderly, familiar—is structured in these ways by our consciousness. This insight of course precedes phenomenology. It was first articulated by Kant, who as mentioned in the previous chapter argued that our knowledge of the world is shaped by the necessary categories of the mind. We can never know or perceive the world as it truly is in itself, an insight that provoked longing among Romantic interpreters of Kant. Phenomenology, however, demands that we bracket questions about the ontological status of the world in itself in order to regard the world as phenomena and examine how it appears to us. Sartre experimentally imagines such a bracketing, exploring how it might look when our habitual meanings fall away, when "being-in-itself" before us is deprived of its usual meaning and experienced instead only in its phenomenal qualities. Being becomes not tree roots or trolley car seats, but heavy or light, sticky or smooth, heaving with life or cold and inert, and above all indifferent to our attempts to understand it. Sartre explores the consequences of the fact that it is we who order the world, by our language, practices, and cognitive habits, into a set of relations familiar to us. *Nausea* is a philosophical-literary experiment that attempts to illustrate the contingency of the world as we know it.

Yet the novel is also existential. If the appearance of the world is contingent for Sartre, the same is true of ourselves, and of our social roles. We tend to think of ourselves as having an essence, a sort of character that defines us, one by which we may feel we can be recognized, to which we might refer in explaining ourselves or our actions. But such a view of oneself leads to "bad faith," to which a number of characters succumb in Sartre's novel. The so-called self-taught man whom Roquentin sees regularly in the local library defines himself by his humanism. When Roquentin asks him about the very people he claims to love, the self-taught man cannot tell him the color of their eyes. He prides himself on his self-directed learning, but it turns out that he is reading books in alphabetical order, failing to choose, to develop his own perspective on any topic. The local doctor Rogé basks in self-satisfaction at being a highly "experienced" man and is regarded by the towns-people as such. But he fails to realize that, Roquentin muses, such experience might amount to but a long accumulation of errors or illusions. Another character frequenting the local café, Monsieur Achille, is content to be defined by others as a "crazy loon." His bad faith lies in accepting his role defined by others and acting it out.

Roquentin's own self-reckoning occurs when he realizes that his past memories and adventures had long served to justify his life. But he comes to see that these, too, are merely reconstructions from the past, dissolved into the words he has used to retell them. Roquentin finds relief from the nausea only when, listening repeatedly to a jazz song, he comes to embrace contingency as the source of freedom and creativity. He abandons his research project—the biography of an aristocrat active during the French Revolution—and resolves to write a novel instead.

Just as the outsider status of Dostoevsky's underground man influenced Rilke and Sartre, it is echoed in the literary works of

Camus. The protagonist of Camus's novel *The Fall*, Jean-Baptiste Clamence, is a self-described "judge-penitent" who, perched at his nightly haunt in Amsterdam translating between foreigners and the Dutch barman, judges the sins of others while nursing his own guilt. His contention that "anyone who has considerably meditated on man . . . is led to feel nostalgia for the primates" suggests the influence of Kafka, who in his story "Report to an Academy" depicts an ape evolved to the intelligence of the average European man. But in his moral confession Clamence echoes the underground man's moral failure. Just as the underground man had failed to come to the aid of the young prostitute, Clamence eventually reveals his own failure, some years before, to intervene as a young woman on a bridge jumped to her death. The critical mirror Clamence holds up to humanity will turn out to reveal, in stark outline, his own fall.

Camus achieved international fame with his novel *The Stranger* (*L'Etranger*), the protagonist of which is an anti-hero immune to conventional meaning. At the novel's opening Mersault is unmoved by news of his mother's death, an event which he considers to have made no change in his life. The day after he buries his mother, he goes swimming, takes in a comic film, and sleeps with his girlfriend. Later in the novel, Mersault shoots a man on the beach, explaining in his murder trial only that the sun pained his eyes.

Here Camus departs from Dostoevsky's *Crime and Punishment*, where Raskolnikov attempts to rationalize crime by reference to his exceptionality and by calculating the social benefit that could be gleaned from the proceeds. Mersault offers no justification for murder, only a description of the sun beating down on him. "It was the same sun as on the day I buried Maman and, like then, my forehead especially was hurting me, all of the veins pulsating together beneath the skin."

While Dostoevsky's anti-hero comes to accept his guilt and hold out for religious redemption, Camus's Mersault rejects any abstract values. Only when he faces execution does Mersault wake up to his existence, enlivened not by fear or regret, but by a surge of elation, recognizing that he has been happy all along. Although Mersault comes to feel solidarity with human beings in our common finitude, the ethical implications of his crime remain unexplored. Yet Camus's novel masterfully envisions how existence can be affirmed even as it loses all human meaning.

The political implications of the colonial situation in *The Stranger*—that the victim is an Arab man shot in Algeria by a descendant of French colonists—are skillfully considered in a recent work, *The Mersault Investigation* (2013) by the Algerian writer Kamel Daoud. The novel revisits the events of *The Stranger* from the perspective of the victim's brother Harun, thus personalizing what to Mersault was merely an anonymous incident. While the Arab characters are unnamed in Camus's novel, Daoud gives the victim a name, "Musa," illuminating by implicit contrast the practices of European colonialism which contextualize the events of Camus's story. Despite its implicit critique, Daoud's novel affirms Camus's existential themes, particularly its vision of absurdity. When Harun himself kills a Frenchman in the wake of Algerian independence, the precise timing of the act will determine whether he is to be considered a revolutionary or a murderer. As if he were a reader of Camus, Harun compares his own fate to that of Sisyphus, and like Mersault, demands freedom from religious dogma in coping with the consequences of his crime.

Camus followed Dostoevsky in offering a murderer as anti-hero. This theme, transported to the context of segregated America, was explored by Richard Wright in *The Outsider* (1953). Wright's novel suggests the impossible pursuit of freedom, and even of meaning, for a protagonist struggling in the context of brutally oppressive racism. Cross Damon, a highly and overly conscious individual, feels himself to be capable of freely endowing the world with meaning, yet pursues his freedom in reckless and violent ways. When he is himself dying from gunshot wounds, Damon experiences an epiphany of sorts. Recalling Dostoevsky's solution for Raskolnikov, Wright has Damon remembering the words of his mother that "life is a promise" given by God and without that promise, "life's nothing."

All of these writers contend with the problem of absurdity. In Camus's *The Stranger*, the public, the press, and the authorities cannot understand the nature of Mersault's crime. The murderer admits his guilt, yet recognizes the contingency involved. His friend Raymond, having earlier provoked hostilities with the victim, happened to hand Mersault a gun. Only because it was so hot had Mersault wandered toward the stream where the victim was waiting. He cannot say why, after firing the first shot, he kept on shooting. Instead of offering an explanation that might help to exculpate him, Mersault merely describes the sun which had beaten down on him mercilessly that afternoon. There is no motive for Mersault's crime, and yet a motive must be found, not only for the prosecutor to secure a capital sentence, but for the deed to be comprehended by the public.

Mersault's only virtue may be telling the truth exactly as he sees it. He turns out to be more honest than his prosecutor, who, in order to explain the crime, characterizes Mersault as monstrous. Mersault's failure to show emotion at his mother's funeral, that he there smoked and drank café au lait, are cited as evidence against him. In his cell after the verdict, Mersault ponders his fate, considers the absurdity of the guillotine machine, which forces the condemned to hope it is in proper working order, so that the death is painless. For a moment Mersault tries to conceive a way around the inevitable, and he pours out his objections in a burst of anger against the chaplain who tries to make him repent. Yet the novel ends with Mersault's ecstatic realization of blissful contentment.

Absurdity, as expressed in Camus's novel, has little to do with the topsy-turvy, random, or irrational promoted by modernist avant-garde aesthetics—some manifestations of which as we will see can be linked to existential themes. We have seen that absurdity as Camus conceived it arises from our need for meaning and its conflict with the silence of the world. Sometimes the course of events that shape human lives seem not only without inherent meaning but contrary to or against any possible sense or purpose. This is true of Mersault's crime: he is guilty, but not in any way that can explain his deed, and there is no way around his execution. Camus suggests in the novel that, since death is the inevitable ultimate end for all of us, life is tinged with absurdity. To the priest, Mersault rages:

From the dark horizon of my future a sort of slow, persistent breeze had been blowing toward me, all my life long, from the years that were to come. And on its way that breeze had levelled out all the ideas that people dried to foist on me . . . All alike would be condemned to die one day; his turn, too, would come like the others'. And what difference did it make if, after being charged with murder, he were executed because he didn't weep at his mother's funeral, since it all came to the same thing in the end?

This evocation of death underscores the rejection of any worldly meaning that might assuage our need to explain our life and our suffering.

While Sartre complained that Camus's novel offered no ethical perspective, Camus expressed in other works a fundamental commitment to ethics, grounded in love for others. In *The Myth of Sisyphus* Camus argues that absurdist reasoning affirms the rights of others to life. Since, as self-reflective beings, we are capable of deciding not to live, our every breath is an affirmation of life. While being alive, we cannot justifiably denounce life as a value. Camus suggests that maintaining one's own life involves also an affirmation of other lives: "The moment that we recognize the impossibility of absolute negation—and merely to be alive is to recognize this—the very first thing that cannot be denied is the right of others to live." This does not provide an extensive elaboration of how to live, but identifies its basic ethical fundament: "From the moment that life is recognized as good, it becomes good for all."

We can see the implications of this perspective in Camus's novel *The Plague*. A doctor who is fighting a bubonic outbreak in the Algerian city of Oran refuses to accept a priest's religious dismissal of the death of a child. While the priest accepts the death as an expression of divine love beyond human understanding, the doctor holds that the only appropriate response to such meaningless suffering is to rebel against it. The plague in the novel can be read as an allegory for the Nazi occupation of France, for Camus himself was active in the Resistance, and this establishes a political dimension to the novel. This historical context makes all the more exigent Camus's affirmation of the value of joy in life itself and his ethical demand to promote the well-being of others.

Beauvoir engaged concrete existentialist problems in her works of fiction and regarded literary works as equally capable of exploring "metaphysics" as any philosophical argumentation. In Beauvoir's novel *All Men Are Mortal*, the protagonist Fosca, like Kafka's hunter Gracchus, cannot die. Echoing Heidegger's notion of being-toward-death, Fosca discovers that the prospect of death is necessary for human beings to maintain a commitment to life's value. In an early short story, "Marguerite," the protagonist is a young woman breaking free, as Beauvoir herself did, from the restrictions of her religious upbringing. The naïve Marguerite ventures into Parisian nightclubs, experiments with vice, risk, and unconventional love. Infatuation with her wayward brother-in-law Denis and his avant-garde spirituality leads to heartbreak. In the wake of these experiences, she comes to rediscover life on her own terms, learning "to look things straight in the face, without accepting oracles or ready-made values."

In her novel *She Came to Stay,* Beauvoir explores Husserl's idea of phenomenological constitution. Beauvoir shows how reality comes to life for—or in phenomenological terms, is "constituted" by—a human consciousness. From the perspective of the protagonist Françoise, "her presence revived things from their inanimateness." Yet *She Came to Stay* is predominantly dedicated to the exploration of social conflict, figured through the sexual rivalry between two women characters attached to the same man, the actor Pierre.

The situation was loosely based on a triangular relationship Beauvoir and Sartre, when in their thirties, had with a former student. When at the end of the novel Françoise kills the younger Xavière, it is to expunge her own guilt at sleeping with Xavière's young boyfriend in revenge for the intrusion on her relationship with Pierre. In the novel Beauvoir offers an explicit adaptation of Hegel's notion of the human subject as both for itself (free desiring consciousness) and in itself (an object in the world that can be acted upon, even negated, by others), and of the dialectic between "master" and "slave" in the struggle for recognition. In the murder scene, Françoise wonders, "But how was it possible for a consciousness not her own to exist? In that case, it was she who did not exist. She repeated, *She or I*, and pulled down the lever."

In *The Ethics of Ambiguity*, Beauvoir argues that some ambiguity always remains between our own subjective freedom and its objective limits—including the subjectivities of others. As she writes: "The for-itself carries nothingness in its heart and can be annihilated, whether in the very upsurge of its existence or through the world in which it exists." Françoise's refusal to cope with such ambiguity is disturbingly explored in *She Came to Stay*. Although Beauvoir later expressed ambivalence about the novel's tragic ending, it dramatizes the quotation from Hegel which serves to introduce the novel: "Each conscience seeks the death of the other."

Sartre is likely to have been influenced by Beauvoir's novel as he described, in a famous chapter of *Being and Nothingness*, the annihilating "look" of the other. Such conflict is illustrated in Sartre's most famous play, *No Exit*, with its well-known proclamation that "hell is other people." Three condemned souls find themselves trapped together in a room for eternity, each needing a recognition from another that will never be granted. While Sartre claims that human freedom is absolute, it would seem that the cooperation of others may be required to realize freedom even in the most fundamental task of self-recognition.

Franz Kafka is among the writers whose radical departures from realism extend the reach of existentialist thinking. In Kafka's stories and novels, the most banal scenes of everyday life are uncannily transformed. In the story "The Metamorphosis," the traveling salesman Gregor Samsa, tired of the daily grind, wakes up one day to find himself transformed into an insect. He is eventually killed by a wound from an apple thrown by his father, and swept out with the garbage by the maid. In Kafka's story "The Judgment," George Bendemann, a successful young businessman whose aging father suddenly condemns him to death by drowning, puts up no fight and jumps from a bridge. In "A Country Doctor," the protagonist is called out in the middle of the night to attend to a sick patient. He ends up rather bafflingly undressed by the villagers and placed in bed with the boy whose putrid and inexplicable wound he cannot heal. The doctor finds himself attempting to reach home with unearthly horses that move so slowly he may never arrive. In the novel *The Trial*, Josef K. is arrested without charge on his thirtieth birthday at his rented lodgings. He spends a year in fruitless pursuit of his case, only to be killed "like a dog" by officials one year later, the charges against him having never been revealed. Humorous or disturbing, and always estranging, these fictions reconfigure ordinary life in absurd ways, provoking confusion through images of extraordinary clarity. While profoundly influential for existentialism, however, all of these works may appear to cast doubt on one of its principal claims: that we are free to shape our nature, to determine our own essence.

The problem of freedom is explicitly posed by a parable told within the text of *The Trial* (also published independently as "Before the Law"). Nothing prevents a man from the country, having wasted his entire life waiting to gain access to the law, from entering the doorway. Yet inexplicably, he never does so. When the doorkeeper shuts the door, he tells the man that the entrance was made "only for you." In the novel's last chapter Josef K. seems to expect, and yield to, his own murder. How is freedom to be exercised against external obstacles as well as those within, if the source of power cannot be clearly identified? Kafka's narrative seems to illuminate the problem of freedom in the negative, forcing readers to question whether we are free at all, and, if so, why freedom may elude us.

While Camus identified absurdity as a metaphysical condition, and Kafka wove a fictional atmosphere of the absurd, the idea has been more immediately related to aspects of human experience. For black American writers in the era of segregation, it has been argued, everyday life was charged with an absurdity borne of racial oppression. W. E. B. Du Bois, famous for his theoretical and political writings, wrote a short story, "The Comet" (1920), which can be interpreted in this light. Du Bois depicts a black bank employee Jim who, having been sent to an underground vault to retrieve some papers, survives a catastrophe initiated by the collision of a comet spewing poison gas. For a brief while Jim appears to be the only survivor, and only in these conditions can he dare to enter a restaurant on Fifth Avenue and partake of a meal, having to walk literally over the dead bodies of the white patrons. Jim's freedom and his liberated relationship with a white survivor are short-lived, however, as other survivors appear and re-establish racial segregation. Du Bois's story suggests that only a total apocalypse could wipe out the poison of racism. Well over a decade before the reflections of Sartre and Beauvoir pondered the ontology of freedom, Du Bois illuminated its contingency—its dependence on the social and political conditions that make up the situation of the existing individual.

Chester B. Himes, an African American writer, engaged the concept of absurdity for a memoir, *My Life of Absurdity*. In 1955 Himes found himself so impoverished that he had to pawn his typewriter, while knowing his novels were selling at every newsstand. Upon this situation he reflected that "my life itself was so absurd I saw everything as absurd." Himes understood this as a communal condition, for "realism and absurdity are so similar in the lives of American blacks one cannot tell the difference." The very summer Himes pawned his typewriter, Emmett Till, a fourteen-year-old black boy, was lynched in Mississippi. Till had been accused by a white woman of whistling at her (she would later admit that she had lied), and his murderers were acquitted. Himes concluded that existential absurdity—and here a despairing rather than hopeful sense—may be inextricable from the concrete and often violent denial of freedom oppressed people have suffered.

Absurdity is but one of many existentialist themes in Ralph Ellison's novel *Invisible Man* (1952). The protagonist, downtrodden by racial oppression, falls down a manhole during a riot. After it is covered by white police officers, he decides to live underground, finding there a long-forgotten basement section of a building. Unwilling "to accept the harsh nature of reality," as Ellison himself described his protagonist, he burns over a thousand lightbulbs, and, as he listens to blues music, analyzes the social invisibility inflicted by racism.

Ellison spoke of the "existential tradition" in black American life that emerges from the blues and spirituals, and he was directly influenced by T. S. Eliot's use of the blues and jazz in *The Waste Land*. His protagonist's underground predicament also literalizes Dostoevsky's metaphor, and yet in a Kafkaesque twist, mirrors precisely the irrationality and cruelty of his society. In the end, Ellison's underground man emerges into society with a new understanding that "even an invisible man has a socially responsible role to play."

In this respect Ellison rises to greater literary heights than Sartre, for whom responsibility to others, while lauded in philosophical manifestos, was scarcely envisioned in his literary narratives. Solidarity for Sartre is a logical extension of the self's absolute freedom, to be expressed through political activism. Ellison achieves the concretization in literature of both the predicament of a specific character within racial oppression and a felt communal responsibility, as he put it, for "the essential unity of human experience as a whole." While Sartre envisions subject-object dichotomy as a metaphysical framework for social conflict, Ellison envisions the agony of coming to terms with, and transcending, a heinous historical oppression.

Sartre recognized the value of what he called "engaged literature" in publishing Ellison's contemporary Wright in *Les Temps Modernes*. The protagonist of Wright's short story "The Man Who Lived Underground" (first published in 1944), much like

Ellison's, resonates with Dostoevsky's underground man. Wright was inspired by a story he had read in *True Detective* magazine about a man who lived under the streets of Los Angeles for over a year, subsisting on goods he was able to procure through stores' connections to the sewers. While rooted in this real-worldly example, Wright had counted Dostoevsky as his model for writing since his youth. Wright both literalizes and transforms Dostoevsky's metaphor of the underground to express a uniquely African American experience.

In Wright's rendering, the protagonist Fred Daniels, a black man falsely accused of murder, disappears down the city's sewer system and makes his home there. Gradually he loses his sense of identity. He finds a typewriter and begins to write but, after so much time alone, he cannot for a time remember his own name. Paradoxically, through his own estranged innocence, the protagonist comes to think about guilt as a general human condition.

Existential themes can be found in a number of other literary works that might not be typically associated with any philosophical movement. In Herman Melville's *Moby-Dick*, Captain Ahab's obsession to find the whale that had maimed him has been read as a struggle to cope with a universe bereft of God, to pursue to the brink of the abyss the limits of human suffering. Virginia Woolf depicted characters more joyously coming to terms with their individual consciousness, as in this passage from *The Voyage Out*: "The vision of her own personality, of herself as a real everlasting thing, different from anything else, unmergeable, like the sea or the wind, flashed into Rachel's mind, and she became profoundly excited at the thought of living." We have mentioned the profound vision of happiness that ends Rilke's *Duino Elegies*. His poem "Archaic Torso of Apollo" too depicted enthrallment, in this case with an ancient work of art which seemed to speak directly to the viewer: "There is no place that does not see you. You must change your life." The positive implications of Rilke's most famous poem are several: that one is not indifferent to the world but relevant to it, that change is possible, and that one is oneself the agent of change.

While the literature associated with existentialism often explores anxiety or despair, it is often also exuberantly affirmative. New unexplored possibilities are opened up when old ways of thinking are swept away. Rilke's speaker in "Archaic Torso of Apollo" is wonderstruck by a divine creative power that seems to surge through the ancient artwork he regards. The sculpture presumably sits in a museum, torn from its temple. It could be experienced as a lifeless piece of stone—after all it is but a fragment, missing head and limbs, all the rest having to be imagined by the viewer. Yet it is resplendent with intense vitality, and by the end of the poem it seems to speak to the viewer personally. Rilke's ingenious turn to the second person (and in German the informal, intimate "Du") in "you must change your life" means that in the moment the speaker is addressed directly by the statue, the reader is addressed directly by the poem. The affirmation in this directive is afforded by creative works—the visual art, as the object of the speaker's vision, and the poem itself, which conveys it to the reader.

We have seen that both the problems and possibilities of human existence can be intimately explored in literary forms of description. Novels, stories, plays, and poems made the themes of existentialism available to vast and varied audiences, often addressing the situation of the individual reader directly. The works of literature mentioned in this chapter are but a few of the many that expressed and provoked existentialist thinking. Whether inspiring, illustrating, or expanding existentialist philosophy, such works manifested the salience and urgency of its central concerns. The next chapter will explore some of these concerns in light of the living dimensions of existentialism.

Part III

Existentialism in Living Dimensions

6 | THE SELF

All existentialist thinking begins with the fact that a human being experiences the world through a first-person, subjective perspective. The special nature of this perspective means that it cannot be interchanged with any other, as this personal dimension makes experience one's own. Despite the ever-changing flow of our consciousness and the inevitable fragmentation or dispersion of its content—as we shift attention, develop, change, remember, and forget—we may recognize ourselves as relatively stable anchors of such experience. Reflecting on this first-person perspective or subjectivity affords us the sense of a self.

Existentialist thinkers insist on the irreducible nature of subjectivity, the basic perspective of a self. But they also consider critically what a self might be or not be, and the discrepancies among their views may be puzzling. Some affirm an inward self (Kierkegaard), while others describe the self as always outside itself, extended in its interactions with the world (Heidegger). Some may vigorously defend the self's intrinsic autonomy (Sartre), while other existentialists paint a more ambiguous picture of freedom hardwon (as could describe, in different ways, the self of Dostoevsky, Nietzsche, and Beauvoir).

Existentialist thinkers agree on a few core ideas concerning the self, however. For all of them the self is not a thing or object, but an activity. The self always exists in relation to something other than itself. For all existentialist thinkers, the self is never complete but always a process of becoming. All consider some kind of turn to self or reflection as the basis of an individual's choices and commitments.

No philosopher has thought more extensively about subjectivity and the self than Kierkegaard. Although writing under a number of pseudonyms, Kierkegaard wrote philosophy in the first person in order, as he put it, "to make a turn away from inhuman abstraction to personality." Like characters in a novel, these pseudonyms are constructed personalities that allow Kierkegaard to imagine different points of view about how to live. Needless to say, Kierkegaard did not advocate all of the perspectives his characters were meant to embody. With these figures, rather, Kierkegaard could communicate indirectly about possible forms of self to cultivate with his readers who must choose for themselves.

Kierkegaard defines the self as a "relation that relates itself to itself." This definition might sound terribly dialectical—we have noted that his thinking develops in critical response to the philosophy of Hegel. But Kierkegaard goes further to argue that this self-relating relation must also relate to something other which constitutes it. While we might think that a self could find fulfillment through integrating successfully with the world or with society, Kierkegaard thought that the self must be fulfilled at a still higher level. This requires the achievement of what Kierkegaard called inwardness, the state of relation Kierkegaard thinks is necessary for an authentic life.

We can explain this most clearly, though in a roundabout way, through Kierkegaard's conception of the three stages of life. These are not temporal stages the self would inevitably pass through, as from childhood to adulthood to old age. These phases rather signify distinct attitudes and commitments the self can take to existence, ways a self can live.

At the aesthetic stage of life, the self relates primarily to the immediate moment, or to the reminiscence of past moments. The aesthete may feel content in enjoying the sensuous pleasures of existence, whether directly in the here and now, or collected and savored in memory. Needless to say, one can remain an aesthete forever, never progressing to a further stage of self. The aesthete is illustrated by the figure of Johannes the Seducer, pseudonymous author of the diary contained in Kierkegaard's massive work, *Either/Or*. The seducer is in effect a collector of experiences. While pursuing the experiences and effects of falling in love, and of convincing the beloved of his sincerity, the seducer coldly rejects any commitment that a love relation would entail. According to Kierkegaard, life at the aesthetic stage conceals a state of despair, for the aesthete lives from his own point of view only. The self must move beyond himself in order to be further realized.

Reaching the ethical stage, the self would connect with human society and subordinate personal desires to a common good. This stage is illustrated by Judge Wilhelm, another pseudonymous author in *Either/Or*. The judge advises against the stance of the aesthete. Instead of collecting various experiences, the judge thinks, the self should engage in meaningful commitment. Since commitment indicates constancy toward the same object or other, this requires a special form of repetition. An example is found in marriage, through which one does not make a commitment only once and for all, but rather must affirm, over and over again, commitment to a particular someone other than oneself. Judge Wilhelm also advises that happiness cannot be won if it is based on external factors, such as wealth, recognition, or beauty, since all of these are subject to loss. What we can rely on is our own commitment to the good, no matter what the circumstances. While at the ethical stage we need not wholly give up the aesthetic pleasures, these ought to be subordinated to, and serve, the ethical life. Only then will the self be truly free of life's contingencies.

Although it is an advance over the aesthetic stage, the ethical stage of life is still not sufficient for the full realization of the self. In Kierkegaard's view we must take a more radical step, indeed, an unmediated transition to a higher stage of being. We must be willing to be singled out, over and above the universal, in order to relate to the very source of our being. We must relate not only to something other than ourselves that we know and recognize, like another person, or society in general, but also to something we do not know, cannot recognize, and cannot explain. This unknowable other must be accepted as the very ground of our own selves. For Kierkegaard, the highest stage of self requires a relation to God. The achievement of the religious stage demands a qualitative change, a transformation of the self. This occurs through a radical decision that must be made in inwardness. Kierkegaard writes: "When someone is to leap he must certainly do it alone and also be alone in properly understanding that it is an impossibility." What does Kierkegaard require for such a leap? Says Kierkegaard, "The leap is the decision. . . . I require a resolution."

As mentioned in an earlier chapter, this leap is not a matter of cozy, comforting belief. It cannot be achieved by merely accepting the supposed certainties provided by the church. Nor can one simply convince oneself through reasoned argument that God must exist. According to Kierkegaard, whatever God would be worth believing in must exceed the self's comprehension, for it is an absurdity for a finite being to claim any relation to that which is eternal. The relation in which we can ground our self-relating cannot therefore be rationally secured but demands decision and risk. We cannot of course force faith, but we can cultivate a state of "infinite passion" toward what we recognize is objectively uncertain. This is the full meaning of inwardness, the highest state of subjectivity, in which we would recognize ourselves as alone before God, exposed in ultimate risk. The leap to believing presupposes, then, the highest relation to one's own singularity as a self.

Other thinkers associated with existentialism offer more ambiguous assessments of the self. Dostoevsky's view of the self both affirms the freedom of the self and advocates selflessness as the highest virtue. As we have seen in reference to *Notes from Underground*, Dostoevsky criticized the Enlightenment concept of rational autonomy. In his view, the Enlightenment self, grounded in reason, would exclude emotion and passion as inessential, and personal relationships would be external to the self's core. In its claim to universality, Dostoevsky thought, Enlightenment thinking diminishes the importance of individuality, while at the same time promoting separation and egoism. In rejecting this Enlightenment vision of the self, Dostoevsky advocated the annihilation of the "I" in favor of a selfless, Christian openness toward others. Yet he also vigorously defended the self—or the cultivation of the subjective point of view—and insisted on the self's freedom, in harmony with Enlightenment thought.

Contradictions in Dostoevsky's thought may be mitigated when it is recognized what exactly he meant by selflessness, as well as what he meant in promoting a free self. The achievement of the kind of selflessness he had in mind demands the highest development of the individual personality. Such selfishness would not entail slavish subordination of oneself to another, but the overflowing fullness of a self so inwardly nurtured that it would need no reassuring boundaries. The religious aspect of this view of the self is affirmed in the philosophy of Marcel. The fundamental ambiguity of Dostoevsky's position was also echoed in the philosophy of Nietzsche, who was critical of the Christian ideal of selflessness.

Nietzsche's assessment of the self can be found in a number of works, including *Beyond Good and Evil*. There Nietzsche describes human consciousness as subtended by drives and instincts. Rather than merely accepting the idea of free will at face value, he considers the attraction of that which we move toward, the repulsion of that away from which we move, and the emotion and thinking involved in any willed action. Willing, he wrote, "seems to me to be above all something complicated, something that is a unity only in name." Any self would seem to be at most an effect of these and related affects, none of which are mastered by an individual's conscious will.

On this view the self is not, as it were, a captain steering its ship, but more like a bubble bobbing about helplessly on the waves. Nietzsche's caricature of the illusion of free will may be interpreted as a polemic encouraging a healthy skepticism about our human pretensions. Nietzsche doubts that our rationality is all it has been cracked up to be, that what we take to be our clearest convictions and decisions are untroubled by unconscious urges or natural instincts. The argument is compelling if we consider the extent to which we are not in control of all of the thoughts that occur to our minds, of all the feelings that course through us. It is difficult to say with any certainty whether it is pure judgment, or other less conscious impulses or prejudices, that drives choices and actions in every case. Despite this skepticism about the self, in the same text Nietzsche promotes "free spirits" who think for themselves. And in the essay "Schopenhauer as Educator" Nietzsche praises a self that takes charge of existence. Nietzsche declares: "We have to answer for our existence to ourselves; and will therefore be our own true pilots, and not admit that our being resembles a blind fortuity." Nietzsche describes the strong self as one who is overflowing, with generosity toward others not a matter of weak subordination but an expression of abundance. His work *Ecce Homo* is subtitled "How One Becomes What One Is." Nietzsche describes the prospect of creating ourselves as a work of art. While he expresses skepticism regarding any rational core of the self, Nietzsche constantly encourages choice and decision in our self-becoming, thus promoting the idea or goal of an authentic, freely chosen, and cultivated self. That we can become what we are, and shape that becoming as a work of art, would require a role for freedom.

Twentieth-century existentialist thinkers embrace the concept of a self in contrast to a tradition that would ascribe it any predetermined essence. Adapting Husserl's notion of intentionality, Heidegger argued that the self is not a thing contained in some interior, but an activity. The activity of the self, since it is always moving beyond the self toward the objects of its regard and concern, is described as transcendence. For subjectivity always moves outward toward and in the midst of the world. Because we are "fallen" into the world, however, we are often not "ourselves." We may be absorbed by worldly distractions or caught up with the perspectives of others. The self must wrest free of this state of fallenness in order to come into its own, as it were as a self.

Following this phenomenological trajectory, Sartre also insisted that consciousness is out there, in the world. The self is not a thing but an activity. Drawing from Heidegger, Sartre denied the self any intrinsic character or essence. But in Sartre's vocabulary, the self is nothing, or nothingness, for it is never a thing or a fixed state, but an activity, and this includes the power of negation. The self's distinction comes from its being not the world, but rather a consciousness of the world. Such negation is involved at every level of consciousness, including our basic recognition of things: an inkwell is not a table, and I am not any of the objects I so cognize. For Sartre, any unity of the self is not a given, but a task to be accomplished through its projects. Because the self has no given essence, it is essentially free. What Sartre regards as the absolute freedom of the self, however, has to be negotiated with his acceptance of the fact that the self always finds itself in a situation. The self must, in other words, always interact within a specific world the self did not create.

It may be difficult at first to see what these varying accounts of the self have in common. We can say that for all of these thinkers, the self does not have a predetermined nature. The self is not a given core of our being that must be discovered but an activity to be manifest through action, decision, or commitment. We cannot choose the situation into which we have been thrown or the physical substrate of our existence, but we can choose how we respond to these given factors. For some existentialists, like Sartre, the self's freedom to so choose is absolute; for others, it is more ambiguously entangled in circumstance. But all of these thinkers pay tribute to the courage required in self-realization. Existentialists regard the self not as the basis or starting point for our existence, but its achievement.

For existentialism, the self is also a distinctly human phenomenon. Whatever the nature of the self, it would be as "selves" that we are distinct from animals. A turtle returning to the beach where it was born, a puffin flying thousands of miles to return to its nest, a polar bear defending its cubs all act from instinct. In promoting their survival, so far as we know, they are governed by an innate, evolved set of capacities and characteristics that define their being. While many animals undoubtedly have a degree of self-awareness, they do not, so far as we can tell, reflect on the nature of their efforts or question their trajectories in light of other possibilities. In their activities they would seem to be at one with what they are and do. Animals, presumably, do not agonize over their options, puzzle over the meaning of what is there before them, or wonder about their own existence. Only human beings—and Nietzsche mocked us for this—need a reason to be, or demand that their existence be justified.

Of course, we too have instincts, as Nietzsche pointed out, and it is likely that we share considerably more in common with animal beings than we have traditionally supposed. Yet our particular capacities to consider multiple alternative possibilities, to reflect on our own thoughts and actions, will all contribute to the experience of being a self. In particular, human beings manifest a distinctive level of self-awareness. As not only "in itself," but also "for itself," a human being chooses this or another course of action, this or another project, and so establishes new qualities and values.

Of course, in transcending the given facts and circumstances—that is, interacting with, and changing the given state of things around us—we may not always foreground our reflection. We may actively take initiative or respond more passively to what we feel to be the forces of circumstance. As you go through your life you may stumble in the dark, feeling the way as you go along. Alternatively, you may act according to a grand, clarifying vision. Or you may oscillate between blind improvisation and well-reflected habit. Yet even when you are not explicitly thinking about yourself as you act—and for the most part you would not be so doing—you relate to yourself in and through your endeavors. You may pause to question what you are doing and why, worry about the next step to take, or consider the options from a personal point of view. This capacity for relating to yourself is an important condition for self-hood, for being a self.

Taking our clue from these existential approaches, we can think about the self in more detail. Of what does a sense of self consist? We mentioned first of all how the self includes experiential specificity. What Heidegger will call *mineness* is the sense that whatever is happening in my field of awareness is happening to *me*, that *I* am the subject of this perceiving, thinking, acting, doing, undergoing. Second, from the further explicit act of *reflecting* on our own specific experiences emerges a distinct relation to ourselves. This self is never directly manifested but is a first-person orientation, or an idea that attends when we present to our own minds, in reflection, the current flow of our thinking, acting, and being, and compare it to other moments. Given this temporal structure, third, the self has a relative *continuity*. While this may be more or less durable, over time we accumulate experiences, exercise particular tastes and preferences, develop memories and habits. We can compare our current experiences to past ones, and we can also bring those forward into our projections toward the future. Even Sartre, for whom the self is radically free, understood the importance of a fundamental project that gives the self an overall orientation in living. Finally, we do not only passively receive impressions and thoughts but also, through free *initiative*, actively contribute to the world, in part shaping our experiences. We steer ourselves in this direction or that, make choices and exert our will in accord with or against our circumstances. Despite the various approaches to the self among existential thinkers, all of them address these qualities of mineness, self-reflection, continuity, and free initiative. Yet none of these qualities are absolute. All are subject to qualification.

Nietzsche's polemic regarding the self, mentioned above, appears to attack the certainty of our first-person perspective. Nietzsche said famously that the "I"—as in "I think, therefore I am"—is but a fiction of grammar. How can I be sure it is I who is doing the thinking? he asked. Are my thoughts, desires, and so forth truly mine, or is some force of nature, such as instinct, thinking through me? Contemporary philosophers may challenge the idea of the self on similar grounds: that it is simply a grammatical mistake to think that because I recognize myself involved in experience, that there is a "self" that is mine to be noticed therein.

Yet on closer examination, Nietzsche's challenge may not be principally a rejection of the mineness of the self but more of its continuity as a distinct and originating entity, and of the free will we so self-assuredly attribute to the self. For it is unmistakably the case that, even if drives or instincts are coursing through me as I think, I experience them from a first-person perspective. At the very least I would be one to whom or through whom these are coursing and aware, at least, of their subjective effects. Under ordinary circumstances, it seems human beings generally have this first-person perspective, and Nietzsche does not seem to be challenging this fact of human experience.

Nietzsche's critique nevertheless invites us to scrutinize this aspect of self and may bring to light ways our sense of first-person specificity or mineness is reliant upon sources of our experience that come from elsewhere than the conscious mind. While we may, with Descartes, meditate in an empty room, even in this sequestration we are engaged with a world, albeit a broken-off fraction of it. Any suspension of the world would be an abstraction from a prior state in which we are occupied or preoccupied with it. Ordinarily our experience is filled with innumerable perceptions and thoughts that come to us from without. They are my experiences, to be sure, but can the "me" in that configuration be absolutely segregated from the content that is not me?

Whatever Cartesian meditations I may engage, existentialists tend to argue that I could not be myself without a world to experience and with which to interact. My self is extended through my projects and activities, and even my perceptions. After a long gray winter, I step out into a fine spring sunlight. I feel its warmth and light not only with my skin and eyes but in what feels like much of my being, as if the sun were spreading through me. I do not confuse the sunlight with myself, or my bodily sensations with my whole mental life, and yet in the moment it is not possible to say where I am completely separate from these. I do not merely "have" my body, to use Marcel's distinction, but *am* my body. Marcel's distinction between being and having highlights the extent to which embodiment, as our connection to the physical world, is crucial to selfhood.

Where then precisely does this self begin, and where does it end? The spatial metaphor of the inner life, so important in Kierkegaard's thought about the self, is meant to describe that dimension of personal reflective experience invisible to others. Though they could guess or imagine from looking, no one else can feel exactly my feeling as I stand there in the sunlight. The interior we may experience is, however, not contained inside us like water can be said to be inside a jar. Even Kierkegaard, with all his inwardness, described the self as a relation. If to be in the world means that we and the world are connected, how far can our self-reflection venture without leaving the realm of self?

For it would seem that, in our experience, even our "innermost" feelings are not entirely contained within us. Any joy we feel does not stay with us alone, but rebounds across our field of perception. On the basis of inwardly felt joy, we are prone to take a greater delight in the world around us. Rilke wrote in the *Sonnets to Orpheus* of joyful experience of mundane things. In the taste and smell and color of ripe fruit, for instance, one may sense the course of nature, both the blossoming of life and its waning. Here a joyful moment is inextricable from the sensation of the fruit and perhaps from the fruit itself as I know it. Would not the self too change if, by a change of circumstance, I were never to feel the sunlight again, or if I would irrevocably lose the sense of taste of such delights? A radical change or loss in our outward perception would surely involve an unmistakable alteration of the so-called inner life.

Traditional philosophical depictions of the self have made it difficult to conceive the self as we actually experience it in existing, and existential descriptions are meant to counter that tradition. Descartes described the core of the self as contained within the mental sphere, excluding the extended things of body and the world. The self was a continuous, self-transparent, predominantly rational core of mind embedded with innate ideas. In contrast, and somewhat adapting Kierkegaard's notion of the self as a relation, Heidegger argues for the self's "ecstatic" structure. The self in this view is, as the word literally denotes, outside itself. Rather than its inward relation, Heidegger illuminated the self's dynamic interactive relations to the world around it. The self is existence, Dasein, the "being there" or "being here" (Dasein can mean either), a relation which illuminates the "there" or "here" as meaningful. The self in this sense is a nexus of involvement in a given place and time, distributed across its practical engagements, and tied up with the others with whom one dwells. This distribution is described as the self's transcendence, its incessant going-beyond itself through its activity.

Insofar as existentialists affirm the self, it is not one closed up in an interior. In the wake of Heidegger, Sartre argued that "precisely this being-beyond-itself, this absolute flight, this refusal to be a substance is what makes it be a consciousness." Consciousness cannot be located in any interior but must be found outside, in the world, among others. "It is not in some hiding-place that we will discover ourselves; it is on the road, in the town, in the midst of the crowd, a thing among things, a human among humans." Or as Merleau-Ponty put it: "I am from the start outside myself and open to the world." Even Kierkegaard's inwardness, echoing an Augustinian interior, is achieved only in being open to something so radically other that it transcends the self's capacities to understand. "Mineness," then, while an unshakably first-person perspective, must be elaborated in the activities or commitments of existing toward something other than the self.

The complications of mineness also pertain to the process of reflection. For if the self is not an inner entity fixed in some interior, self-reflection is not straightforward. My self is not easily manifest when I turn my thoughts to think about who or what I am. While the demand to know ourselves goes back to Socrates, the latter never explained what it is exactly that we would be examining when we turn to ourselves. The mind as we attempt to find it in reflection is elusive. Marcel Proust brilliantly describes the inherent uncertainty of one's own mind, since "it, the seeker, is at the same time the dark region through which it must go seeking."

Do I ever catch hold of myself when I reflect, and if so, how long can this catching myself in the act be sustained? Further complicating self-reflection is the fact that, when we try to characterize our own self, characteristics of our personality or intellect tend to come to mind, aspects of our physical being, such as our gender or ethnicity, facts about our lives and activities. But while these features may contribute to what we are, many of them can change. They do not quite capture our uniqueness, or exhaust our possibilities or the meanings we might give them.

The extension of the self beyond has another sense in existentialist thought. We are always more than our particular lives have manifested. We are not only our actualities but our possibilities. Jaspers called this being-more our "Existenz." Recognition of *Existenz* avoids reducing the self to an object that can be accounted for, wholly known, or described. There is always a further encompassing horizon surrounding the self's perspective and that of which it is aware.

Continuity, another of the self's features, must also be qualified in existentialist terms. The ecstasis ascribed above to the self in its dispersion across perceptions and projections also pertains to its temporal structure. To be a self requires some connection between my experience of the present and the past. Yet this is a precarious connection, and it is often broken.

For most selves, memory is only inconsistently reliable. Some experiences are well remembered, but others are forever forgotten. What is foremost in our concerns right now may give way to other concerns and priorities, or may cease to concern us at all. We may feel very different now from the person we were at an earlier stage in life—at times we might scarcely recognize our earlier self. We may gradually change over many years, or, should we experience a traumatic or dramatic event, we may change radically overnight. Any self is subject to alteration, continuity, rupture, and change.

Different people may experience their sense of self differently. The contemporary philosopher Galen Strawson points out that different selves may have more intermittent or more durable senses of continuity. Some people may feel consistently over a lifetime a relatively stable self-conception. Others may feel radically different or even alienated from who they may have been at various stages of their lives. The existential view that one never fully *is* a self, but always a process of *becoming* one, can accommodate this difference. The continuity of self is not absolute, only ever relative, never completed or fixed. The self is always, as it were, in progress.

Yet existentialists reflect differently on this potential continuity. Kierkegaard argued that the continuity of the self has to be won by repetition, by a commitment to an idea or a project or a beloved ever renewed, again and again. For Heidegger such continuity must be gathered by the authentic self, awakened in light of finitude to its own singular being. Sartre has perhaps the most radical view in privileging the present over the past: nothing that I have been determines what I am now. All that exists is the present. Nevertheless, Sartre recognized some existential continuity in major projects by which we may define our lives.

The self extends into the future through its expectations, projects, and goals, and into the past through memory, habit, and received cultural inheritance. While our expectations create horizons of potential meaning, we also sometimes recollect the past that is otherwise always slipping away from us. In the most authentic moments, according to Heidegger, we come to recognize our ecstatic nature—that we are never finished or complete, because our most extreme possibility, death, is the end of all our possibility. When we confront this fact, we may look toward our future and back upon the past as illuminating the present moment in a new light. We may, Heidegger argues, gather ourselves authentically. We recognize our specificity especially through recognizing our finitude: that our self is finite, that we have only one existence endowed to us, that our allotted time is ours alone.

Of course, in grasping our past and projecting our future, we are subject to the availability of memory and the facility of our imagination. We may also select elements of the past that seem most important for our projected journey. Nietzsche would advocate gathering up only those aspects or that degree of our past that can be taken up in a life-affirming way. For Nietzsche authenticity does not mean merely faithfulness to the facts, but future-directed creativity, and this may require forgetting as much as it requires remembering. In his essay "On the Uses and Disadvantages of History for Life," Nietzsche promoted the value of forgetting insofar as it may enable us not to be encumbered by the past, and to maximally seize the possibilities of present and future.

If the qualities of mineness, reflection, and continuity are qualified, so too is the initiating spontaneity, or the freedom of a self. While all existentialists (even Nietzsche, despite his critique) directly or indirectly credit the self with a capacity to freely initiate action or choice, this is not equivalent to an unqualified command of our liberty. Even Sartre, who famously argued for the absolute freedom of consciousness, had to admit the importance of circumstance as the situation within which freedom can be exercised.

Sartre is perhaps existentialism's most categorical defender of the self's freedom, and his famous descriptions of freedom are found in *Being and Nothingness*. There he wrote that "man cannot be sometimes slave and sometimes free; he is wholly and forever free or he is not free at all." As a subjectivity, "I am absolutely free and absolutely responsible for my situation." Clearly there are difficulties with this view, since Sartre recognizes that one will have been thrown into a world, and into factical conditions, which one did not choose. It is certainly problematic from a political standpoint to equate the responsibility of one who is born at liberty with that of another born into slavery. Marcel charged that Sartre's theory debased freedom by seeing it everywhere in humanity.

To make better sense of Sartre's position, however, we must suppose a distinction he makes between two kinds of freedom.

There is empirical freedom, my liberty with respect to the material world, to move about within, or manipulate or obtain what I want from it. Distinct from this is freedom to choose, including choice in the interpretation of my reality, of the factical situation at hand. The self is not absolutely free insofar as it is just a part of the world, but it is absolutely free as consciousness *of* the world. Since consciousness is always transcending toward possibilities, it is never wholly fixed, or wholly determined, by any given reality. The non-coincidence of the self and the world, by virtue of the special nature of consciousness, provides this freedom.

Even so, Sartre's position is radical. Even if I am being tortured, Sartre argued, I can choose fidelity to or betrayal of my loyalties. Even if I am contained in a tiny physical space, he would say, I can negate these walls that constrain me and imagine vastness. So long as I am conscious, my consciousness is never compromised by the world, for it is other to the world. Sartre's position, particularly in the example of torture or real enslavement or imprisonment, seems implicitly to rely upon an underlying division between the mind and the body, between consciousness and the physical world, between the in-itself and the for-itself, and from a contemporary perspective it is clearly insensitive to the influence of physical and social factors on the mind.

All the same, Sartre's position follows in some respect an idea articulated decades earlier by W. E. B. Du Bois, which was influential in the milieu of African American literature Sartre was reading up to the publication of *Being and Nothingness*. In *The Souls of Black Folk*, Du Bois presented the idea of double consciousness. This describes how an oppressed person—he was writing about the situation of black people in segregated, post-slavery America—may have a dual relationship to him- or herself, experiencing the self as a "twoness." In the empirical, material, and social world one's freedom may be burdened and restricted by oppression. This involved, as Du Bois wrote, "a sense of always looking at one's self through the eyes of others, of measuring one's soul by the tape of a world that looks on in amused contempt and pity." Yet one was also aware of oneself as inwardly free—and it is this inner freedom that allowed one to maintain dignity in the face of oppression.

Despite his apparently absolute examples, Sartre understood that whatever freedom the human being has, it is always a situated freedom. Freedom must always be manifest within a given set of circumstances. This embeddedness in a concrete situation is referred to as our "facticity." The self's freedom to act is relative to the world in which the self can act, and the way it appears to us is influenced by our capacities relative to it. Yet it is Merleau-Ponty who recognized the importance of facticity in terms of our embodied life. Mountains appear high because "they exceed my body's power to take them in its stride." I can imagine the mountain as tiny, thus "negating" its appearance to my consciousness, as Sartre might say, but I cannot make it so in reality, just by exerting my will. I can endeavor to climb the mountain, too, but my freedom to do so will be situated within the constraints of my physical capacities, my preparedness for the task, and even the weather, and my freedom to exert my will in this activity will come up against, and be relative to, the height of the mountain itself.

Because of the self's intertwinement with the world, it may be impossible to determine exactly how much the self, when acting, exercises freedom, and how much is encouraged or even determined by the circumstances at hand. When I undertake to act, I am aided or obstructed by the world. As Merleau-Ponty wrote: "In this exchange between the situation and the person who takes it up, it is impossible to determine precisely the 'share contributed by the situation' and the 'share contributed by freedom.'" While this appears to stray from the popular version of existentialism advocated by Sartre, it is confirmed by Beauvoir, who devoted a study to just this difficulty. In *The Ethics of Ambiguity*, Beauvoir described an inherent ambiguity in the human condition. Even when I freely act, she pointed out, the effects of my action establish a new situation which constrains me in further action.

When we take embodiment into account, the picture of the self is more complicated than Sartre's absolutely free consciousness would suggest. As we recall, Marcel cautioned against philosophy's overly intellectualized view of self, a view he thought was initiated by Descartes. The "I" or cogito of Descartes is, Marcel argues, merely "indeterminate" and "concerns only the epistemological subject as organ of objective cognition." Descartes ignores the "vital" need of such a subject to ask about its own being. Precisely against the Cartesian position, Merleau-Ponty analyzed the extent to which our mental life arises from and remains inseparable from our embodied life. Beauvoir and Du Bois point out that the body is inextricable from the self through the social interpretation or projection of sexual and racial difference.

Existentialist thinking centers on the dimensions of the self we have outlined in this chapter. Our first-person perspective, the reflection by which we can consider it, the continuity of experience across place and time, and the freedom with which we initiate action are all subject to qualification. The mineness, reflection, continuity, and initiative are all explored by existentialist philosophers as inextricable, if complex, features of our subjectivity. None of these dimensions of the self could be wholly explained in the third person, as empirically describable facts, without reference to our experience of them.

Despite a number of differences among them, all of the thinkers we have associated with existentialism agree that the self is not a static thing. The self is not a thing at all, but a dynamic relation of being, doing, and experiencing that uniquely pertains to human consciousness and emerges through the life of the human subject. The self has no permanent essence, is no bounded interior immune to the vagaries of world, materiality, and time. Just as the physical body is ever-changing—in its growth, movements, interactions, and capacities, at the systemic as well as at the cellular level—so too is the self. The self is never a finished product, but a process of becoming, responsive to the whole context of embodied life and its ongoing interaction with the world. We can lose ourselves, in a manner of speaking, by unreflective absorption in the world around us, or by identification with some fixed essence remote from our self-generated possibilities.

Existentialist thinking about the self can help us to come to terms with some apparent contradictions in our human experience of being a self. We may feel at times to be not quite ourselves. We may as selves become dispersed in our worldly attentions, or instead gather ourselves to ourselves in inward reflection. What may feel to us as "inner" experience is neither bounded nor enduring. Yet we can describe in existential terms how we can both feel awareness of some kind of inner life, while also always within the world with which we interact.

7 | OTHERS

Other selves are not merely present among us but constitute an existential dimension of our world. Others enable our physical survival, the development of language and culture, but equally crucially, they contribute to the full reality of a human self. For others who share our form of consciousness also recognize us as subjects, as selves. They share our human condition and contribute the intersubjective texture of a fully human world. As others may also dismiss or deny our subjectivity, however, existentialists characterize the relationship between self and other in diverging ways.

Existential consideration of others often begins with recognizing the ontological distinctiveness of consciousness, its categorical separation from any other consciousness. They point out that one self has no direct awareness of the consciousness of others, of their subjectivity or first-person perspective. This separation can be in part overcome through care or cooperation, or it can yield longing and desire, conflict or competition between self and other. A number of existentialists consider the problem in terms of recognition: if others cannot know my consciousness directly, how can they affirm my subjectivity? How can I affirm the subjectivity of others? Alternatively, how might others objectify me, in effect denying my status as a subject?

Some existentialists start from the self's isolation from others in accounting for social life, an isolation encapsulated in the philosophy of Descartes. As we know, Descartes presents the standpoint of the isolated *ego cogito*, or the "I" who is thinking. From such a standpoint in the *Meditations,* Descartes methodically doubts the existence of the rest of the entire world. Other people too are caught in that skeptical sweep, when Descartes describes observing what appear to be men outside the window, insisting that he cannot be sure that they are not merely automatons in coats and hats. Just as Descartes conceives of animals mechanistically, so too might another human body turn out to be a soulless machine.

Husserl accepted Descartes's assumption that we cannot know the minds of others directly. Yet Husserl also wanted to explain our experience of their being other subjects in the world alongside us. For despite Descartes's exercise of doubt, we do not generally experience what we take to be automatons but others whom we take in the first instance as conscious, experiencing subjects. Husserl's theory of intersubjectivity describes in phenomenological terms how I might know other minds indirectly, by way of analogy with my own. For others appear to me not as inert bodies or static objects, but as feeling and thinking as I feel and think. I take them to be conducting their actions in ways that mirror my own conduction of action. Husserl argued that, on analogy with our own self-experience, we infer in the phenomenon of the other a conscious life. I cannot perceive the mental life of another, but I analogically "apperceive" that the other is conscious.

Other subjectivities also contribute to the experience of a shared intersubjective world. Another person looking toward me from the other side of the table will have a perspective on the table and the room that is different from my own. My own experience is enriched by my implicit awareness that should we trade places, my perspective and that of the other will be interchanged. I will see what the other just saw before, and the other will see what I have just seen. This interchangeability applies not only to the perception of individual objects but to all kinds of experiences, and gives me the sense both of a common world and of the multiple perspectives we can take on it. We may not only inhabit transposable perspectives at the table, but we also share food that diminishes as we each partake of it. Such experiences allow for the sense of inhabiting a shared world.

Heidegger's theory of Dasein as being-in-the-world, extended through its worldly projections, offered a more radical alternative to Cartesian solipsism than Husserl's solution of apperception. If Descartes thinks of the thinking self as contained within an essential isolation, Heidegger conceives of the self as embedded in the world and ontologically connected with others. One of Dasein's modes of being is *Mitsein*, or "being-with" others, which, Heidegger argues, is more "proximal" than any experience of my own individual being. This means that at any given point in my existence I am more likely to be preoccupied with others than I am with myself, or embracing my individual existence. Even what appears to be a form of self-absorption can be first of all a concern with others in the form of competition with or envy of them, or wanting others' attention or approval. According to Heidegger, authentic singularity of the self must be wrested from this everyday being-with, and become a more authentic form of *Mitsein*.

The solutions of Husserl and Heidegger to the isolation of the Cartesian ego are both rejected by Sartre, whose account of social interaction emphasizes how others may pose a threat to the self. Sartre bypassed Husserl's analogical solution to the problem of other minds posed by Descartes. He further defended the Cartesian view of the solitary self against Heidegger's critique, arguing that with his theory, Heidegger overlooked the fundamental fact of singular consciousness. In *Being and Nothingness* Sartre radicalized the existential implications of a lone consciousness by integrating it with the master-slave dialectic of Hegel.

In his account Sartre starts precisely where Descartes began, with doubt. The physical appearance of the other before me carries with it no immediate evidence of consciousness. It is but the error of a certain prejudice that other human bodies have minds like I do, as Sartre wrote:

> It remains always possible that the Other is only a body. If animals are machines, why shouldn't the man whom I see pass in the street be one? What I apprehend on this face is nothing but the effect of certain muscular contractions, and they in turn are only the effect of a nervous impulse of which I know the course. Why not reduce the ensemble of these reactions to simple or conditioned reflexes?

Following Descartes, Sartre argued that the self has no intuition of another's soul. The body of the other remains to me a pure exteriority. The other remains as external to my mind as two distinct objects are from each other, as an inkwell is to a book.

Sartre progresses from doubting the existence of the other to elaborating an inescapable, ontologically rooted antagonism between self and other. The Hegelian dialectic of master and slave describes a fundamental conflict of self and other, in which the other's very existence as a subject is a threat to my own. According to Hegel, the relationship between master and slave (the German terms *Herr* and *Knecht* can also be translated as lord and serf) is not a one-way relation of power. Rather the two figures are correlated, since the master needs the recognition of the slave to maintain his position of dominance. Thus, not only is the slave subordinated by the master; the master, too, is threatened in his own position by the slave.

Sartre wove this master-slave conflict into the Cartesian vision of the isolated cogito. Just as Descartes saw the men outside the window as potential automatons, others might see me merely as an object. But in so seeing me, Sartre figures, the other has objectified me, reduced me to a mere "in itself," like a thing, or a slave. Sartre thinks that by being able to objectify me, the other consciousness is a threat to my subjectivity.

Given these views it is not surprising that the paradigmatic example of self-other relations for Sartre's philosophy is shame. Sartre describes (in the first person) a self apparently alone with itself, making for some reason a vulgar gesture, and subsequently realizing that someone has witnessed it. One cannot experience shame in solitude, simply reflecting on oneself, but only in being gazed at by another. For as Sartre writes:

> Shame is not originally a phenomenon of reflection. . . . [I]t is in its primary structure shame before somebody. I have just made an awkward or vulgar gesture. This gesture clings to me; I neither judge it nor blame it. I simply live it. I realize it in the mode of for-itself. But now suddenly I raise my head.

Somebody was there and has seen me. Suddenly I realize the vulgarity of my gesture, and I am ashamed.

The other, Sartre goes on to say, mediates between the self's unreflective awareness of self and a reflective self-awareness. One imagines how the other may see oneself, or as Sartre puts it: "I am ashamed of myself as I appear to the Other."

Sartre holds shame to be an inevitable situation, an inescapable fact of the human condition. It is not anything particular that the other must do to put me into this position. It is simply the existence of the other as another consciousness that, in coming upon one's own, leads to one's objectification. "By the mere appearance of the Other," he writes, "I am put in the position of passing judgment on myself as on an object, for it is as an object that I appear to the Other." In keeping with the motif of shame, Sartre likens the existence of the other to the religious concept of original sin, or a fall from grace: "My original Fall is the existence of the Other."

Moreover, Sartre understands the "look" of the other to manifest an antipathy that can annihilate one as a subject by fixing one as an object. He offers another example (again in first person) of peeping through the keyhole of a door while motivated by "jealousy, curiosity, or vice." When another self comes upon the peeper suddenly, and regards him in this act, the unselfconscious activity is transformed into a self-reflective, self-objectifying shame. But the peeper also becomes an object in the regard of another, a situation confirming not his own freedom but the other's:

For the Other, I am leaning over the keyhole as this tree is bent by the wind. Thus for the Other I have stripped myself

of my transcendence.... [My consciousness] acquires a nature
by the sole fact that the Other confers on it an outside. . . .
I grasp the Other's look at the very center of my act as the so-
lidification and alienation of my own possibilities.

The outrage against the self in this scenario consists both in the act
of witness and in the ability of the other's free consciousness to fix
or identify the self with the act that is witnessed. One becomes,
for the other, one so acting—an object to which a quality is
attributed—thus losing one's freedom from any essential nature.

Relations with others are also competitive in respect to resources
to obtain from the world. Sartre uses the example of walking in a
public garden toward the only available chair and seeing another
coming from another direction doing the same. Not only the
chair, but this other is depicted as an object for the subject, and
as a rival for the resource of the chair. Sartre goes further to argue
that the very existence of the rival challenges the subject's own existence as the center of the universe, a shift which, as Marcel puts
it, "undermines the centralization operated by myself."

While admitting that it is of course perfectly true that we
do compete for resources, Marcel argues that Sartre sees such
situations too one-sidedly. Sartre predicts in the encounter between self and other only a threat, an invitation to conflict,
leaving wholly unconsidered that one self might gladly give up
a chair for another who may be wearier. Nor does Sartre suppose
that the other, in an act of generosity, might gladly yield the chair
to oneself. Sartre never considers the situation as an opportunity
for either or both subjects to exercise civility, gallantry, decency,
or kindness.

The situation in the garden is not a serious conflict, but the stakes are raised when Sartre compares the denial of one's freedom by the look of the other to a form of metaphysical slavery. He writes:

> Thus being-seen constitutes me as a defenseless being for a freedom which is not my freedom. It is in this sense that we can consider ourselves as "slaves" in so far as we appear to the Other. But this slavery is not a historical result, capable of being surmounted, of a life in the abstract form of consciousness. I am a slave to the degree that my being is dependent at the center of a freedom which is not mine and which is the very condition of my being.

Any dependence of the being of self on another's freedom is condemned here in polemical terms. Others attribute a value to oneself, make one into the instrument of their own possibilities, or as Kant would say, they may reduce one to a means to their own ends. While Kant's moral philosophy issues the categorical imperative in order to prohibit just such a reduction to mere means by one self of others—and we have seen that Sartre at times affirmed the Kantian perspective on the universality of freedom—Sartre regards this danger as intrinsic to being a subject among other subjects. Among others, I am no longer being-for-itself but being-for-others. The danger of objectification is, he says, "not an accident but the permanent structure of my being-for-others."

The situation of being-for-others who may enslave the self in some way is compared to a Kafkaesque nightmare. Sartre likens being-for-others to the situation of Josef K. in *The Trial*, who is arrested for no apparent reason, cannot discover it, and is eventually murdered by nameless others.

> That gloomy, evanescent atmosphere of *The Trial*, that ignorance which, however, is lived as ignorance, that total opacity which can only be felt as a presentiment across a total translucency—this is nothing but the description of our being-in-the-midst-of-the-world-for-others.

Here opacity describes the others whose consciousness I cannot access; translucency describes one's own self-consciousness. Their interaction is a state of gloomy ignorance. Sartre sees Kafka's novel, along with the master-slave dialectic of Hegel, as capturing not only the structure of interpersonal oppression but the oppressive nature of social life itself.

Some subjects have enslaved or do enslave others, of course, and Sartre's account brings the resources of philosophy to bear in understanding that tragic human experience. One might engage the Hegelian master-slave dialectic to describe particular forms of social oppression, as Beauvoir did in *The Second Sex*. Yet identifying such a structure as a universal feature of the human condition as Sartre does neglects the crucial factors of actual oppression that motivate domination or objectification of the individuals of some groups by those of others.

In *Black Skin, White Masks* (1952), Frantz Fanon uses the same existentially adapted Hegelian dialectic to describe the problem of social recognition. Like Du Bois in the context of racially segregated America, Fanon outlines the divisive effect of oppression in the consciousness of a black person—in this case, of French-colonized Martinique. Fanon identifies the structure of oppression in the context of a historically specific racist oppression, where the oppressed class is given an "inferior status within a colonial order" and as such must struggle for recognition of worth. In such a situation, he writes,

> Man is human only to the extent to which he tries to impose himself on another man in order to be recognized by him. As long as he has not been effectively recognized by the other, it is this other who remains the focus of his actions. His human worth and reality depend on this other and on his recognition by the other. It is on this other that the meaning of his life is condensed.

An analysis of the relations between oppressor and oppressed in such a context would have to take into account its historical and political realities, and its racial particularization, as Fanon does in his analysis.

Yet if, as Sartre suggests, the ontology of oppression is intrinsic to our life among others, how can it ever be overcome? Sartre's account of being-for-others neglects more positive possibilities such as caring, cooperation, and respect. In contrast, Fanon suggests that respect for the other's humanity is possible, and that such mutual respect can break with the dialectic of oppression: "The only way to break this vicious circle that refers me back to myself is to restore to the other his human reality. . . . The other, however, must perform a similar operation." Despite his devastating exposure of the effects of racist oppression, Fanon insists that the human being is "an affirmation" who can say "Yes to life. Yes to love. Yes to generosity." At the same time there must also be refusal: "No to man's contempt. No to the indignity of man. To the exploitation of man. To the massacre of what is most human in man: freedom."

As one of Sartre's fiercest critics, Marcel issued a sharp critique of Sartre's individualism, suggesting first of all that "Sartre's world is the world as seen from the terrace of a café." As Marcel characterizes, "A café has the immense advantage of indifference: I and the other people who come to it are independent of one another." Against what he sees as Sartre's solipsism, Marcel advocates interdependence. Where Sartre sees competition for resources, Marcel sees opportunity for cooperation. Where Sartre sees love as appropriation, Marcel sees it as a chance for presence and fidelity. Where Sartre sees receiving gifts as entrapment, Marcel sees it as a form of trust. Even shame, in which one can see oneself as another might see one, can be a helpful reminder to check oneself or to conduct oneself in a better way.

In keeping with his social ontology of conflict, Sartre also has a negative view of the phenomenon of gift-giving. Giving and generosity are not, as might be supposed, forms of submission to others, but rather the opposite—ways of dominating them. "To give is to appropriate by means of destroying and to use this act of destruction as a means of enslaving others," Sartre writes. "Generosity is, above all, a destructive function" and is nothing more than a "frenzy of possession." To give is "destructive appropriation," and indeed to give is "to enslave." Likewise, Sartre conceives of receiving as incompatible with freedom. While Sartre may be right that some forms of apparent generosity work to manipulate or render the receiver dependent in some way, he overlooks the possibility of altruism or even, more simply, graciousness.

One can give in manipulative ways, but also in creative, generous, gracious ways. For Dostoevsky, the self can be generous, not as a matter of subordination to the other but of overflowing fullness from within. Even receiving another's gift can be done with generosity. In his essay "Testimony and Existentialism," Marcel offers the notion of "creative receptivity." One receives a gift not merely as a transfer of a thing from self to other, but recognizes another giving something of themselves, and receives it with imaginative gratitude. For in the giving and receiving, the thing undergoes transformation. For example, one may receive the bedraggled flowers offered by a child as if they are inestimably valuable. The giving enriches the gift, just as giving enriches the giver, while the experience also offers an opportunity for community and creativity on the part of the receiver. Rather than subordination, Marcel argues, there is an "accretion of being" in one who receives. Giving and receiving are related to trust, not forms of opposition. Rather than domination, Marcel finds communion.

From this very different existential rendering of the self-other relation we can return to the question of other minds posed by Descartes. Beauvoir, while accepting the Cartesian starting point, nevertheless sees the individual as coming together with others. In *The Ethics of Ambiguity* we read:

> It is rather well known that the fact of being a subject is a universal fact and that the Cartesian *cogito* expresses both the most individual experience and the most objective truth. . . . [Yet] for existentialism, it is not impersonal universal man

who is the source of values, but the plurality of concrete—
particular men projecting themselves toward their ends on
the basis of situations whose particularity is as radical and as
irreducible as subjectivity itself. How could men, originally
separated, get together?

But are we in every case so separate as Beauvoir claims? While
Descartes and his philosophical inheritors recognize rightly that
one cannot know another's mind directly, one nevertheless can
feel and respond to them as if one does so. If one witnesses another hurting, one is likely to experience a feeling of empathy and
therefore connection. Some others may live alongside one sometimes so closely that it may be difficult to draw, in psychological
terms, the exact boundary between oneself and another. While
contemporary philosophy of mind will account for this in terms
of "theory of mind" (where one self will have an implicit working
theory that others are thinking) or simulation theory (where one
simulates in the mind what they witness another experiencing),
an existential description of this situation is given in the notion
of being-with.

Being with others may be experienced inauthentically, if,
as Heidegger puts it, one loses oneself to the "they-self." In this
mode, one is for the most part and most proximally not oneself,
but anonymous others. In this case the self fails to distinguish itself from others. One may get caught up in gossip, turning this way
and that to catch others' opinions. One can lose one's own sense of
self when "going along with" the crowd.

While insistent that the self must wrest its singularity away
from others, Heidegger at least allows for the possibility that

communal life can be experienced authentically—a prospect, however, that Heidegger does not elaborate upon at length in his writings. He does describe a mode of being-with that does not take away the sense of individuality of the other but rather frees the other for such individuality. We can image being-with as authentic even through moments of intense empathy with or admiration for others. We may care for others in ways that are inextricable from our sense of self while still recognizing our individuality. We may take joy in communal activity, as when a single voice melds with a great choir. The experience of love may make us feel, at least in moments, at one with another soul.

Perhaps the most positive account of others in existentialist thinking is offered by Marcel, who developed some of his ideas in response to what he regarded as the hostile vision of Sartre's philosophy. While Sartre sees others as a threat to our freedom, Marcel regards others as manifesting the mystery and splendor of being. Marcel affirms relations with others, whether strangers or others to whom we make commitments or to whom we feel responsibility.

Marcel describes the disposition we must have in order to avoid reduction of others to an object or a mere function. He calls this disposition "creative fidelity" or presence. Marcel writes of "that inward realization of presence through love" for the other. To be present to others is a form of selfless generosity that cannot be calculated or verified. Presence does not involve a dialectic that inevitably devolves to oppression, but remains an open attitude to the other, and an affirmation. To be present for others means being available to them, regarding others in all their complexity and possibility as mysteries rather than problems to be solved.

Marcel advocates in daily life being there for others as one in whom they can confide, from whom they may seek reassurance. Presence can be offered in a look, a smile, a handshake, an intonation, in genuine listening, through which we might offer not only attentiveness and conscientiousness, but making room in one's own view of the world for the specificity of the other. In presence, our understanding resists becoming closed off by the accumulation of our own experience and the categories that arise from it. When these remain permeable and revisable, Marcel thinks, we avoid being captive by the anxiety of self-encumberment. We realize our freedom in light of openness to others, a realization that may protect against despair of an objectified world, one without mystery or meaning.

If Sartre's account of self-other relations is grounded in an ontology of oppression, overlooking more positive dynamics between human beings, Marcel's analysis may seem naïve from the perspective of the oppressed. But the same could not be said of Fanon. Despite his penetrating analysis of racial injustice in a colonial context and its devastating effects, Fanon holds out hope for overcoming the master-slave dialectic that grounds oppressive relationships between self and other.

> It is through self-consciousness and renunciation, through a permanent tension of his freedom, that man can create the ideal conditions of existence for a human world. Superiority? Inferiority? Why not simply try to touch the other, feel the other, discover each other?

Fanon's position suggests a rapprochement between the ontology of oppression and an ethics of recognition and mutuality.

To his credit, and despite his rather negative vision of intersocial relations, Sartre also regarded the freedom of others as indisputable and indeed as demanded by the self's own freedom. To recognize oneself as free is to recognize freedom as a universal condition, according to Sartre. Both Sartre and Beauvoir, while regarding conflict as inherent to the ontology of the subject, argue that the freedom of one subject implies and demands the freedom of other subjects. As Beauvoir writes in *The Ethics of Ambiguity*: "To will oneself free is to effect the transition from nature to morality by establishing a genuine freedom on the original upsurge of our existence. . . . [B]y turning toward this freedom we are going to discover a principle of action whose range will be universal." Any defense of my own freedom implies that of all others.

> An ethics of ambiguity will be one which will refuse to deny *a priori* that separate existants can, at the same time, be bound to each other, that their individual freedoms can forge laws valid for all.

On the same basis Camus demands ethical rebellion against the oppression of others. In this case one may take up the cause— even if that means against other antagonistic others—for others' freedom.

8 | WORLD

We have seen that from an existentialist perspective, the self is inseparable from the world. So too is the world—or the world as it is for us—inseparable from human experience. Existentialists challenge claims to absolute objectivity about the world. They reject any god's-eye view of reality.

For the existentialist thinker, a world is not merely a collection of all the material stuff that is there but rather a lived phenomenon. The world for the existentialist thinker must be experienced from within, as it were. Even the earthly substrate of our world, according to some existentialists, cannot be exhaustively accounted for only by measuring and objectively analyzing it. The being of things, the presence of world, the very fact that there is a world here for us, are sources of existential wonder.

This does not mean that existentialists deny us any objective view of the world. Yet they recognize that since we are always involved in the world, any objectivity to be achieved is qualified by that involvement. Existentialists recognize, as Marcel put it, that "knowledge is contingent on a participation in being for which no epistemology can account because it continually presupposes it." The "world" is a sphere of involvement within a totality that cannot be made wholly objective.

Scientific thinking must aim to eliminate any private influence on our observations. Its achievements require taking a third-person, impersonal point of view on material reality. Some existentialists, particularly Jaspers, appreciate the importance of scientific efforts to transcend partiality, yet they would challenge the exclusive claim by any one domain of knowledge to total truth about the world. Of course, scientists themselves have abandoned claims to absolute objectivity, recognizing that the very fact of observing a phenomenon changes it. They may also admit that directions of inquiry, interest taken in this or that aspect of the world, reflect particular concerns and scientific priorities. What is at one time regarded as categorical truth may be later revealed to be partial or limited in some way.

In contrast to scientific thinking, existentialist thinking concentrates on the world as it is experienced by us, and how it matters to us—from the human and personal point of view. "More than objective knowledge," writes Camus, "it is the experience of the world that makes it intimately my world." This experience and this intimacy imbue the very notion of a "world" with existential value, while it is also possible to become alienated from the world, to feel it defamiliarized and strange.

Some aspects of the world cannot be understood at all without including a first-person perspective. Experiential phenomena such as perceptions and emotions can be studied in objective ways—as firings of neurons, for instance, or as chemical processes in the brain—but these phenomena cannot be fully grasped without lived familiarity. First-hand knowledge of things and practical know-how can be described abstractly, but their meaning is experiential in nature. In order to grasp some phenomena, we must have occasion to have been personally involved at one time or another. Decision making, curiosity, commitment, interpersonal conflict, love, altruism, and inspiration are a few examples. These elements of conscious life experienced from the first-person perspective are as much a part of the world for the existentialist as are trees, buildings, streets, rocks, or the earth itself.

The world is a totality not only of things but also of meanings and potential meanings, while the always partial, sometimes fragmentary nature of our experience also calls this totality—and these meanings—into question. Accordingly, the world may be experienced in a number of existential registers. We may be alienated from the world, or fall into indifference; we may find it absurd, or we may encounter it in a mode of awe. We are always attuned to the world in some way or other, and this attunement belongs to our being-in-the-world.

Heidegger's most significant contribution to existentialism may be his concept of being-in-the-world. The dashes, of course, are meant to show the inseparability of our being with the world we are in. While all other beings—stones, trees, human-made objects like tables and pencils—simply are, the human being exists in a unique way. For our relation to the world around us, what we make of and do with it, contributes to what we are, to our Dasein. From this perspective, a consideration of the world entails questions about human existence and the human self.

As we have seen, existentialists argue that we are never just reposing inside ourselves, or simply there among other things as things are, but are rather always extending toward the world through our activities, involvement, and interpretation. We come from a particular worldly place and time, but we also transcend this particularity, while transforming the world we are in. We express and elaborate our existence through our projects, through those things in the world which we are aiming to understand, which we enjoy, transform, manipulate, use, arrange, admire, or create. We are connected to the world not only biologically—in light of the air we breathe, the water we drink, the food we eat, the place we shelter—but through a whole network of activities and concerns. The world takes shape for us through what we do in the world, though this relationship between our activity and the world may remain implicit and unreflected in ordinary experience.

We can take the phenomena of the equipment that belongs to a human world. Heidegger's famous example in *Being and Time* is the hammer. Our activity with the hammer manifests implicit worldly relations, interconnections among things that belong to our world. We implicitly engage these interconnections when we take up, for example, the nails that must be pounded into wood, when we consider the factory or workshop where they were made, the forest from which the wood came, the people who may use the table to be constructed, the meals and conversations and everyday activities that may take place around that table. Unless and until the hammer breaks, we may scarcely notice how things are interrelated in this worldly arrangement.

The world is a usually unconsidered, implicit network of meanings in which we exist, and their surrounding horizons. It includes the ever-changing configuration of things around us, which shift as we move toward or away from them, work to preserve or change them. We may not usually notice the world in this way, going about our everyday business. Should the hammer—or whatever tool we are using—break, however, we may notice the network of relations with the surrounding world the tool itself and the activity with it had established. Some of the relationships that make up the worldly arrangement of things become explicit to awareness when there is a break in the circuit of relations.

While this everyday experience may not lead to any deep thinking about the world, Heidegger regards it as an impetus to begin to contemplate our being-in-the-world. When habitual expectations are unsatisfied or break down, we may begin to notice the world in a different way. Of course, such attention to the world can be then further elaborated in creative ways. Apart from phenomenological philosophy or existential contemplation, we may write poetry or tell stories, make artworks or films or videos, take photographs, all of which can present the world as a realm of explicit reflection.

As being-in-the-world we do not merely absorb the world's data for anonymous processing—though that is one potential mode of abstract regard—but remain constantly interconnected through our projects and concerns. We never face the world in complete neutrality but always find ourselves disposed within the world in a particular way. The phenomenon of attunement describes that color or particular cast through which the world is experienced by an involved human subject. Heidegger employs the notion of "attunement" to indicate a quality of receptivity that, since it is constituted through human interests and concerns, belongs to our every encounter with the world. As Heidegger puts it, "In attunement lies existentially a disclosive submission to world out of which things which matter to us can be encountered."

Attunement, then, is a structure of awareness of the world, specifically toned or modulated through our mood, and through which we disclose various possibilities within the world. Specific moods, such as anxiety or joy, are not only pre-cognitive affects or emotions but also existential orientations that disclose the world in certain ways. A mood is not just a feeling, then, but includes an atmosphere that extends across self and world and contributes to our interpretation of them. In everyday life and for the most part, we are aware of our moods primarily through coloring they give to the world, in a given circumstance and at a particular time. Objects in the world around us look inviting or discouraging not only due to their objective features but according to our own faring, for they are prospects for our potential activity, enjoyment, or avoidance.

Our specific moods may be as shifting as the weather, changing like the light in a sequence of Impressionist paintings. The world will look different to us depending on whether we feel inspired or discouraged, content or disaffected, energized or defeated, and we will be influenced in our moods by physical pain or comfort, hunger or satiety. We can be aware of these orientations in moments of self-reflection, but in the ordinary activities of life they remain largely unregarded, since it is the world as much as ourselves that they disclose. Sometimes we are aware of our own moods primarily through how other things look to us at the time. Heidegger suggests that "the mooded nature of attunement constitutes existentially Dasein's openness to world." Ultimately the world is revealed as that context of existence for the being to whom being is a question.

This description of the world in terms of human involvement can be seen as an existential adaptation of Husserl's phenomenological notion of constitution. Regarding the world phenomenologically, we bracket any ontological interrogation of its being as it may be apart from its appearance, and regard the world precisely in its appearing, as phenomena. The world phenomenologically speaking is a correlate of consciousness, such that consciousness "constitutes" it through intentionality. But that does not mean that the world is the product of consciousness, or that the world only exists for our perception. Rather, it means that phenomenology recognizes the contribution of consciousness to the world's appearance to us.

The notion of constitution helps to explain how acts of consciousness register, for example, the specific relations that make a beautiful landscape appear as a harmonious whole. We recognize that it is from our own perspective that the landscape, or the world in general, appears as it does. We can abstract from this perspective and gain objective knowledge about the world—for example, in studying the landscape's structures and measuring its underlying, for instance geological, features. In that case then the world is known by way of abstract thinking generated through and beyond a prior constitutive familiarity.

As Husserl saw it, an objective understanding of the world is not lost through phenomenological thinking. Rather, phenomenology attempts to account for the constitution of objectivity, how an intersubjectively verifiable account of the world is enabled by abstraction from lived experience. In "The Origin of Geometry," an appendix to his *Crisis of the European Sciences*, Husserl considers the concepts of geometry and mathematics, for example, as arising from experience in and with the physical world. While Descartes regarded such ideas as innate to the mind, Husserl conceived of them as generated by abstract thinking on the basis of empirical experience. Although there are no perfect triangles in nature, the concept of such may have emerged by abstracting from our ordinary measurements in lived space.

If we only ever begin with partial views of the world, how do we arrive at a concept of the world as a whole? Husserl argued that a "world horizon" forms the general experiential framework for our perception and knowledge of the particular objects we perceive and think about at any given time. We do not ever see the totality that makes these things belong to the world as a whole, but they are encompassed within this projected, but implicit, horizon. In terms used frequently by Beauvoir, the "totality" that is the world we experience is always experienced by a human subject from a "detotalized" position. From any given moment and place we perceive or think about only a fragmentary part of the world, but we make sense of this within the context of a projected whole.

At the moment, for example, I am thinking about a number of existentialist concepts. Right now, at the same time, I·hear some music playing from a radio in the background. I see my computer screen and the coffee cup from which I've been sipping, the tables in the café, a view through the window of an expanse of green and some bare trees from the square outside, a few people walking about under a bleak mid-winter sky. These and any other objects of my perception and thought at the moment are just the tiniest fraction of the world. Even if I put these together with all of the things of the world I have ever experienced and thought about, it would all together still add up to but a minuscule fragment of the world as a whole. Yet at every moment I am aware that every bit that I experience belongs to such a whole. I do not experience my partial glimpses as broken-off fragments but as part of the world itself, of one fabric with an implicit whole world.

While these phenomenological notions of the world horizon and the lifeworld describe our sense of world-belonging, existentialists also explore our sense of fragmentation. Nietzsche proposed a vision of the world in which detotalization wins out against any projected totality. Nietzsche gave serious weight to the fact that we have only ever a tiny slice of the world in our view, and pointed out that we ever only occupy but one perspective alongside innumerable other perspectives and possible perspectives. How then could we adjudicate among differing points of view? Nietzsche was suspicious about ideas of totality, for they might lead us to idealize the notion of a unified reality above and beyond all appearances. For this reason, Nietzsche seized on the notion of the partial perspective as the very truth of appearances.

Nietzsche's perspectivism affirmed the multiplicity and difference, discrediting any idea of world as it would be apart from, or behind, these various perspectives. Perspectivism arises, as he puts it in *The Gay Science*, "when we cannot reject the possibility that life may include infinite interpretations." For Nietzsche the world should be affirmed even in its unstable, often conflicting appearances. Such a view allows for the "rich ambiguous character" of the world. Although Nietzsche recognized its terrifying aspect, he suggested that if we could accept such a vision of the world, we ought to be able to accept any fate that would befall us.

The threat of fragmentation, however, is more hauntingly described by other existentialist thinkers. We can feel alienated from the world, for even in everyday life we may not always feel at home. We can experience the world as contrary to our most urgent needs and desires. The very fact that human beings have developed a profound sense of inner experience may sometimes place us at odds with the world around us, particularly in the context of the decline of traditions which explain such inwardness as part of a providential design for our lives. Existentialists have a lot to say about a world experienced as inhospitable, as estranging.

We might question why there is a world at all in the first place. The Young Man character in Kierkegaard's *Repetition* demands to know:

> Where am I? What does it mean to say: the world? What is the meaning of the world? Who tricked me into this whole thing and leaves me standing here? . . . How did I get into the world? Why was I not asked about it?

Rather than the unconsidered background to all that I experience, or its unifying horizon, the world may suddenly appear to us as conspicuous and strange.

Heidegger described this as the experience of the uncanny. Our being-in-the-world results, he explains, from our having been "thrown" into a world. By this he means that we are born into a world already full of activities and things and meanings, none of which we had any say about. Continuing the trajectory of that thrownness, we tend to "fall" into the world, usually absorbed with the tasks of living, invested in our attachments, preoccupied by various distractions. If we are phenomenologically awakened, as a student of Husserl might become, we may come to regard the world as a correlate of our constitutive intentionality. Yet we may suddenly find ourselves ill at ease in what had been so familiar. We may suddenly feel there to be a chasm separating us from the rest of reality.

The German word for uncanniness, *Unheimlichkeit*, is literally the state of not being at home. For Heidegger this uncanniness in which the world comes to be cast is brought about by anxiety about death—by becoming suddenly aware of the possibility of nothingness, of becoming nothing. I look up from all this worldly stuff and it may dawn on me that my being is precarious, and more, that I will at some point simply cease to be. What may most shock me is not the thought of my own ending, but that the world will simply go on without me. Not just death itself, but the contrast between the world's being and the idea of my not being, can prompt anxiety.

The theme and title of Sartre's most famous novel, *Nausea*, suggest repulsion from the world. Roquentin finds himself at odds with a world exposed in its bare contingency. From the standpoint of his nausea, the world in its fleshy materiality and shifting contours is experienced by Roquentin as repellent. Even Roquentin's own face is described as a foreign mass of flesh, his hand as strange as the claw of a crab. The material objects he confronts, the landscape and cityscape of Bouville, the social world of its inhabitants, are all subjected to what one critic describes as an acidic reduction of meaning.

Again the critic is Marcel, who argues that the cost of Sartre's emphasis on the absolute freedom of consciousness is a "negative enlightenment" about the world to which it belongs. Sartre's categorical division, even opposition, between consciousness and the rest of being is problematic for Marcel. Of the illness indicated by the title of Sartre's novel, Marcel writes: "Nausea is, at bottom, the experience of contingency and of the absurdity which attaches to existence as such." Marcel offers, in contrast, a reverent account of world as a source not of alienation but of reverence.

Before turning to a more reverent attunement to the world, we can consider the fact that of course the world is not always a hospitable place for the human subject. If the physical world does not fit my hopes and desires, and my personal finitude provokes anxiety, the social dimension of the world also poses difficulties. The world we share with others does not always promote human freedom. Dr. Martin Luther King Jr.'s interest in existentialist philosophers arose from what he saw as their common diagnosis of the threat of fragmentation.

King wrote that existentialists all recognized that "history is a series of unreconciled conflicts and man's existence is filled with anxiety and threatened with meaninglessness." The human world is fraught with antagonism. Undoubtedly the experience of oppression—the political and social denial of one's intrinsic freedom, for instance, in circumstances of racist segregation in which King wrote—may radically amplify this sense of fragmentation. Acknowledging existentialism's influence on his own intellectual and spiritual journey, King found that existentialism's "perception of the anxiety and conflict produced in man's personal and social life as a result of the perilous and ambiguous structure of existence is especially meaningful for our time."

Alienation from the world comes in many forms, and a number of literary depictions concern the problems wrought in the modern world in particular. Of course, the modern world brings innumerable improvements in the human lot—such as medicines, communication technologies, and widespread education—and an expansion in our capacities to explore the world. Despite such advantages, Dostoevsky's underground man and Rilke's Malte, discussed in earlier chapters, both experience the modern world in an attunement of alienation. Both authors diagnose the modern human being as essentially at odds with the world. In the underground man's case, the overrationalization of modern society repels the self-aware mind. To Malte, anonymity and rootlessness caused by urbanization and technological alienation from nature make the world inhospitable. Marcel too, for all his attunement of wonder, worried about the aspects of the modern world that threaten to reduce human beings to mere functions of production and consumption.

A sense of existential alienation from the world may also arise in response to the modern scientific perspective on the physical universe. Having once regarded itself as the very purpose of creation, Western humanity may be pained to feel insignificant in a vast, godless cosmos. Nietzsche described a cosmic perspective, pointing out how minuscule and petty human beings and their concerns seem once you look at the world from the point of view of the stars. From a cosmic perspective we, and the entire planet which comprises our worldly home, are just specks of dust in a universe so vast as we can scarcely even imagine its size. Nietzsche could not yet know that it takes over 46 billion light years to reach the edge of the observable universe alone. It is still unknown how far the universe may extend beyond that boundary of observation.

Science allows us to consider the world without illusions—in particular without the illusion that the world is made especially for human life and its particular needs. Yet some existentialists' reservations about the domination of a scientific perspective reflect not only their interest in first-person phenomena, but also their anxiety over what Max Weber called the world's disenchantment, an anxiety they shared with their Romantic predecessors. Reducing our sense of the world—including all human phenomena—to that which can be entirely accounted for by science would leave us existentially adrift, our personal existence undernourished. In *The Myth of Sisyphus*, Camus writes:

> In a universe that is suddenly deprived of illusions and of light, man feels a stranger. His is an irremediable exile, because he is deprived of memories of a lost homeland as much as he lacks the hope of a promised land.

Existentialists argue that while it can offer knowledge about the world, science cannot account for the world's meaning to us. The existentialist thinker explores the consequences for us of explaining the world in exhaustively scientific terms.

Going beyond the rejection of a total scientific explanation of the world, some existentialists seem to depict the world as wholly unpredictable or absurd. As Marcel complained, Sartre's *Nausea* depicts a world melting down into chaos. "Absurdist" literature seems to depict a distorted and even deranged world. We have mentioned Kafka's example of Gregor Samsa devolved to an insect, and in a famous absurdist play, *Rhinoceros*, Eugene Ionesco depicts inhabitants of a small town turning into that animal. Yet these are not served up as realist descriptions but as literary metaphors, and it is their contrast with the ordinary appearance of the world that provokes readers to wonder about it. Existentialist philosophies of absurdity likewise do not necessarily endorse an irrational vision of the world itself but allow for an irresolvable contradiction between the world as objectively known and its human interpretation.

While there are many literary inspirations for an absurdist philosophy, it was Camus who formalized this idea, in *The Myth of Sisyphus*, as an existentialist insight. Again, it is not the world itself Camus described as absurd but the mismatch between the needs of human consciousness and the world it seeks to understand. Given the nature of our consciousness, we cannot but ask after the meaning of the world and our place in it. Yet no matter how we look at it, even from a scientific perspective, the world offers no answer. According to Camus, "the absurd is born of this confrontation between the human mind and the unreasonable silence of the world."

Camus interprets the ancient Greek myth of Sisyphus as expressing an awareness of the absurd. The gods, to punish Sisyphus, force him to roll a boulder up the mountain, only to watch it fall down over and over again, for infinity. There is no meaning to this toil, and its results are ever undone, yet it must be undertaken over and over. The analogy to human life in the modern world is poignant. According to Camus we cannot find any guaranteed meaning to human existence, though we expend so much effort to live and to keep on living. Human beings explore the unknown, erect skyscrapers, write books, and raise families. We journey to work and home, to the grocery shop and back in a regular rhythm, for many decades to keep ourselves and our loved ones alive. Without an afterlife, the results of all our efforts eventually end in a dust-heap. The meaninglessness of human life in such a perspective can extend to our feeling about the world itself: what purpose is a world in which any final end is unachievable?

Sometimes the most dramatic worldly events seem not only without meaning but contrary to any possible sense or purpose. Natural disasters—erupting volcanoes, earthquakes, tsunamis, and droughts—have wiped out cities and even civilizations. The world we know may be torn apart by the chaos and destruction of war. Each individual life is vulnerable to disaster and despair. Camus was only a year old when his father was killed in a battle in the Argon forest, nine days after the Armistice of World War I, the war that was "to end all wars." Camus's own untimely death— in a car accident, with a ticket in his pocket for the equivalent train journey he did not take—is often cited as expressing the central concept of his own philosophy. These unnecessary tragedies may give rise to a sense that the world itself, this one refuge of our existence, is absurd. But this is, again, only shorthand for the mismatch between our expectations of meaning and the lack of any meaningful explanation the world and its happenings may offer.

The sense of the absurdity of the world may be provoked even in the most ordinary circumstances. Our lives may be so regulated by the demands of getting by that the repetition of the most mundane tasks can seem absurd. Camus describes the humdrum of everyday experience:

> Rising, street-car, four hours in the office or the factory, meal, street-car, four hours of work, meal, sleep, and Monday Tuesday Wednesday Thursday Friday and Saturday according to the same rhythm—this path is easily followed most of the time. But one day the "why" arises and everything begins in that weariness tinged with amazement.

We may look up from our habitual comings and goings, our efforts and labors, our moments of repose. We may suddenly question the purpose of this rhythm, and then ask after our own purpose, and perhaps the purpose of the world itself. Camus suggests here that we do not need any special provocation to come to question the world. We need not even confront the idea of our own death after which the world will go on as before. We can simply take a step back from the rhythm of our lives and wonder what it is all about. Camus reckons with this possibility head-on:

> I don't know whether this world has a meaning that transcends it. But I know that I do not know that meaning and that it is impossible for me just now to know it. What can a meaning outside my condition mean to me? I can understand only in human terms.

Camus concludes that we must not look for the world itself to harbor meaning, but to ourselves for a source of meaning's creation.

Camus realizes that one might be tempted to respond with nihilism. Since the world itself yields no meaning, it might be said that nothing matters, one may as well do nothing or anything at all. Against such slippage into nihilism, Nietzsche suggested that even in the face of a meaningless world, affirmation is not only possible, but the only truly healthy response. It takes courage to affirm existence just as it is, and to create despite its futility from a cosmic point of view. Echoing this affirmative vision of Nietzsche, Camus insisted that happiness is possible in the face of the absurd. He argued that we should interpret even Sisyphus as happy. We can get beyond nihilism by seeing in the absurd, as Camus wrote, a "lucid invitation to live and to create."

Beyond fragmentation, alienation, and absurdity, the existentialist may also regard the world an attunement of wonder. Though recognized as not made for our use, the world may be felt to include us and may be experienced as splendorous. Despite Camus's own thesis of absurdity, his descriptions of nature, of the elements, of everyday life sometimes overflow with affirmations of the world experienced in sensuous glory. Here the existentialist does not oppose or objectify the world but accepts the world just as it appears, in a state that may be described as awe. Camus writes:

> And here are trees and I know their gnarled surface, water and I feel its taste. These scents of grass and stars at night, certain evenings when the heart relaxes—how shall I negate this world whose power and strength I feel?

And again:

> At the moment, my whole kingdom is of this world. This sun and these shadows, this warmth and this cold rising from the depths of the air. . . . When am I truer than when I am in the world? My cup brims over before I have time to desire.

Despite its silence to our demand for meaning, the world as Camus describes it can fill the self with satiation and contentment.

Marcel too emphasizes the mystery and wonder of a world that evades exhaustively rational explanation. The wondrousness of the world does not register in analytical knowledge. But the fact that the world is ever only grasped through a detotalized perspective, he thinks, allows room for our intervention and creativity. At the same time, although we have no epistemic grasp of its higher unity or totality, we may sense the world in its wholeness through a kind of existential intuition. What Marcel calls the "overflowing richness of reality" should be experienced as "something positive, as a kind of glory." If Sartre often depicts the world in opposition to the existential subject, Marcel affirms its being as a glorious gift.

While we must also aim to regard the world objectively—that is what our evolved rationality is for—we do not have to reduce our understanding of the world to this dimension only. In Marcel's terms, while "first reflection" regards the world only in objective terms, a "second" form of reflection recognizes the irreducibility of being to an objectively solvable problem. This second reflection, recognizing the mystery encompassing the world's being, is beyond the boundaries of knowledge proper. Jaspers called this dimension the "encompassing."

To recognize the mystery of being, that which encompasses our world and makes any world possible, is not to deny reason and knowledge but to recognize that the world is a manifestation of a greater dimension that will always exceed our objective grasp. To regard the world existentially is, as Marcel puts it, to recognize "that knowledge is, as it were, environed by being, that it is interior to it in a certain sense." Despite the existential interest in uncanniness and absurdity as a potential response to the world as we see it, existentialist thinking too touches upon a more generous receptivity to the world. Even Rilke, as the author of Malte who found the modern world alien, and as poet of angelic abandonment, encourages just such a view of the world. Echoing Nietzsche, Rilke writes:

> We have no reason to harbour any mistrust against our world, for it is not against us. If it has terrors, they are our terrors; if it has abysses, these abysses belong to us; if there are dangers, we must try to love them.

This sense of generous acceptance of the world is, too, crucial to how we treat the world. The implications of an existential sense of the world will bear upon our relations to the earth.

9 | EARTH

There are good reasons to think of nature, or much of living earth, as in contrast to the human. To begin with, only human beings, so far as we know, have existential concerns, anxieties, and philosophies. Not only our language and ideas, but much of human practice distances us from the natural world. Once human beings learned to conquer many of nature's challenges, many humans have regarded nature primarily as a resource to be exploited. As human civilization expands, non-human nature is crowded out.

In two centuries since the advent of the industrial revolution, our relation to nature has become disastrously imbalanced. Producing and consuming on a mass scale, we have polluted the earth's atmosphere. We have exploded mountains, flattened forests the size of whole countries, clogged the oceans with plastic. We have contributed to climate change through the persistent burning of fossil fuels and the eradication of forests, and we are heading for catastrophe as a result. The use of our existing nuclear weapons could lead to human extinction and the extinction of much of the life on the planet, and yet we continue to build more. The difference and distance between the human and the non-human have led not only to our alienation from nature but to the very endangerment of the earth itself as a living planet.

This situation familiar from current news would not seem, at first glance, to be in any significant way challenged by a philosophy centered on human existence and individuality. Indeed, existentialism has been criticized for its anthropocentrism and egocentrism. Sartre for one often described nature as a threat to human subjectivity and freedom. Yet other existentialist thinkers, particularly Nietzsche, Camus, and Heidegger, along with the poet Rilke, urge concern for the earth, critically rethinking our role in nature. Before considering ecologically oriented existentialism, however, we might first look again critically at the philosophy of Sartre, the limitations of which become starkly apparent when we consider the question of non-human nature.

Like all thinkers described as existentialist, Sartre begins with the fact that human consciousness is unlike anything else in the universe. As a self-aware capacity for initiating action of our own will, consciousness is considered exclusive to human beings and the source of our freedom. In Sartre's philosophy, nature is, at best, merely an object, or potential object, for human consciousness. When nature is appreciated—as when we regard a beautiful landscape—Sartre credits human consciousness with establishing relations among its various elements. This view is in part sanctioned by the phenomenological notion of constitution. Yet not only is beauty, for Sartre, judged by the beholder; it is constructed in the eye of the mind. While a beautiful landscape may provoke in many of us a feeling of awe or reverence for the natural world, for Sartre such beauty is but an occasion to celebrate human exceptionalism.

Sartre's thinking goes further, disparaging nature, especially living nature, as repulsive or hostile. The earthly is mere in-itself, to be resisted or overpowered by the for-itself, for even merely as matter, nature seems a threat to the sovereignty of consciousness. In *Nausea*, Roquentin describes the mute being of material existence as "hateful." For him the root of a chestnut tree appears repugnant, an oozing serpent. He finds nature redundant, dumb, and existentially void: "What good are so many duplicates of trees?" he asks. "Those great clumsy bodies. . . . They did not want to exist, only they could not help themselves."

Sartre himself describes in somewhat more neutral terms the starker landscapes of mountains and seas with their flat horizons. But even here the relation is oppositional. In *Being and Nothingness* an effort to climb a mountain is "a way of appropriating the mountain, of suffering it to the end and being victor over it." Sartre imagines the human subject exercising power over and against nature in the mode of such appropriation:

> This mountain which I climb is myself to the extent that I conquer it; and when I am at its summit, which I have "achieved" at the cost of this same effort, when I attain this magnificent view of the valley and the surrounding peaks, then I am the view; the panorama is myself dilated to the horizon, for it exists only through me, only for me.

With the Cartesian ego as his starting-point, Sartre would take such monuments of the natural world as its possession.

Attending this philosophical attitude was Sartre's own personal disgust for nature. In her memoirs Beauvoir reported that Sartre "loathed" the countryside, feeling at home only in cities, "at the heart of an artificial universe with man-made objects." He preferred the human body clothed—even those of the lovers he ardently pursued. Sartre would eat only foods processed by human effort, their natural form disguised. Fruit was acceptable to Sartre only when made into preserves—when he could not recognize the natural source. A stunning contrast is found in Rilke's *Sonnets to Orpheus*, whose speaker savors ripe fruit as "double-meaninged, sunny, earthy, present," affording as it does for the speaker rich "experience, sensation, joy." While Sartre's Roquentin is bored by the redundant awkwardness of trees, for Rilke's speaker in the sonnets a tree is an emblem of transcendence.

We must look beyond Sartre to other existentialist thinkers, then, to understand the scope of more generous relations to nature in an existentialist light. The first existentialist philosopher to reconsider our relationship to nature in an ecological way was Nietzsche, whose thinking was in part devoted to revalidating the realm of becoming, that of earthly experience long-disparaged by Western philosophy. Nietzsche rejected any philosophy that favored eternal ideas "beyond the stars" over the changing natural world around us. Nietzsche argued that whenever we regard truth as wholly transcendent, beyond this world and time, the earth is thereby devalued. This history of philosophy since Plato had led to the denigration of the earth in favor of timeless ideas. In the name of Christianity, Augustine rejected the life of the mortal body and its worldly attachments in favor of an eternal afterlife. Descartes followed suit by understanding the essential human mind as isolated from all else, even from the human body, and by distrusting the world as known by the senses.

In contrast, Nietzsche not only promoted the truth of appearances as experienced in and through embodied life, but affirmed nature itself. The protagonist of his novel *Thus Spoke Zarathustra* implores his followers to remain "true to the earth." Nietzsche rejected the idea that our rational capacities render us radically distinct from the rest of nature. While we are uniquely self-conscious, and perhaps—from Nietzsche's perspective—overly intellectual, human beings are also shot through with nature, with the impulses and drives of organic life. We are not primarily rational idealists but physiological beings. For Nietzsche this means we are earthy, natural organisms as all other animals are. In this vein Zarathustra promotes a future manifestation of humanity evolved not away from our natural origins, but as the very "meaning of the earth."

Nietzsche was one of the first philosophers to contend with the impact of Darwin's *On the Origin of Species* (1859). Nietzsche took notice of Darwin's explanation of human life as connected, through evolution, to all living beings via a single primogenitor. Thus Zarathustra acknowledges the human being as having evolved from apes—while yet challenging human superiority as a fiction or human prejudice. "Once you were apes, and yet the human being is even now still more ape than any ape," Zarathustra declares. This view is echoed elsewhere in Nietzsche's writings, when it is hypothesized, somewhat comically, that the human being may be considered but a limited phase in the evolution of the ape.

Yet Nietzsche envisioned a program of further evolution for human beings who might make some effort to overcome what he found to be the sorry state of the human species. He thought that if all of nature is dynamically evolving, there is no fixed essence that determines once and for all what we are. The human being could go further, not just by struggling for existence and self-propagation, but by striving to become something better, striving for a more vital existence, one more harmonious with the natural world of becoming. In other words, Nietzsche appropriated evolutionary thinking toward an existentialist project compatible with fidelity to the earth.

It may be paradoxical that to achieve this self-overcoming self-creation, we must overcome anthropocentric thinking, and abandon human hubris. Nietzsche begins an early essay "On Truth and Lies in an Extramoral Sense" with an ironic fairy tale meant to expose the delusions of anthropocentrism.

> In some or other remote corner of that universe which is dispersed into innumerable twinkling solar systems, there was once a star upon which clever beasts invented knowing. . . . After nature had drawn a few breaths, the star congealed, and the clever beasts had to die.

Human beings are, of course, the "clever beasts." The point of this imagined zooming out to a cosmological scale is to displace the anthropocentric perspective on which much of the Western tradition had been founded. Nietzsche then shifts to the perspective of the smallest animals, exposing the specificity, and limitedness, of human cognition. He points out that "the insect or the bird perceives an entirely different world from the human." Nietzsche's perspectivism would prohibit the human perspective, over that of insect or bird, from becoming the criterion of any absolute objectivity.

Nietzsche further challenges the superiority traditionally granted the human being, again by contrast to an insect. The bee constructs its hive with wax produced from material gathered laboriously from nature. Humans, with all their philosophy, merely fabricate our idea of reality "from far more delicate conceptual material, which the human first must fabricate from himself." This conceptual fabrication, Nietzsche charges, misleads the human being about the nature of reality and truth. While the bee makes something real from real raw material, what we fancy to be the "really real" underlying all appearances—Plato's forms, Kant's in itself—is only a hubristic illusion.

While Nietzsche did not fully anticipate the environmental disaster that would ensue in the century after his death, he recognized the disastrous consequences of human hubris. In *The Genealogy of Morals* he wrote that "hubris is today our entire position on nature, our violation of nature with the help of machines and the ever so thoughtless ingenuity of technicians and engineers." Zarathustra is haunted by the soothsayer's description of a wrecked earth that has become a graveyard. In this vision of environmental disaster, the fruits of the earth have turned foul and poisonous, the fields dry and ashen, wells empty, and even the sea has retreated. Zarathustra laments: "Oh where is there still a sea in which one could drown?—thus rings our lament—out across the shallow swamps."

This warning will be echoed by Rilke in the *Sonnets to Orpheus*, whose speaker describes modern human consciousness as opposing nature through fragmentation, taking "piecework and parts as though it were the whole." In the machine age, Rilke suggests, human technology distances us from nature but also from ourselves. Machines are not merely our tools but distort and weaken the human beings who set them to work against the natural world. In the machine age, carving up nature for our use, we end up producing and destroying in equal resolve. As an alternative, Rilke promotes a more authentic relationship to nature he thinks may be figured in poetry.

Rilke's poetry, along with that of Hölderlin, inspires Heidegger's later thinking, devoted largely to reconceiving the human relationship to the earth. While in *Being and Time* Heidegger was primarily concerned with understanding the human constitution of world, in "Origin of the Work of Art," Heidegger adds "earth" as the world's counterpoint. While world is constituted through human life and practice, earth does not yield entirely to human efforts to reveal it. Earth withholds and withdraws while also becoming manifest through the struggle of expression in our worldly efforts.

Heidegger tends to think of the problem of the earth in the sense of a local German *Heimat* or homeland, and thus veers at times into repugnant nationalist politics. Yet Heidegger's thought turns eventually to ways to dwell on earth "poetically" rather than aggressively. He hopes that we can learn to dwell poetically upon the earth with an awareness of our special, sheltering relationship to Being itself. Heidegger's promotion of the stance of *Gelassenheit*, loosely translated as "letting-be," is issued in the wake of a searing critique of modern technological exploitation of the earth.

In an essay called the "Letter on Humanism," Heidegger criticizes the anthropocentrism of existentialism—particularly the Sartrean variety with which his own philosophy came to be associated. Heidegger admits to some residual anthropocentrism in his own articulation of Dasein's relation to world in *Being and Time*. Shifting his concern to thinking of earth and our dwelling on it, Heidegger came to draw upon poetry for ways to "reveal" the earth in a non-exploitive way. A more original relation to the earth—a more authentic grasp of being—is enabled, he thinks, by poetry. For the poetry may describe an intimate connection with nature without the illusion that its revealing is complete or definitive.

Another essay, "The Question Concerning Technology," is credited with first bringing philosophical attention to the human manipulation of nature by modern technological means. Heidegger is the philosopher most inspiring for "deep ecology," an ecological perspective which holds the earth and nature as intrinsically valuable apart from the resources they offer for human life. Heidegger criticized modern technology for "enframing" the earth for human use and exploitation. Heidegger's citation there of Hölderlin—that "where danger grows, is the saving power"— holds out hope for the possibility of poetic stewardship of the earth, or of being. Such poetic dwelling would involve a more reverent relationship to being itself. It could be achieved not primarily through abstract conceptualization but through lived existence of authentic human communities.

German existentialist thinkers, of course, do not have a monopoly on reverence for nature. While concerned primarily about human authenticity and spirituality, Marcel develops his case for a more wholistic relation to nature in his work *Man against Mass Society*. There Marcel criticizes technological reduction of the lifeworld, where persons and natural objects are manipulated as things. Reckless mastery of nature leads to our ignorance of the sacred, the mysterious, the transcendent, such that we lose our native wonder in being. Marcel's concern extends to wonder in nature. In contrast to the abstracting and exploitive features of modern existence, Marcel defended the "feeling for the natural" in human life and in our experience of the world. Marcel argued that a healthy relation to nature, both the nature within us (or bodies) and outside us, can foster vitality and creativity, respect for diversity, and a sense of wonder. Rather than isolation from the non-human, existential authenticity should foster harmony with the natural element of ourselves and with the surrounding natural world.

Reverential regard for nature also abounds in the writings of Camus, particularly in his literary writings. The seascape and the desert, descriptions of birds, trees, insects, and lizards, the elements of air and water and light, whether described in the form of memoir, essay, or novel, were fundamental to Camus's thinking. While Sartre regarded the beauty of nature as an achievement of the human mind, for Camus, nature's beauty exposed us to nature's difference from us. But again, in contrast to Sartre, this difference of nature is regarded reverently rather than with hostility. Camus describes the natural world as dense with otherness.

> At the heart of all beauty lies something inhuman, and these hills, the softness of the sky, the outline of these trees at this very minute lose the illusory meaning with which we had clothed them, henceforth more remote than a lost paradise.

Both Sartre and Camus recognize that human consciousness projects meaning onto nature. Yet while Sartre criticizes the inherent meaninglessness of nature leaving only the human realm with value—with Roquentin's irritation, cited above, at the multiple iterations of trees—Camus turns the tables on this assessment. Camus locates the problem of meaninglessness within human consciousness itself, admiring the natural world for its lack of need for any explanation of being. Camus writes:

> If I were a tree among trees, a cat among animals, this life would have a meaning, or rather this problem would not arise, for I should belong to this world. I should be this world to which I am now opposed by my whole consciousness and my whole insistence upon familiarity. . . . And what constitutes the basis of that conflict, of that break between the world and my mind, but the awareness of it?

When we accept the difference between the mind's need for meaning and the world's plentitude without such meaning—when we accept absurdity—we may regard nature otherwise than in hostile difference.

Nature is not segregated from human life and habitation, for Camus, but ever-present even if at the margins of our world. Camus writes longingly about natural life, for example, at the edge of his native city of Algiers, at twilight.

> On the hills above the city there are paths among the mastics and olive trees. And toward them my heart turns at such moments. I see flights of black birds rise against the green horizon. In the sky suddenly divested of its sun something relaxes. A whole little nation of red clouds stretches out until it is absorbed in the air. Almost immediately afterward appears the first star that had been seen taking shape and consistency in the depth of the sky. And then suddenly, all consuming, night.

Such meditation on nature yields something like an alternative to the mind's demand for meaning. Consider how Camus describes the sounds of nature penetrating the silence at sunrise:

> . . . the figured bass of the birds, the sea's faint, brief sighs at the foot of the rocks, the vibration of the trees, the blind singing of the columns, the rustling of the wormwood plants, the furtive lizards. . . . A magpie preluded briefly, and at once, from all directions, birds' songs burst out with energy, jubilation, joyful discordance, and infinite rapture.

Contemplations of such phenomena are not merely descriptions of Camus's surroundings, merely records of his own personal experiences, but contribute to the substance of his philosophy. For Camus, it seems, our metaphysical distance from nature, which nevertheless surrounds us invitingly, gives exigency to the question of the purpose of our lives. But it is also nature, without needing reasons of its own, that seems to offer reason for being. Or rather, in the absence of reasons, the consolations of surrounding nature seem to promote the happiness Camus suggests we may embrace in the face of absurdity.

10 | BEING

In describing the living dimensions of existentialism, we have inevitably touched again and again upon the notion of being. "Being" encompasses all the other dimensions we have outlined here—self, others, world, and earth. Insofar as all of these exist, one might say that they partake in being. As an ontological designation—a philosophical concept pertaining to what is and to the existence thereof—being has many manifestations in existentialist thinking. Yet it is also the most difficult to define, and it is on this topic that the existentialists are most diverse and often obscure.

Being, as existentialists understand it, evades the grasp of objective thought. While we can of course engage the concept in philosophical discussion, the term "being" points to what can never be rendered wholly an *object* of thought. Jaspers considers the basic experience of considering the existence of what is. He comes upon the problem that

> whatever becomes an object for me is always a *determinate* being among others, and only a *mode* of being. When I think of being as matter, energy, spirit, life, and so on—every conceivable category has been tried—in the end I always discover that I have absolutized a mode of determinate being, which

appears within the totality of being, into being itself. No known being is *being itself.*

While thinking tries to grasp being as such, it may only end up amplifying one of its dimensions. The sense pervades existentialism that being brings us to the limit of thought.

Needless to say, in their thinking of being, existentialists depart considerably from the philosophical tradition. Our discussion of the rise of existentialism began with the distinction between being and non-being, the contemplation of which led to the founding of Western philosophy. Plato's metaphysics arose in contending with this distinction, and thinking through the problem of permanence and change. The ancient Greeks conceived of being as the plentitude of what truly is, that which exists in full presence. For Plato this meant above all the eternal forms or ideas, the ever-unchanging truths. The tradition from Parmenides to Plato onward—overriding Heraclitus's vision of ceaseless becoming—favors the permanent ideal over the ephemeral and changing world we know and experience through the senses.

Existentialists engage the idea of being, yet without excluding the change and ephemerality that falls short of the ideal of eternal presence. They see unchanging being as an empty idea, for what exists emerges into being and passes away—an emergence and passing without which existence is only thought in the abstract. We have seen how the Heraclitean concept of becoming, as it were, between being and non-being, plays a crucial role in existentialist thinking, particularly as it is revived by Nietzsche. While existentialists continue to refer to "being," they consider that being, insofar as it is the existence of what exists, is necessarily becoming, or subject to change.

We can think of being not as an object or a thing but in a verbal sense, not merely what exists but the primordial activity of existing as well as bringing to exist. Phenomenologically speaking, being makes what is—or beings—appear. Existentialists refer to "being" sometimes interchangeably with, and other times in distinction from, "existence." Beauvoir, like Sartre, differentiates being and existence. Beauvoir for example describes the ontological modality of the human being as "lack of being, but this lack has a way of being which is precisely existence." When they are distinguished from one another, existence can indicate the factical being of one concretely existing, as opposed to all being as such.

While this may still sound terribly abstract, in everyday life we are familiar with the term "being" in our own name for ourselves. The "human being" among all other animals is designated as a certain kind of being, as one that is. This is reflected in the existential terminology of our human "being-in-the-world." The awareness of our own being, or being here (or there), is also encapsulated in Heidegger's concept of Dasein (being here, or being there), as discussed earlier in this book. Our own being is but one manifestation of being as such, though a special one, since, as Heidegger writes at the outset of *Being and Time*, it is the human being for whom being is a question.

Apart from our own being, the notion of being is also engaged in other senses. For we also notice the being of other beings. Existentialists try to understand how the human being might have a special role in "revealing" being—and in describing this, Sartre and Beauvoir borrow the language of Heidegger. Apart from our own being, being is always immediately present to us as something, as particular beings. This tree, this sunset, this landscape, this animal or stone or house or person do not merely exist but exist *as* the particular thing they are. The phenomenological notion of constitution suggests that it is from the standpoint of human beings and because of our human standpoint that things appear as something, as particular beings, rather than only undifferentiated matter. We further "reveal" them by understanding or regarding these beings in a certain way, in a certain context, in connection with a particular activity, and so on. Our way of understanding or regarding a tree, for example, may reveal it in a variety of ways. The tree may be understood as the familiar everyday source of shade during our walk home from work or study, and quite differently if we are looking to find a source for firewood, or another if we endeavor to analyze the tree scientifically, or regard it aesthetically as a part of a landscape. In each case we would participate in revealing the tree in a distinctive way, as the being that it is.

Yet we might also, Heidegger argues, become aware of the very existence or Being of beings, of that which issues them forth as existing. In writing poetry about the tree, or in meditation upon the tree before us, we can experience a sense of wonder that it is there before us, that it exists at all, in the first place. In that way we may have a sense of its belonging to, or manifesting, being as a whole. We would have a sense of what Heidegger called the "Being of beings." Although we cannot capture Being as such in thought, we may become aware in some way of that which makes particular beings be.

The so-called ontological difference between Being and beings is a central distinction in Heidegger's philosophy. This difference is often rendered in translation by capitalizing "Being" as such ("das Sein"), in contrast to a merely particular "being" that is ("das Seiende"). (This strategy of course works only in translation, because all nouns are capitalized in German.) Heidegger argues that the human being is special in being the one being that asks about its own Being, reveals beings, and has a special relationship to Being as such.

While Heidegger investigates the problem of Being through the special particular human being in *Being and Time*, his philosophy thereafter becomes increasingly concerned with Being apart from its manifestation in particular beings. The later Heidegger thinks in fact that human beings, once awakened to a sense of Being, have in modernity come to "forget" Being. Heidegger traces the history of this forgetting all the way back to the idealism of Plato, for whom Being is an object of rational thought and a concept of full eternal presence. Heidegger thinks that we have reduced Being to a direct object of thought—reduced Being, if you will, to the status of a (particular) being. We have, furthermore, come to regard natural beings not in their Being but simply as resources to be manipulated. We have forgotten our role as revealers and stewards of Being, having objectified everything before us as reducible to our measurement and manipulation.

Heidegger experiments with different ways to try to articulate our sense of Being. Heidegger sometimes writes of how "there is" something or "there is" being. The German phrase for this is "es gibt" which means, literally, "it gives." Where in English one would say "there is much wildlife in this area," in German one would say "es gibt," or "it gives," such wildlife. Heidegger capitalizes on this peculiarity of phrase in order to suggest the generosity of Being, of that which literally gives (us) beings and gives Being to the beings themselves. Being brings beings forth, and yet in so manifesting beings, Being itself, or Being as such, withdraws. This withdrawal of Being explains why it is so hard to think being: it does not manifest itself for us to perceive or understand on its own, but is thinkable only through particular beings that are there for us to experience.

In his writings after *Being and Time* Heidegger repeatedly emphasized the elusiveness of Being. Although we can, as Heidegger would put it, formally "indicate" the Being of beings, and refer to Being as a concept, we cannot make it the direct object of our thought, for it always evades our attempt to grasp it directly. Other existentialists describe Being in similarly evasive terms. Jaspers calls Being the "encompassing." The encompassing grounds all possible knowledge but can never itself be directly known. Marcel has a similar way of describing being as that which evades our cognitive grasp. While we regard beings as that which we can know, or as problems which we can eventually solve, Being is otherwise. Rather than a problem, Being is, Marcel argues, an "ontological mystery."

Levinas, although a critic of existentialism, often engages its ontological sensibilities, and his engagement of the vocabulary and themes of existentialism evidences its influence on his philosophical development. Just as Heidegger wrote of the "es gibt" or "it gives" ("there is") as a mode of understanding being, Levinas wrote of the *il y a*, which, followed by a noun, functions similarly in French to denote the existence and presence of something. But Levinas also thought that we can become aware of Being without its reduction to a direct object of my knowledge or perception. Sometimes we seem to be haunted by Being, as in the experience of boredom or insomnia, or whenever the pressure of existence seems oppressive. While Heidegger validates the notion of Being positively, Levinas writes of our mental effort to escape from the oppressiveness of Being—an escape, he argues, provided by our relationship to others.

Levinas's turn against existentialism was directly aimed at its fascination with Being. Existentialists, he thought, obsessed about Being, over and above what Levinas thought should occupy philosophy's first or perhaps only concern, namely, ethics. Levinas entitled one of his most important books *Otherwise Than Being*. Here he argued that the thought of Being that characterizes philosophy from the ancient Greeks to existentialism offered a kind of totalizing thinking that excluded the radically "other."

Instead of Being, Levinas thinks, we should conceive of our relationship to the other human being, a relationship which precedes any interest in Being. The other is the one for whom—since the other is not myself—I cannot account, and yet the one who provides the condition for any possible ethics. It is not Being but the alterity or difference of others that most evades us and yet should occupy philosophical thinking. Ethics, Levinas argues, should be first philosophy, over and against any interest in Being. Despite his critique, existentialist concerns—the problems of the self and the self's responsibility, the relation of subjectivity and otherness, and above all the question (even if in negative) of Being—remain central to Levinas's thinking.

Part IV

Existentialism in the Practice of Life

11 | ON IMITATION, INSPIRATION, AND AUTHENTICITY

How does existentialist thinking relate to our concrete experience? What does existentialism look like in practice? We have seen that existentialism is varied in its approaches to the questions of existence, that it is diverse and broad in scope. The ways of life to which its insights may be relevant are as potentially numerous as the individuals who may experience them. Indeed, since they are particular to the ones living them, existentialist lives should be just as diverse as they are alike. Strictly speaking, there is not one existentialist approach to life but *approaches* to life, not one existential way to live but existential *ways* of life.

Yet while defying reduction to a single template, existentialist thinking can be mined for possibilities of relating to our shared human condition. We can say at least in formal terms what existentialist lives would exhibit in common. They would involve clear-eyed reflection about freedom and choice, demand courage and creativity, and eschew predetermined, externally imposed meanings, making room for invention in our actions and values and sense of purpose. They would entail some recognition of responsibility for what we are and do and affirm by our actions.

But can we say anything more concrete about existentialist ways of life? This chapter and those which follow present some of the ideas of existentialism that pertain to concrete experience and practice. We can begin with the idea of authenticity, as that relates to looking to models—sometimes to the lives of existentialist philosophers themselves—for inspiration.

Existentialism is enjoying a resurgence of late, with a number of popular accounts providing existentialist advice concerning the authentic life. Whatever merits some of these may have in explaining the philosophy, they tend to present the life of one or other of its most famous adherents as the paradigmatic model of existentialist authenticity that ought to be imitated. Such a model may be attractive to readers looking to escape the inauthenticity or purposelessness of the world as they see it. Any of us may wake up to feel that our lives have become stuck in patterns that no longer feel freely chosen, no longer representative of what we feel we are or wish to be. Existentialist philosophers, with their unconventional ways of thinking and sometimes of living, and their profound understanding of the human condition, may seem an obvious place to look for inspiration.

Kierkegaard's admiration for Socrates stemmed from the idea that the ancient philosopher's views were reflected in all his activity. We know that Socrates lived his philosophy in often provocative dialogue with others rather than writing down his thoughts in solitude. He famously accepted death rather than cease his activities. Yet one can find inspiration in Socrates, as Kierkegaard did, without holding philosophical debate live in public (instead Kierkegaard wrote privately under pseudonyms) and while steering clear of public trials and poisonous substances. That Kierkegaard spent much of his own relatively short life at his writing desk did not diminish the vitality and force of his own philosophy.

It may be obvious that imitation of the lives of others would be problematic for any vision of authenticity. In an earlier chapter on the self, we saw that to live as an authentic self involves seizing one's individual existence as an individual—whether in light of finitude, or before God, or in deliberate self-evolution, or as a self-reflective consciousness in distinction from any externally determined essence. One who lives authentically resists defining oneself primarily in the eyes of others, and freely owns up to one's choices. Being an individual, recognizing one's singularity, would surely preclude imitating the lives of others. Even inspiration one draws from others must be assimilated to one's unique point of view.

Yet some imitation is unavoidable in human life. Imitation underlies human capacities for communication and social cooperation. Aristotle pointed out that imitation is natural to us, and that imitation is how we learn. As children we learn to speak by mimicking the speech of those around us, and this no doubt is how we acquire many of the skills we need to survive. Inspiration, through which our own imagination may be sparked by the ideas or achievements of others, also involves some degree of imitation. Much of human achievement—in philosophy, art, literature, music, invention, and scientific inquiry—has proceeded through individuals rehearsing, responding to, redressing, and reviving the ideas of others, interpreting them in a new light, and going beyond them. Like imitation, inspiration is essential to every level of human culture. But the inspiration one might draw for existentialist living could not mean following a program devised from the life of another. From an existentialist point of view there are a number of problems with accepting any blueprint or formula for living.

First, some lives led by the thinkers and writers we now associate with existentialism are either unremarkable from an observer's point of view—that would more or less describe Kierkegaard—or ethically problematic. The figure of Kierkegaard reminds us that much of what characterizes the authentic life may be expressed inwardly, or in quiet reflection, decision, and commitment. These aspects of lived authenticity, unadvertised, may be unrecognizable to others—they may remain opaque even to Kierkegaard's most avid readers. The example of Socrates notwithstanding, sometimes the most authentic acts may be the least flashy or dramatic or publicly advertised.

The ethically problematic case, in respect to the failures of one existentialist thinker in particular, ought to be addressed head-on. Heidegger spectacularly failed to live up to the model of authenticity he so brilliantly described in *Being and Time*. Authenticity in Heidegger's philosophy meant seizing one's particular singularity in confronting one's finitude, and as a result, freeing oneself from merely belonging to, and echoing the views of, a mass mentality. In a moment of vision, as Heidegger described it, one hears a call of conscience that comes literally from nowhere or from "nothing." Although it may provoke anxiety, this call need not plunge one's Dasein into an abyss but can make one aware of the possibilities of ecstatic being. In responding to the call, one realizes that one is not a fixed essence but exists in a sense outside oneself. One recognizes one's own existence as projected through possibility, transcending toward a world that one has a stake in revealing and role in realizing.

An authentic response to that call involves wresting oneself from identification with the anonymous "they" and recognizing one's own unique self as a being whose essence is being-possible. In absolutely singular finitude, authentic Dasein faces one's own future and present, and recovers the past, as illuminated by possibility. That this past is also the past of others and may involve a cultural history does not diminish the singular call Dasein experiences in a state of authenticity.

This inspiring model of authenticity—in one of the most brilliant analyses of human individuality in the philosophical canon—stands in stark contradiction to Heidegger's own decision to join the Nazi Party. Fascist ideology typically involves an exclusionary definition of national identity, aggressive self-assertion of that group against others, and submission to authoritarian or dictatorial power. All of this radically diverges from any idea of an authentically individual self.

While Heidegger publicly disagreed with the Nazis' fanaticism for ideas about race and biology, he nevertheless, as a university rector in the early 1930s, enacted some of their policies (though he evaded others). Many of Heidegger's defenders—including the philosopher Hannah Arendt, a Jewish former student and one-time lover of Heidegger who after the war reported on the Nuremberg trials—saw Heidegger's as a personal error, short-lived and unrelated to his philosophy. Yet although he quit as rector after a year, stopped going to party meetings, and later admitted his involvement with National Socialism as the greatest stupidity of his life, Heidegger maintained his membership until the party was dismantled at the end of the war. He never apologized for it. For the rest of his life he stayed almost silent on the subject of the Holocaust.

Furthermore, there are clear resonances between certain moments in Heidegger's writings and nationalist ideology. For example, in a later section of *Being and Time*, Heidegger described the "historicality" of a "Volk" or a people as an elaboration of authentic temporality. If some readers hesitate to link this, written in 1926, to a nationalist narrative concerning the supposed destiny of Germany that unfolded in the following decade, Heidegger himself pointed to that passage to explain the connection between his philosophy and nationalist politics. Yet any insistence on the exclusive authenticity of a people seems to miss the mark of existential individuality rather widely. Jaspers, a one-time colleague, found Heidegger's involvement with the Nazis baffling for a philosopher who had so brilliantly revealed the structures of authentic Dasein. After meeting with him in 1933, Jaspers denounced such alliance with the fascists as a "deceptive mass intoxication," clearly at odds with authenticity as Heidegger himself defined it in *Being and Time*. Should they choose to engage his thought, readers must decide for themselves to what extent Heidegger's idea of authenticity can be separated from his politics.

Earlier in this book it was noted that the political and moral disaster of German politics in the 1930s and early '40s contributed to the rise of French existentialists, who in sharp contrast were involved at some personal risk in resistance to fascist occupation. For good reason, then, advertisements for the existential life tend to rely upon the biographies of Sartre and Beauvoir. We know that, for their time, they were famously unconventional. While not beyond reproach, there is much to admire in their lives, not least their personal courage to live in freedom as they saw it. Such courage was needed particularly by Beauvoir who, as an unmarried woman in an open relationship from the 1920s onward, would have existed in far more serious breach of social convention than the bachelor Sartre. They both contributed generously to important social movements of their time, and their activism tirelessly promoted the freedom of others. But imitating Sartre or Beauvoir as a model would miss the point of the particularity of each individual existence upon which existentialism insists. While illuminating universal aspects of the human condition, such as freedom and finitude, existentialism encourages individual choice and creativity in one's singular relation to possibility. Each life is unique and authenticity is achieved in taking up its possibilities on one's own terms.

Of course, it may happen that an original idea, or an original approach to life itself, emerges precisely when one attempts to venture beyond a significant or even overwhelming influence. We can take the example of the inspiration Nietzsche found in the philosopher Schopenhauer. As a university student in Leipzig, Nietzsche discovered Schopenhauer's work *The World as Will and Representation*. The young Nietzsche became enthralled to find a "master," indeed a "demi-god" of philosophical thinking. He paid tribute in an early essay, "Schopenhauer as Educator," declaring: "I am one of those readers of Schopenhauer who when they have read one page of him know for certain that they will go on to read all the pages and will pay heed to every word he ever said."

Such devotion issued from a mind desperate for a higher form of inspiration than Nietzsche felt the culture of his time seemed to offer. Nietzsche went on to describe "my joy and amazement when I discovered Schopenhauer: I sensed that in him I had discovered that educator and philosopher I had sought for so long." When, at the age of twenty-five, he moved to Basel to become became professor of philology, Nietzsche hoped to infuse the discipline with Schopenhauerian spirit.

Nietzsche looked to Schopenhauer for guidance, both in the philosopher's writings and in his experiences of life, for as he wrote, "I profit from a philosopher only insofar as he can be an example." The young Nietzsche was certain that "this example must exist in his outward life, not merely in his books." Nietzsche thus praised Schopenhauer for his honesty, his joy, and his consistency. As Nietzsche imagined him, Schopenhauer wrote for himself alone, not to please his readers. He thus cultivated himself as an individual, "single-hearted and unaffected," without much reliance on society or the state. He was, in Nietzsche's estimation, unconstrained by public opinion. Despite Schopenhauer's radically pessimistic description of existence, which Nietzsche would later come to criticize, he found in Schopenhauer a joyful figure, a joy he attributed to the clarity with which he could conquer difficult thoughts and face reality unencumbered by fear. Schopenhauer's consistency arose from the strength and quality of his mind, but also from clarity and personal courage. Nietzsche admired how Schopenhauer manifested not only in writing but in his bearing toward life the "productive uniqueness" each of us bears "within him as the core of his being."

Nietzsche found many ideas in Schopenhauer to shape his own thinking. The explorations of a will within nature and of the depths and physiology of the psyche, the association of aesthetic experience with truth, the interest in Eastern religion and philosophy, all reflect Schopenhauer's influence upon Nietzsche's thought. Yet despite, or perhaps because of, the intensity of his early admiration, Nietzsche came to assert his independence from Schopenhauer's philosophy. Some of his most important insights were developed precisely by advancing a critique of Schopenhauer.

Nietzsche's ecstatic affirmation of life, for one, can be read as a rejection of Schopenhauer's pessimism. Nietzsche above all rejected the latter's devastating conclusion that it is preferable not to have been born at all, and that one can find salvation only in turning against the will to live. Nietzsche's perspectivism and his rejection of systematic thinking can also be read as a reaction against the closed and encompassing nature of Schopenhauer's metaphysics, though it also reflects a rejection of the systematic idealism dominating philosophy in the nineteenth century.

Beyond philosophical differences, Nietzsche was aware of the need to forge one's own path for thinking as well as living. His whole philosophy comes to affirm individuality, and the creativity and courage it takes to think for oneself. In the same text devoted to praise of Schopenhauer, Nietzsche writes: "No one but you can build the bridge upon which you alone must cross the stream of life, no one but you alone."

The implications are clear regarding existential philosophy: we cannot look to the lives of the philosophers as models by which to shape our own. But the same would be true of taking anyone's life as a model, whether those of artists, thinkers, political leaders, saints, entrepreneurs, inventors, or others we may admire. While we may learn from and be inspired by exemplary lives, by manifestations of creativity or genius or exceptional goodness, authenticity demands shaping one's life in one's own way, as an individual.

Any manifesto pretending to offer a single model of how to live authentically or indeed "existentially" is therefore bound to self-contradiction. Even in that early essay reflecting on his philosophical influences, Nietzsche wrote: "One repays a teacher badly if one remains only a pupil." Whichever personality we may come to admire, existentialist thinking suggests we ought to find our own voice in response to the challenges and opportunities of existence. We are to face our choices with fresh consideration. We are to choose without the reassurance of following any already established path. We are to venture, as it were, off-piste.

12 | ON SEEKING AND TAKING (AND GIVING) ADVICE

If we are not to look to existential philosophy—or indeed to any philosophy—for a manifesto, this does not mean that we should not seek or take advice about existential matters, or find inspiration where it is helpful. We may seek advice for an experienced assessment of the matter, or solutions we may be unlikely to think of. Others may have more relevant experience or can illuminate something familiar by a new perspective. Existentialism would, however, highlight individual responsibility in both choosing the influences we seek out and the decisions we ultimately take.

For Sartre pointed out that there is already a manner of choosing involved in the sources we choose to seek out for guidance. In his famous lecture "Existentialism," defending the philosophy from its various critics, Sartre offered the example of a young philosophy student who, during the war, came to him asking for advice. The student asked whether he should join the French resistance against the Nazi occupiers, who had already killed his father and brother, or stay at home with his mother who, already twice bereaved, would be left wholly alone and helpless should he come to harm. Sartre appreciated this example because no formula from traditional ethical theories—whether biblical commandments, the Kantian categorical imperative, or utilitarian calculations of numerically greatest happiness—could resolve the young man's difficulty. The young man had to choose without the help of any pregiven rule or formula. Sartre writes:

> By what authority, in the name of what golden rule of morality, do you think he could have decided, in perfect peace of mind, either to abandon his mother or to remain with her? There are no means of judging. The content is always concrete, and therefore unpredictable; it has always to be invented. The one thing that counts, is to know whether the invention is made in the name of freedom.

As Sartre saw it, there was no passing off responsibility here to any higher authority. Even if the young man were following orders, he would be responsible for that choice to do so.

Sartre recognized however that the young man's predicament illuminated something very important about human ethics from an existentialist perspective. We may ordinarily think that our values dictate our actions. If something is important to us, so we may presume, we will act accordingly. Sartre argued the opposite: any values the young man may hold are not the cause, but the result, of his choices. Should he join the resistance to avenge his father and brother, or appease his national loyalty, these would be the predominant values his actions affirmed. Should he stay with his mother, the value of loyalty to one who had borne and kept him would predominate and define his values at that point. The value itself cannot guide but is rather expressed by and manifested in the action. Our actions are not determined by, but create, our values. Our emotions too do not serve up ethical justification. In any action, Beauvoir writes,

> It must therefore be understood that the passion to which man has acquiesced finds no external justification. No outside appeal, no objective necessity permits of its being called useful.

Should the young man then consult a priest or alternatively an atheist philosophy professor? Sartre insisted that we contribute to our decision by choosing the sort of advice we invite. Whether one consults a conventional authority or visits a fortune-teller, one has already contributed to shaping the vision of possibilities from which to choose. One is responsible for the presentation and interpretation of the advice on offer and whether or not one will act on it.

I was once asked by a former philosophy undergraduate a question of what turned out to be significant gravity. The student had taken some of my classes, including one which convened the semester of the attacks against America on September 11, 2001. The student was exceptionally bright, and after graduation and despite a scholarship to a doctoral program, joined the military—to a significant extent in response to those events that had taken place at such a formative time in his studies. After the end of a first tour in the army, the student wrote to me asking whether he should sign up again for another tour or accept a position in the reserves, noting that, if it were the latter, he would not have a voice in where he might be assigned should he be called up. I did not know how to answer this former student's letter, knowing that his future well-being, even his life, could depend upon the answer. I prevaricated, and I did not answer in time, which I realized when I received a further letter from the base to which he had been ultimately stationed. I wrote to wish him well, of course, but I regret very much never properly answering that important letter. He had taken my class on existentialism, so he would have known the view that to ask me was already to generate value in whatever direction he thought I might advise. At the same time, when I found out that he had been fatally wounded, I felt remorse for my failure to give him an answer.

While the existentialist approach does not offer the security of being assured what to do in advance, it credits the individual with freedom to choose and with productive generation of values. We do not know how the young man may have felt about Sartre's advice, or whether my former student would have taken any advice I might have given. We do not find out in Sartre's essay what the young man chose to do in the end, as we do in my student's story. But undoubtedly the responsibility for choices—insofar as they prescribe both consequences and the values appropriate to the act—would not have been lost on either of these young people.

One of Rilke's most interesting works of prose is a series of letters he wrote to a young poet who admired the elder poet's work and initially sought advice about his own poems. Over the course of their correspondence the young poet sought advice about all sorts of other matters. Rilke's answers, now published as *Letters to a Young Poet*, offer advice about not only poetry but about solitude, intimate love, about being a soldier, and loneliness. Despite his generous encouragement and often specific advice, Rilke was aware of the difficulty of advising precisely where it is most important. He closed one letter with this thought:

> But finally I want to add just one more bit of advice: to keep growing, silently and earnestly, through your whole development; you couldn't disturb it any more violently than by looking outside and waiting for outside answers to questions that only your innermost feeling, in your quietest hour, can perhaps answer.

Whether or not this counsel was helpful for Rilke's interlocutor, it is in keeping with an existentialist perspective. In his letter Rilke at once affirms the young poet's decision to seek out an established poet for advice and the necessity to turn to himself, to allow his own conviction to develop from within.

I wish I would have thought to send on Rilke's words to my former student, and admitted that I simply had no idea what to advise him. I might have learned from Rilke how I might have affirmed a person's own "innermost feeling" and growth, without intervening in his decision at all.

13 | BEING IN THE CROWD
ANONYMITY, CONFORMITY, AND INDIVIDUALITY IN MODERN LIFE

If you have ever commuted to work on a packed subway train or inched your car forward in rush-hour traffic, you may have feared your individuality submerging into an indistinct mass. Holiday-time shopping in a crowded superstore or languishing in a slow queue may provoke a similar feeling. It hardly helps that the barista serving your coffee may scribble your first name onto the cup, though scarcely looking at you and perhaps feeling equally diminished by the exchange. Then there is the experience of time spent online, where much communication is mass-circulated and anonymous. One may be one of thousands or even millions following, "liking," or reposting the same images and ideas. Central to the idea of authenticity is the idea of being an individual, or being oneself. How can one be "oneself" within a crowd, or in a culture of the "masses"?

Many of the existentialists were concerned with how an individual may be oneself in the modern world. Kierkegaard, Nietzsche, Heidegger, Rilke, and the existential social theorist Georg Simmel were particularly skeptical of modern mass culture and feared that it endangered human individuality. These existential thinkers could not have anticipated globalization, the proliferation of mass production and consumption, or the data-driven anonymization of life that characterize our world today. Yet they witnessed the early manifestations of mass culture and were concerned by what they saw.

Kierkegaard's criticism of the mass mentality, of life spent in and among the crowd, issued a response to concrete cultural developments of his time—quaint as they may seem in comparison to mass culture today. For example, in 1844, in a swiftly urbanizing Copenhagen, a pleasure garden called Tivoli opened just outside the city walls. For an entrance fee one could enter a vast venue of entertainment, spectatorship, and voyeurism in which people wandered and mixed, all drawn toward spectacle and the new activity of seeing and being seen. The park drew 10,000 visitors on its opening Sunday, equivalent to a tenth of the city's population, and in its first summer, over 300,000 visitors, or a third of the population of the entire country. While many were delighted with such developments, Kierkegaard was not. In response, Kierkegaard famously wrote that "the crowd is untruth." It is not difficult to think what he would make of massive entertainment parks and mega shopping malls, in which people are ushered through by the thousands or even millions, with everything for consumption itself mass produced.

Nietzsche linked mass culture to conformism. Insisting as he did on individuality, Nietzsche was critical of those who it seemed to him lived in unreflective deference to the conventions of mass society. He urged his readers to assert their individuality over and above fear of others' opinions, common habits, and lazy conformity. He complained that some modern people "seem like manufactured goods" and advised:

> Human beings who do not want to belong to the mass need only to stop being comfortable; follow their conscience, which cries out: "Be yourself!" All that you are now doing, thinking, and desiring is not really yourself.

Nietzsche recognized of course that differentiating oneself from others can be painful—an experience familiar to anyone who has suffered the peer pressures of adolescence. Yet it is likely that for most of us, conformity of some sort or another may remain a pressure our whole life long. We may not even be fully aware of this pressure, for modern life, as Simmel wrote, offers a myriad of "stimulations, interests, uses of time and consciousness" which "carry the person as if in a stream, and one hardly needs to swim for oneself."

In some respects, the worries of Kierkegaard, Nietzsche, and Simmel about social conformism may be outmoded today. The societies of those likely to be reading this book would be more diverse in social terms than in those worlds of the early existentialists. Precisely in the context of mass consumption, cultivating one's individuality, being special or distinctive, has become a mainstream aspiration in contemporary life. Despite this, it would be untrue to say that we have escaped the pressures of the crowd. An existentialist critique of culture may be as uncomfortable for readers of today as it was for those in previous centuries. Our social landscapes are increasingly dominated by outlets of homogeneous corporate chains. Mass production and consumption pertain not only to products but also to lifestyles and ideas. Fashion promotes the ideal of individual style, yet most producers aim to sell their products in mass quantities, and idiosyncrasy is promoted primarily as a brand. Social media may exacerbate pressures to conformity by parading experiences for competitive consumption, quantifying and tracking popularity, and exploiting the ever-dreaded fear of missing out.

Yet criticisms of the anonymizing nature of modern life and its social institutions were expressed by existentialist thinkers and writers already early on in the twentieth century. Rilke's *The Notebooks of Malte Laurids Brigge* (1910) opens with a description of the "factory-like" death prepared by the hundreds at the Hôtel Dieu across from the Paris lodgings of his protagonist. There, Malte observes, patients are passive conscripts awaiting not their own personal death, but an anonymous death defined as it were by the institution. Later in the novel Rilke depicts Malte himself as a faceless patient of a modern clinic where, with little personal interaction, he is submitted to electroshock therapy and let back out to wander a city full of strangers.

Kafka poked fun at life in the modern economy, and our conformity to its repertoire of expectations. We recall that in *The Metamorphosis*, Gregor Samsa, a traveling salesman, wakes up one morning to find himself an insect. Crucially, Gregor's grotesque physical transformation is not his most urgent preoccupation. Rather, Gregor obsesses over the prospect of getting himself and his case of cloth samples to the train station on time. With multiple legs, antennae, and a dome-shaped exoskeleton in which he can scarcely maneuver, Gregor worries above all about disappointing his boss and the deputy clerk who, having waited in vain for him at the station, shows up at the Samsa household to demand his appearance for work.

More than on his own disastrous condition, Gregor reflects on his life as a traveling salesman among other such traveling workers. He naïvely admits that while he detests the work, his family has come to depend on his income, in part to pay off a debt his father had incurred (he later discovers it had been eliminated long before). There is, incidentally, a hospital across the street from the Samsa home, visible from Gregor's window. Yet it does not occur to anyone that Gregor might need help, so predominant is the common obsession about Gregor's missing work and offending any visitors with his new, grotesque form. In his treatment of Gregor, Kafka was not merely mocking the workaday person, though he was surely prompting his reader to consider why Gregor so submissively maintained a life so drudging and failed to become his own self.

Kafka himself agonized over demands to conform to a modern mode of existence. After reading much philosophy and graduating in law, he labored at an insurance company, visiting factories and writing risk and accident reports, while longing instead to live as a literary writer. Only in painful conflict with his father could Kafka evade pressure to take up management of an asbestos factory, a prospect he dreaded. With torturous ambivalence, against the expectations of bourgeois society, he broke off an engagement to be married, as it would have demanded of him a life prescribed by the institution. While he resented these pressures, Kafka transformed them into fuel for his literary imagination.

Undeniably, some critics of modern culture seem to harbor elitist preoccupations. Rilke's concern for the singular individual belies some anxiety about distinction from the masses. Like Heidegger, Rilke condemns the "sham things, dummies of life" of mass-produced objects, but leaves unmentioned how helpful some of them might be to the ordinary person. In the novel, Malte's pain over the loss of his family's landed estates, their houses, belongings, and servants expresses nostalgia for an old aristocratic world set apart from the urban crowd, a world Rilke himself enjoyed primarily as the guest of wealthy patrons.

In his nostalgia Rilke echoes his philosophical predecessors Kierkegaard and Nietzsche, both of whose philosophies have been criticized as elitist. Kierkegaard's cultural commentary on the crowd has been criticized as anti-democratic. For the anonymity of the crowd, Kierkegaard complains, obscures among other things the distinction between teacher and pupil, master and servant. More severely, in some of his writings Nietzsche promotes the idea of an "overman" (the German term is *Übermensch*), literally the person who rises above the (average) human, above the "herd" instinct, and who may be capable of monumental acts. Nietzsche's notion of the "will to power," as an extra-rational force that can be channeled to different ends, validates the strong over the weak, the courageous over the meek. In this context Nietzsche's preference for the exceptional risks diminishes the value of the ordinary person who lives as one of the many.

Yet these thinkers considered the achievement of individuality a universal human possibility. Kierkegaard suggested that the singularity of every human being binds us together as commonly human. Kierkegaard wrote in *Works of Love* that faith, which above all singles one out, allows one to embrace all individuals in their "human similarity" before God. Despite Nietzsche's promotion of the extraordinary person, he frequently confesses his deep reverence for the individual. He wrote that every self is "a unique miracle." An artistic perspective on the individual sees the possibility that "by being strictly consistent in uniqueness, he is beautiful, and worth regarding, as a work of nature." Nietzsche advocated that everyone be themselves—that is, to become what they aim to be. Such individuality should be possible, in principle, for everyone who has or musters the courage to nurture it.

Moreover, not all visions of the modern crowd are negative. Charles Baudelaire, a nineteenth-century French poet influential for many existentialists, celebrated the endless attractions and distractions of the urban crowd. Whitman, who could have been an existentialist penning many passages in *Leaves of Grass*, expressed exhilaration in the crowded streets of Manhattan and poetically embraced the tired masses. Walter Benjamin analyzed the popularization of photography and film as forms of art that he thought were inherently democratizing because they could be reproduced endlessly and seen by the crowd rather than only the privileged private spectator. These promotions of modern life and its diversions suggest that one need not be aloof from mass culture in order to prize individuality or indeed to be oneself.

Yet modern life undoubtedly poses challenges for the individual. These challenges were examined by Georg Simmel, an early twentieth-century sociologist steeped in existentialist thinking and whose lectures Rilke attended in Berlin. Simmel analyzed features of modern culture that anonymize the individual in public life and relegate individual self-expression to the private sphere. But that private sphere, or what Simmel called subjective culture, was also shrinking. Simmel wrote:

> The individual has become a mere cog in an enormous organization of things and power which tear from his hands all progress, spirituality, and value in order to transform them from their subjective form into the form of a purely objective life.

The contrast between subjective culture and objective culture allows Simmel to consider how the individual may be protected from dissolution into anonymizing abstraction.

In "The Metropolis and Mental Life" Simmel wrote about the anonymizing effects of the modern urban city. In a milieu so varied and complex as the metropolis, with its "aggregation of so many people with such differentiated interest," external relations are most efficiently organized by reducing the personal aspects of existence. Features of urban life contribute to the "leveling" of the individual—a notion Kierkegaard had written about in "The Present Age," discussed earlier in this book. With mass transportation, personal movement is made efficient. Money brings precision, calculability, and exactness into exchanges. Contracts eliminate ambiguity. Communication technology allows for the uniform transference of news. Imprecision, inexactness, particularity, unpredictability, and contingency are all features of the subjective, emotional, and spiritual life of the individual excluded from the external relationships of modern exchange.

According to Simmel, a metropolitan "mentality" emerges in response to this diminishment of the subjective sphere. Simmel identifies a blasé attitude, coldness, apathy, or even latent antipathy toward others, along with the calculative mentality, as standard defense mechanisms against the leveling experience. On the crowded street, one may pass others in a state of relative indifference, even when others are in need. One may feel less vitally individual when adjusting to the patterns and movements of the crowd. One's own sense of individuality—and individual responsiveness to the world—may be dulled.

Yet one may react against such dulling of individuality. Strivings toward eccentricity and stylistic uniqueness, Simmel argued, may be provoked in some as a reaction against the anonymizing tendencies of mass production and consumption. "In order to preserve his most personal core," Simmel wrote, the individual "has to exaggerate this personal element in order to remain audible even to himself." Simmel identified the cult of personality and the affectations of egocentrism as reactions against modern anonymization. Of course, Simmel recognized that in a modern metropolis one may also experience the advantages of anonymity. In a crowded physical space, there may be paradoxically more mental space to think for oneself. One will observe a greater range of lifestyles in a cosmopolitan setting than in other social environments. But in Simmel's view the excessive focus on the self's own personality may fail to nurture a genuine subjective culture, remaining merely superficial if adequate spiritual, intellectual, or communal resources were lacking.

Despite the critique of modern life among existentialists, they are not wholly nostalgic for a premodern past. Kierkegaard expressed hope that the difficulties of the modern age will provoke the individual to respond all the more vigorously in action, passion, and decision. Part of the "dialectical" character of the modern age, he thought, is that its promotion of anonymity may provoke the individual to respond against the leveling. Nietzsche, too, wrote for an audience of an imagined future and promoted the further evolution of the human species. One meaning of the "overman" is the idea that the individual may go over and beyond the stultifying limitations of the current cultural regime and embrace earthly natural life, living and creating in a vital way. To go beyond the leveling is not to go backward in time but to create a new future. Rilke, too, writes his way toward a poetic transformation of our relation to the natural world and suggests that in a newfound harmony with it—and in giving up wooing the angels, as he puts it in *Duino Elegies*—we might find an earth-bound form of happiness. For his part Simmel does not advocate the elimination of objective culture, but suggests balancing the pressures of anonymization with renewed attention to what sustains the individual. Simmel pointed to positive developments of modern thought, including a turn to pragmatic philosophy rooted in life, art that breaks with tradition and engages new possibilities of form, and personalized explorations of spirituality. All of these thinkers would advocate cultivating a thoughtful relation to ourselves, cultivating our own voices in the midst of a noisy, overcrowded world, while moving forward in our projects, commitments, and actions.

Being an authentic individual in an age of mass culture does not have to mean cultivating isolation from our fellow human beings. Indeed, it may be in a kind of attention paid to others that our own individuality can best flourish. Kierkegaard wrote, "The real moment in time and the real situation being simultaneous with real people, each of whom is something: that is what helps to sustain the individual." Individuality is not for Kierkegaard an end in itself but the basis for authentic relation to others. While the crowd may threaten us with anonymity, we can cultivate our authentic modes of being with others through our recognition of others' individuality as well as of our own. Yet being an individual among others demands real presence, as Marcel described it, including openness to others' differences. While we need to be willing to stand apart, to avoid merely succumbing to others' point of view, we can also consider the creative potential of friendship, of collaborative projects, of love, and of common purposes. Nietzsche, similarly, promoted creative openness and new forms of expression not simply for the purpose of individuality as such. He described a better human future in which individuals could be recognized and appreciated as works of art. While critical of any "herd" mentality, Nietzsche's description of authentic selfhood is not a self-obsessive narcissism. In his view, what one admires and works toward outside of oneself contributes to self-becoming.

Of course individuality may be impoverished if one fails to connect to something other or even greater than oneself. The authentic individual is sustained by authentic relations to the surrounding world. The contemporary philosopher Charles Taylor, interpreting anew the ethics of authenticity, wrote that individualism "both flattens and narrows our lives, makes them poorer in meaning." Trying to achieve authenticity by fulfilling ourselves or our aspirations in neglect of ties to others is a self-defeating proposition, for such would destroy "the conditions for realizing authenticity itself." Authenticity of the self, Taylor argues, must be won in connection with its achievement by and for others.

Individual authenticity need not be recognizable to others in the form of some obvious uniqueness. For Kierkegaard it would be sufficient—and perhaps even the most difficult thing—to become just an individual, a true person, one who "by leaping into the depths . . . learns to help oneself, learns to love others as much as oneself." Kierkegaard argued that those who have understood and overcome the leveling process may not be recognized by others as authentic individuals. They may lack any outward authority "because they have understood the universal in equality before God, and, because they realize this and their own responsibility every moment, are thus prevented from being guilty of thoughtlessly realizing in an inconsistent form this consistent perception." That the highest individuals may be unrecognizable as individuals also prohibits the valuation of individuality from becoming a standard of discrimination. Despite Kierkegaard's critique of the abstracted modern individualist, he writes in *Works of Love* that "one person cannot actually judge another, but the one judging only becomes disclosed himself."

14 | INTO ONE'S OWN, OR ON "FINDING" ONESELF

Each of us may face moments in our lives when we ask about the purpose of our being, about what we live for. We may ask ourselves who we truly are. If we are to be ourselves, as Nietzsche urges, how do we know what this self is? Does authenticity mean finding our true inner nature? Finding what Kierkegaard called "a truth that is true for me" may be taken to be synonymous with finding oneself. But it is important to distinguish finding a purpose, or a truth, an ideal worth believing in or a project to which to devote one's life—all important existential pursuits—from the goal of self-seeking. For the existentialist, there is no such self as one may find. There is only a self that one may become.

The difference is not merely linguistic. The idea that one ought to or even can find oneself may be invoked to justify making a change or setting off on a new course of direction. If one is to find oneself, it must be presumed that the self is not already apparent or known to oneself, that it is perhaps buried within, yet to be discovered. Psychoanalysis and its predominance in modern culture have promoted the widespread idea of a deep interior within each of us that is not ever accessible to direct reflection. This may contribute to the sense that one may need a radical break from or alteration of a present situation in order to discover "who one really is" veiled, buried, or otherwise suppressed. One may long to abandon a job, a relationship, an existing or impending commitment, a long-familiar place, a course of study, or established habits. Instead of the familiar path, one may feel driven to go to unfamiliar places, do new things, explore the world. One may abandon what appears to be a secure plan in order to expose oneself to the unknown.

There may be existential reasons to do any of the above (along with reasons not to). Finding out about life and expanding one's imagination of what is possible, of what might be fulfilling, or breaking from a situation that feels stifling of one's possibilities would be among them. But finding oneself or uncovering a deeply buried inner secret will not count as an existential justification for anything. One cannot find a self. One must become the self that one wants to be. Such becoming is a never-finished task.

The idea of finding oneself has been popularized in modern literature, particularly in the *Bildungsroman* or novel of education, a genre that rose to prominence in the later nineteenth century. In such novels a protagonist may set off on a journey, educational not in the sense of amassing informational knowledge but of gaining an understanding of life. In the process of experience, an inner knowledge is won that cannot be found in books. The resolution of such a novel would involve discovering, or arriving at, a more complete or deeper or more real self. But rather than being discovered, this self is constituted in and through the progress of experience.

Often the journey is not a literal one but the education of the heart, through the thrills and failures of romantic love. The French writer Gustav Flaubert's novel *Sentimental Education* follows a young Frédéric Moreau in and out of Paris, falling in and out of love with a married woman, among other affairs. Fortunes, personal and material, are gained and lost against the backdrop of the Revolution of 1848. One can read the personal fates of the characters as analogous to the political and economic tribulations of the time. Conversely one can see in the historical events an objective turmoil analogous to the subjective turmoil of the self. As a society undergoes transformation, so too does the self, both arriving eventually at a more mature state of being.

A very different narrative of self-discovery is offered in Zora Neale Hurston's *Their Eyes Were Watching God*. The protagonist Janie Crawford, granddaughter of a former slave, recounts her life story. The unfolding narrative presents hopes from her youth as a beautiful but naïve girl disappointed when she finds herself in a series of troubled marriages in which she is mistreated and subordinated. In her third marriage, however, prior to which she has become a woman of independent means, Janie finds something of the kind of love she had hoped for as a girl. As a widow she becomes finally fully liberated in spirit. While Flaubert offers a paradigmatic study of the education of the heart, Hurston's novel illustrates brilliantly how, in enduring a difficult fate and overcoming illusions, one might, as it were, come into one's own. Needless to say, Janie's is a self hard won.

A now classic adaptation of the *Bildungsroman* genre is Jack Kerouac's *On the Road* (1957). This famous *roman à clef,* often associated with existentialism for its advocacy of free-spirited nonconformism, follows a cast of thinly disguised writers and poets from the Beat generation—modeled on Allen Ginsberg, William S. Burroughs, and Kerouac himself. The novel was praised at the time of its publication as "the most beautifully executed, the clearest and the most important utterance" of its generation. The narrative traces the road trips of Sal Paradise (Kerouac) and his friend Dean Moriarty (Kerouac's friend Neal Cassady) through the United States and Mexico, in various stages of intoxication and sobriety. They pursue adventures and seek meaning and evade conformity with a world in which, to quote Sal, "everybody's doing what they think they're supposed to do."

Leaving behind that world, they go off into the unknown to find out what freedom might entail. As Sal eventually says of Dean, "bitterness, recriminations, advice, morality, sadness—everything was behind him, and ahead of him was the ragged and ecstatic joy of pure being." An overriding theme is the escape from tradition and the rejection of conventional life, in order to seize the present with a fully rounded awareness of existence. Yet only Dean seems to embrace his existential freedom in the end. Driving a symbolically important Cadillac, Sal appears to conform to a conventional version of the American dream.

The notion of coming "into my own" is explicitly explored in Robert Frost's wonderful sonnet of that title. The speaker describes staring longingly at a dark wood and imagining entering that forest to become lost there. As the poem begins:

> One of my wishes is that those dark trees
> So old, and firm, they scarcely show the breeze
> Were not, as it were, the merest mask of gloom
> But stretched away beyond the edge of doom.
> I would not be withheld but that one day
> Into that vastness I should steal away.

Frost's speaker goes on to describe escaping civilization for a time, only eventually to be caught up with by one of those who had known and missed him since his departure.

Somewhat contrary to the *Bildungsroman* model, the speaker in Frost's poem does not imagine having changed or become educated, exactly, by the journey into the unknown. Nor is the choice between conformity or not to a world with which he disagrees. Frost's speaker does not imagine having discovered anything particularly new about life, the world, or reality. Rather, the speaker imagines that the one who had found him in the forest would only find in himself more of what he had always been:

> They would not find me changed from him they knew
> Only more sure of all I thought was true.

To become more certain of all that one had thought was true may be to become all the surer of oneself. The scenario echoes a passage in *The Gay Science*, in which Nietzsche implores: "What does your conscience say? You should become who you are." One comes into one's own, in Frost's poem, by going off by oneself and becoming surer of oneself. But is one found in this situation? Or is one's self, yet more sure of itself, created in the process?

While all of these works are ripe for existentialist interpretation, the idea that there would be a self to find as the final end or goal of the experiences they depict would not quite be sanctioned by existential philosophy. For existentialism rejects any inner essential core that could provide a foundation for decision, action, and understanding. The idea of self-discovery is of course closely linked to the existential notion of authenticity, since self-discovery in this sense would require wresting oneself from others' expectations about what one should be or already is. Yet the self that would be presumed to be discovered through experience would be, in existential terms, constituted by that same experience.

The existential interpretation of Socrates and his call to "know thyself" would thus have to distinguish critical reflection on one's beliefs, emotions, actions, and choices from discovery of some inner core. As mentioned earlier in this book, Kierkegaard asserted that prior to Socrates's call to self-reflect the self "did not exist." Sartre is highly critical of the results to be gained from Socratic self-examination, if that means that one aims to discover what or who one "really" is. The idea that authenticity means to go and "find oneself" or to have learned a lot about oneself is nonsense to Sartre because we only are in and through the concrete moment of existing; we are our acts and activities.

In his book *The Transcendence of the Ego*, Sartre argues: "Thus really to know oneself is inevitably to take toward oneself the point of view of others, that is to say, a point of view which is necessarily false." For Sartre, the self, the "me" which we can intend in consciousness, is only a synthetic unity, an ideality of put-together states and impressions that do not add up to an essential "self." There is no self to be found behind, and therefore as the cause of, one's actions, thoughts, and activities. Rather the self is instead nothing but those very actions, thoughts, and activities and the values they establish, and these can never be summed up as an object of wholly captured description. Making any concluding summation about the self would in a sense be to objectify the self, and so deny its very subjectivity.

Of course, existentialists promote forms of self-reflection, and Sartre clearly thinks that an authentic life is going to require some self-scrutiny. As we have seen, Sartre echoes the Stoics in regarding our relation to the world as subject to critical reflection that enables freedom in our relation to it. One's life can be given a unified trajectory by one's choice of a fundamental project, an idea, or truth, for which to live. The severity of Sartre's position in *The Transcendence of the Ego* allows him to support the freedom of subjectivity from objecthood. Sartre sanctions the freedom, within whatever circumstances we find ourselves, to influence who we are and become through our own choices and actions. Once we begin to turn to ourselves as an object of study, or even of seeking, we are in danger of objectifying ourselves and denying our intrinsic freedom. Yet later in his thinking Sartre emphasizes the importance of a primary project, or some consistent goal by which to orient one's self-creation.

Self-discovery is also criticized in Nietzsche's philosophy. While urging us to be ourselves, Nietzsche asks: "But how can we 'find ourselves' again, and how can man know himself? He is a thing obscure and veiled." We cannot find the self as something to uncover that will then yield a basis on which to act. Nietzsche suggests then that we can only find ourselves in retrospect—as Janie does in *Their Eyes Were Watching God*—and not by looking inward, but by gauging what we have done and what we have loved and valued.

This is the most effective way: to let the youthful soul look back on life with the question, "What have you up to now truly loved, what has drawn your soul upward, mastered it and blessed it too?" Set up these things that you have honoured before yourself, and, maybe, they will show you, in their being and their order, a law which is the fundamental law of your own self. Compare these objects, consider how one completes and broadens and transcends and explains another, how they form a ladder on which you have all the time been climbing to your self: for your true being lies not deeply hidden within you, but an infinite height above you, or at least above that which you commonly take to be yourself.

Just as Sartre focuses on action, Nietzsche suggests that what we have aimed for and the heights to which we have aspired reflect who we truly are. In other words, that which above yourself you have admired and toward which you have aimed, that to which you have devoted yourself, will be the measure of who you are. While Nietzsche engages lofty language with his reference to "infinite height," he qualifies this to add that what we aim for need only be above where we take ourselves to be.

Nietzsche's description of broadening and transcending and climbing beyond oneself toward what one admires and loves affirms the view that subjectivity is transcendence. In the most fruitful way of being, we are always becoming, moving beyond, or above and beyond, what is there, and beyond what we already are or may have heretofore become. We can of course deny this movement, cowering in fear of change or of standing apart from others, restricting our own evolution. Or we can direct this process of becoming and transcendence by choosing that toward which we aim, by looking above and beyond ourselves. For the self to be developed is not found within, but in

the direction of that which we choose to love, to devote ourselves to, or to honor.

Nietzsche's metaphors of height notwithstanding, the best of
what one can aim for might in fact be near to hand, within one's
grasp. In this way we can see the speaker of Frost's poem arriving,
through the imagined vastness, right back where he started, with
the same truths, won again in a newfound self-assurance. But the
poem demands of the speaker a venture through "those dark trees,"
into the vastness. Any truths to be won arrive truly for the self on
the other side of the unknown or the uncharted.

It may seem paradoxical that in existentialist terms one can be
said to lose oneself but not to find oneself. Inauthenticity as we
have seen means to be caught up in or refracted through the expectations and ideas about oneself or others, rather than choosing
for oneself. The inauthentic person identifies with some kind of
self-definition—be that hero or coward—as the cause for actions
that person in reality has freely chosen. Authenticity, on the other
hand, means to recover for oneself one's own self-becoming, one's
singularity, and to take responsibility. One is a hero only by acting
heroically, a coward only through cowardice.

When we aim for authenticity, what we may be seeking is not
the self that would be hidden there waiting for discovery. Rather,
the goal of coming into one's own may be to affirm or reaffirm,
by one's actions and one's trajectory of effort, "a truth that is true
for me" and yet that must exceed the self in some way. In finding
this truth one might seek to wrest oneself from any overbearing
influence of one's surroundings, or from others against whom one
may have judged oneself. One should, however, seek not oneself,
but one's capacities and strengths, perhaps within situations one

cannot yet imagine. In finding out what one can do, finding out what one is capable of, one becomes who one is.

Thus the existentialist would not advocate setting out to find ourselves, exactly. Rather the existentialist might say that in what we seek and in the way in which we seek it we are becoming what we are. This is so whether we remain in our familiar world or set off toward new uncharted ones. Neither the familiar nor the unknown has an intrinsic value over its opposite, but only that value which we give it through our attention and our actions, our admiration or esteem, our evasion or our commitment. Only our transcendence toward them determines what our possibilities might be, and what we may become.

15 | I SELFIE, THEREFORE I AM
ON SELF-IMAGING CULTURE

Imagine I have just snapped a photo of myself with my perfect Saturday morning pancakes and shared it online. In the same way, the world may witness me at the beach (bless my trainer!) or celebrating with friends. There I am again pondering a famous work of art (thank you, van Gogh!). There's me lounging at home in cute pajamas, reading a difficult book. Now here I am viewing a rainbow. Or rather, you are viewing the rainbow there behind me, complete with vista, the rainbow and the vista having appeared almost magically for the benefit of my viewers (thank you, nature!). Here I am in a monastery with some photogenic child monks, here I am on a sacred mountain, and in the end, I was able to elbow my way through the sea of selfie-takers up the steps of that famous Roman fountain. Here is evidence of my splendid existence, for all the world to see, posted on social media.

Or it would be so, if I took part in one of the most compulsive features of modern social life. Human beings take over a million selfies every day, and from almost every walk of life. With a camera in our devices at hand, we can turn the lens upon ourselves at any time, in any circumstance, and post the results for all to see. Viewing endless streams of others' selfies, we may feel compelled to evidence in our own right that our lives are interesting or worthwhile, or simply to keep reminding the world that we exist at all.

Emblematic of our contemporary obsession with the self, the selfie phenomenon undoubtedly transforms our ways of being-in-the-world, raising a number of questions we can pose in existential terms. Should we regard selfie culture as a celebration of the self or as perpetuating an unhealthy narcissism? Can the selfie culture contribute to, or only detract from, becoming who we are? Does the compulsion toward selfie taking and posting reveal superficial preoccupation with appearances, or deeper anxieties about our own purpose and importance? Does the relentless documentation of ourselves and our experiences express or induce anxiety about the ephemerality of our lives?

Of course the selfie phenomenon could scarcely have been imagined by the existentialist philosophers under discussion in this book, but it might be worth imagining what they might have thought of it. Admittedly, we do not know much about how they related to images of themselves. As far as I know, there are no extant photographs of Kierkegaard—only artists' renderings. These include the lampooning caricatures penned for a local paper, which rather nastily emphasized his hunchback. Other portraits and drawings, some showing the philosopher at his writing desk, are more reverent. They reveal a broad-eyed, straight-nosed, somewhat brooding but not ungentle face, under a mop of light hair, belying a formidable intellect. But all of these images give us Kierkegaard as seen by an artist, by someone other than himself. Believing as he did in indirect communication and the value of silence about one's immediate experience, it is impossible to imagine Kierkegaard advertising himself or his life directly.

Nietzsche posed for a photographer on nearly two dozen occasions, though a number of these were in his last years when he was ill and no longer in control of his life. A photo taken for his confirmation at the age of sixteen, in 1861, shows a thoughtful-looking youth leaning against a pillar with his hand tucked between the buttons of his coat. It was probably the first photograph he had seen of himself, and although he was glad to have the image and wondered who else would be given a copy he was, like many adolescents, critical of his appearance: "My stance is hunched, my feet somewhat crooked, and my hand looks like a dumpling," he complained. A photograph from 1868, the year before taking up his professorship at Basel, shows Nietzsche in uniform holding a sword—an outfit donned at the request of a friend who was in the army. Nietzsche found the image unappealing, his posture aggressive, and the sword, insisted on by the photographer, superfluous. In a now famous photo taken in 1882 Nietzsche posed in Lucerne, Switzerland, alongside friends Paul Rée and Lou Andreas-Salomé, with the two men pulling a wheelbarrow while their common love interest, a formidable free spirit in her own right, held a riding whip. Other photographs show Nietzsche the professor sporting his paradigmatic moustache in a contemplative and dignified posture. While Nietzsche sent copies of photographs to his friends, this is far from the selfie phenomenon, as he did not have to contemplate their proliferation and circulation in real time to a largely anonymous public.

The French existentialists of the twentieth century however were well-acquainted with the public dispersion of images of the self. Sartre, Camus, and Beauvoir, as we know, were feted as celebrities, attended by fawning photographers. They sat for photoshoots in order to be portrayed in mass-produced, glossy magazines, and their images took on an iconicity that would come to anchor the existentialist style. One wonders, however unattractive Sartre thought himself to be (he called his appearance a "brutality of fate"), whether he would have nevertheless enjoyed the far greater possibilities for distributing one's image today. In the 1970s he participated in a film, *Sartre par Lui-Meme* or *Sartre by Himself*, which presents over three hours of Sartre chain-smoking in his apartment in Montparnasse, talking with friends, including Beauvoir. The film is and is not an extended selfie, as he is asked by the filmmakers about his life. This allows him, as Kierkegaard might have put it, to mirror himself not only in image but in words. Of course, the directorial interview and the input of other interlocutors allow for a multidimensional portrait of the philosopher. Yet Sartre himself savored his celebrity status.

At the same time, Sartre gave grounds for critique of the compulsive self-objectification that develops with selfie culture. The self-commissioned portraits of the well-to-do fathers of the city in the gallery at Bouville, eviscerated by Roquentin in Sartre's novel *Nausea* for their "bad faith" and their smug self-satisfied airs, come to mind. Sartre also protests philosophically at any objectification of the self. Taking and posting a selfie, one is both subject and object at once. Yet once posted, the image invites only an external gaze, capitalizing on the self-objectification of the process. Sartre argues that becoming an object of a gaze presents a danger to one's freedom, in that one will see oneself from the point of view of others who cannot know one's subjective point of view. Not only objectified by others, one becomes an object for oneself. One may come to identify with the series of self-images one has presented to the world, a situation that would mask one's own transcending subjectivity. Marcel too would undoubtedly ascribe to selfie culture a still more pernicious "self-imitation and self-hypnotism" than he found in modern technological culture in general.

The highly mediated nature of selfies may also lead to self-deception. Despite their frequent proximity to real-time events, selfies only appear to constitute immediate evidence of who we are, or how our lives are really lived. Selfies are selected, framed, and frequently edited versions of what we wish to present as our personal reality. They are all posed; they may be technically filtered, enhanced, or otherwise altered to present a stylized image. Despite their measure of irreality, they may contribute to the construction of an ideal self with which a person may strive to identify.

The correlation between individuals' satisfaction with their own lives and their exposure to social media is now a well-studied phenomenon. Even selfies that are enhanced in some way toward an idealized presentation have been shown to have adverse psychological effects on those who take and post them. Recent studies of young subjects show that the posting of selfie images, even flatteringly edited ones, leads to greater feelings of insecurity. Some young people who may be among the most vulnerable to the effects of objectification are known to have undergone plastic surgery to look better in selfies, or even to look more like the edited selfies they have posted. The detrimental effects of selfie culture obtain even when subjects know that the self-images and the life-moments presented do not represent the reality of an actual life but framed and filtered moments. Viewing others' selfies and posting one's own may invoke competition among self-presentations and life-presentations, diminishing the value we attribute to our original experiences, recalling Kierkegaard's description of the externalizing process of envy, values being forged in constant comparison of oneself to others.

The notion of "privileged moments" was explored by Sartre in his novel *Nausea*. Anny, Roquentin's on-again-off-again love interest, had structured her life with the aim of aesthetic and experiential perfection. She had aimed to curate moments to make them just right, to make them seem infinitely meaningful or exclusive or in some other way standing above the humdrum ordinary course of events. In one rather amusing episode Roquentin recalls how his red hair spoiled Anny's curation of her scene. Had Anny been written into a twenty-first-century novel, she might have been a prolific selfie-taker and curator. But just as Roquentin comes to realize that his memories and past adventures cannot define his present reality as a self, so too Anny comes to recognize the impossibility of securing moments of life privileged above reality and its passage through and out of the present. "There are no privileged moments," she comes to realize. Both characters come to regard authentic life only as it is actually lived, not as it is fixed and preserved in memory or its representation.

A further difficulty with the selfie culture is its displacement of presence and of responsibility to others. While social media connects people in many ways, it also isolates individuals from real others while also exposing them to the responses of an uncommitted public. One may post selfies to a select group, or to others anywhere in the world, and may await approval by others, publicly quantified in real time. One may be liked or not, complimented or insulted, affirmed or harassed, and one's affirmations or disaffirmations may be public, too. Anonymity can also provoke aggressive responses in viewers undermining subjects in their own sense of themselves.

Kierkegaard argues that relationships that are carried on primarily through external presentation tend to forgo any bond of inward commitment. In his notion of "reflection" as described in a previous chapter, the self comes to see itself as it were reflected through the eyes of an anonymous public. In such a situation, Kierkegaard would claim, the individual no longer belongs "to himself, to his beloved, to his art or to his science, he is conscious of belonging in all things to an abstraction." If Kierkegaard were alive today, he might describe selfie culture as individuals stuck in a corrosive mode of the aesthetic sphere, abstracted out of all inner reality.

Kierkegaard would, I think, criticize selfie culture for its real-time exteriorization of experiences, its relentless publicization of private life, and its blurring of self-expression and advertising. The "exteriorized caricature of inwardness," he wrote, "is vulgarity and talkativeness." So Kierkegaard criticized the competitive self-exposure of modern society. One markets oneself and shops for others similarly marketed. Some artistic selfies notwithstanding, there is in a selfie typically no presentation of an inner life, but only the self and life as seen on the visible surface. Superficiality is described by Kierkegaard as the loss of distinction between manifestation and concealment. When one lives superficially, everything is laid out on the surface, emptying life of its depth. Kierkegaard could have been describing the selfie culture when he wrote: "Life's existential tasks have lost the interest of reality; illusion cannot build a sanctuary for the divine growth of inwardness which ripens to decisions."

Heidegger, too, would have undoubtedly rejected selfie culture on several grounds, including its anthropocentric hubris and what he would call its technological "enframing" of the self and whatever appears as its background. Two essays, "The Age of the World-Picture" (1938) and "The Question Concerning Technology" (1953), criticized technological modes of pictoral representation. He described any such "enframing" of nature as the mere object of human perception and potential use, stilling in images the changing becoming of nature. In such a relation we have lost sight, he thinks, of the human being as a steward of being.

In these essays Heidegger objected to treating the earth as standing-reserve for human consumption, even aesthetic consumption. He did not know about, or acknowledge, the kind of artistic photography that may cultivate a reverence for nature. He did not acknowledge that the image of the earth from space, which he criticized as a human representational enframing of the world, may enable us to be aware of its global well- or ill-being, to care for it as a whole. Yet Heidegger worried that we have become accustomed to regarding the world as an object to be framed by us. If he could comment on the selfie culture, Heidegger might protest that not only is the human being objectified in the selfie, but so too is the world which becomes but a background for our self-representation.

The selfie culture has in fact impacted how we treat the world's places and people, as the world may be rendered as mere scenery for the exhibition of the self. Hordes of tourists have sought out the best selfie backgrounds, favoring picturesque cobblestone streets or snap-worthy scenes, sometimes causing destruction to local communities. Famous artworks may be barely glanced at by the sea of selfie-takers who treat the art as a background for their own portraits, while those intent on experiencing the artwork for its own sake may hardly get a view. Locals have complained that sites of ancient spiritual value become disrespected by tourist selfie-takers checking off another item on a list of sought-after experiences. Sites of tragic human history, such as concentration camps and memorials to fallen soldiers, have been similarly rendered a stage-set for a self-advertised life.

Other people, too, may become props for one's own self-presentation. Selfie-takers—albeit probably a very small percentage of them—have posed before scenes of human suffering: smiling in front of car accidents, next to sleeping homeless people, even before a teacher suddenly going into labor. One selfie-taker posed in front of a potential suicide as he was being talked down from a bridge by police officers. Animals in the wild have been tracked down, harassed, or shot in order to serve as props for human selfies. Selfie-takers themselves have died while seeking out the most striking backgrounds—precariously balancing on cliffs, swimming among sharks, dangling off of balconies—inadvertently sacrificing themselves, as it were, to a culture of exhibitionism.

Existentialists would likely be concerned about any cultivation of the self that would be based on externalized images. They may be worried that the superficial presentation becomes associated with or stands in for an identity of the self, as a projected personality and image-based narrative takes the place of contemplation, action, passion, and commitment to the world beyond the self. They may be worried that obsession over self-image devalues genuine, in-person experience. For becoming oneself, rather than ceaselessly imaging the self, is the marker of an authentic life.

Even so, some selfies are undoubtedly creative, or engage with some distinguishing irony the dominant culture at large. While many selfie-takers indulge in vanity and ostentation, others may deliberately contest standardized images of beauty or success. Some artists use selfies to convey considered responses to body-image consciousness or to celebrate in some way their specificity, or ethnic or gender identity. A comic celebrity recently posted an image of herself in a decidedly unflattering breast-pump contraption. The image was not only shockingly comical but revealed an unacknowledged complication of many new mothers' lives and senses of self. Many selfies can rightly be considered works of art, of which the self in some manifestation is both subject and object.

We must also consider the experimental value selfie culture might hold. There is mere superficiality, and then there is the play of surfaces. Nietzsche wrote of the masks we all wear, under which there are ever only "more masks." He wrote that "every profound spirit needs a mask," and he understood that masks of some sort or other are inevitable, since everything we project is always subjected to others' interpretations anyway. I doubt Nietzsche would think much of materialism, ostentation, or mere vanity of most selfie culture, insofar as selfies involve crowd-pandering forms of competition and invoke common rather than distinctive measures of valuation. I personally suspect that Nietzsche would have despised the phenomenon for its encouragement of constant but empty self-regard. Nevertheless, it is possible that at least in some cases he might have appreciated in the selfie medium a potential exercise in self-experimentation and even self-creation. Nietzsche might, for example, appreciate that in certain circumstances it may take courage, and not merely vanity, to issue one's self-imagings to the world. The effect of such self-exposure to a potentially unlimited global audience may include a reduction in dependence on the local neighbors Nietzsche tended to think pressed one into the herd.

Any situation where the self is displayed as an object is existentially suspect. Yet it is conceivable that one can present the subject-in-process, the self as becoming, in a communicative way, without necessarily falling prey to self-objectification. One may present oneself in the world such that the latter is not merely a background to be exploited. One may even hint visually at an inner life that cannot be seen in an image. Such innovations, no doubt already underway by some participants, demand creativity of selfie culture and present its existential challenge.

16 | ON BEING AND WAITING (TABLES), OR, THE ROLES WE PLAY

We may take on multiple roles in life, and these may be more or less authentically embodied. Sartre famously argued that a person who takes on a given role too earnestly is inauthentic, comparing such a person to an actor. He presented the example of a waiter who so fully plays the "part" of a waiter that the man would seem to lose any hope of authentic individuality. The waiter imitates the robotic movements that Sartre, observing, associates with the (mere) role or character of a such a person.

Let us consider this waiter in the cafe. His movement is quick and forward, a little too precise, a little too rapid. He comes toward the patrons with a step a little too quick. He bends forward a little too eagerly; his voice, his eyes express an interest a little too solicitous for the order of the customer. Finally there he returns, trying to imitate in his walk the inflexible stiffness of some kind of automaton while carrying his tray with the recklessness of a tight-rope-walker by putting it in a perpetually unstable, perpetually broken equilibrium which he perpetually re-establishes by a light movement of the arm and hand. All his behavior seems to us a game. . . . [H]e is playing at being a waiter in a cafe.

From Sartre's point of view the role of the waiter involves the elimination of individuality and personality that is not tied up with the "ceremony" of public demands. Like other service occupations—Sartre names grocer, tailor, and auctioneer as examples—the waiter engages in robotic actions from which he claims genuine subjectivity is eliminated. One enacts a mere representation, or imitation, of the waiter, or tailor, or grocer.

> It is a "representation" for others and for myself, which means that I can be he only in representation. . . . [T]hat is, imagine to myself that I am he. And thereby I affect him with nothingness. In vain do I fulfil the functions of a cafe waiter. I can be he only in the neutralized mode, as the actor is Hamlet, by mechanically making the typical gestures of my state and by aiming at myself as an imaginary cafe waiter through those gestures taken as an "analogue."

One wonders if Sartre, in such criticisms, did not conceal a certain snobbishness about the service occupations from the lofty position of a public intellectual. All the same, Sartre's attack on the waiter also invites questions about the various roles any of us may play in life.

By becoming, or rather imitatively enacting out that role, the waiter is an example of inauthenticity, according to Sartre. In his movements and mannerisms, attitude and comportment, his subjectivity seems to dissolve into an outwardly prescribed role, one which is merely imaginary. In short, the waiter objectifies himself, presenting as a "contingent block of identity" which he is not. Therefore, he is in a state of bad faith. If it is the case that the waiter fully identifies with his role, using as it were this role as an essence by which to define himself and his choices, Sartre may be right.

Yet it is hard to imagine a life in which one never plays any role at all. Could not the professor, too, also play the role of the professor, presenting as the wise or learned scholar, the authority, the ultimate aesthete? No doubt (according to at least one student who knew him) Sartre himself sometimes played and even exploited the role of the learned mentor, the great philosopher, to great and seductive effect, as he held court in the café or the lecture hall or the jazz club. That in itself is no proper argument against Sartre's view of role-playing, but it does suggest that role-playing may be inevitable for many in social life. Even Descartes, upon whose blank slate vision of subjectivity Sartre admits to basing his own, seems to have mentally played the role, in his *Meditations*, of one sequestered from the world, imagining it scarcely to exist. One wonders if at any moment when absorbed in writing the second meditation, imagining he has no body, Descartes paused over a bit of indigestion. If he had, he would have continued on, in his mind and in his writing, as if he had felt nothing of the kind.

In perhaps an overly purist vision of authenticity, Sartre may have overlooked the very considerable possibility that some role-playing can be authentically creative or even ethical. Parents feeling afraid or defeated by life may feign calm and cheer for the sake of the children in their care. All good parents hide some adult aspects of themselves from children and sometimes have to play the "part" of the good parent in order to be one. Children too may eventually come to play the role of son or daughter, when they'd rather do other things. A person cannot play the same role when being a lover as when being a leader or a colleague or a neighbor. The most successful among us sometimes, in order to be genuinely loved, must allow themselves to be seen as vulnerable. This will differ from the roles they play in moments and modes of success, but if the self is only in and through its actions, one need not choose between the vulnerable and the achieving expressions of the self in order to be authentic.

The idea that one ought to conduct oneself in a single mode, never playing any role, was a rather anti-existential dictate of Plato. In *The Republic* Plato proposes convincing those members of the polis of the essential nature of their souls (allegorically described as bronze, silver, or gold) which would accordingly determine their place in society. Plato rejected poetry and drama because they encouraged citizens to take up multiple roles and to present themselves, in acting or reciting such works, as characters they are not. But imagining others' situations and perspectives may be fundamental to social understanding. Such imagining may allow one to prospect for possibilities for oneself and one's own life.

We noted in the previous chapter that Nietzsche famously celebrated the notion of donning masks and questioned the idea that there would be any single essence as it were beneath them. Nietzsche celebrated the creativity and playfulness of becoming, of experiment, and the diversity of our human experience. Nietzsche at times seems to have imagined himself as his prophet and protagonist Zarathustra, in other moments as his favorite Greek god Dionysus. Nietzsche certainly understood that the human imagination, so long as we do not stifle it, makes us capable of living life at more than one register.

Turning back to Sartre's waiter, we might consider that such roles, though no doubt sometimes drudging, might also be undertaken with genuine interest and joy. One may come across the waiter who seems to play the part of the waiter not only as a genuine profession but also as an authentic art. Such would not be the robotic automaton described by Sartre, enacting subservient delivery in mimicry of the essence of waiterdom. Rather there would be an art of noticing, anticipating, attending, and cultivating occasions for others. It may not be entirely coincidental that many struggling actors take up the role of the waiter for paid work. For the art of acting, too, presenting as the actor does a character in imagined reality, is self-conscious of its mimetic character. Despite Plato's rejection of dramatic mimesis, we might speculate that the more successfully actors take up their roles, the more they might be drawn to wonder who they are in and of themselves. But the actor who makes an art of the medium of acting does not imitate simply in order to pretend to be someone they are not. In playing a role they may creatively express a point of view, bringing to life a work of art. In the final chapter of this book we shall turn to the existential need for creativity, and the idea of life itself as a work of art.

17 | SEIZING THE DAY
THE PRESENT AND PRESENCE

We experience the present moment in vivid actuality, far more vividly, for most people, than the dimly remembered past or the only imagined future. What value does the present have for us? Is it better to live for the present moment or to subordinate our current, fleeting desires for a future goal? How much are we fully present in a given moment to the world before us today, right now, and to what extent should we be? Should we treat the past and past history, experience, or understanding as a guide to our actions in the present? How should we relate to those who are no longer present and to those who are present before us?

Existentialism is often popularly associated with the mantra "carpe diem," an exhortation to seize the day. Vigorous attention to the current "now" may be associated with making a significant change, turning against the course of habit, setting upon a new path. For a number of existentialists, the present is privileged over the past, while the future is valued as the direction of possibility for our present actions and goals. Yet they also tend to consider in what ways the present ought to be negotiated in light of the past as well as the future.

Of course, we may speak of the present in a number of ways. There is, first of all, a temporal sense of presence, captured grammatically in the present tense, as in Shakespeare's phrase: "Now is the winter of our discontent." Now is a moment, an hour, a particular season, and, most expansively, an era or age. In addition to this temporal sense of the present, we are spatially present somewhere. In order to experience what is taking place in the present time, we must be where it is so taking place, to be here at the happening. But the most important sense of presence pertains to one's attention. One can be present in another's life, for example, not simply by being present in time and place, but in paying attention to that other person, being in that person's "here and now" in some sense *for* the other. To be present means to be focused on, and to give something of one's own being to whatever is happening here and now. It may be worthwhile coming to understand how these senses of presence interrelate in existentialist thought.

Nietzsche advocates a primary relation to the present in all three senses. In "On the Uses and Disadvantage of History for Life," Nietzsche warns that too great a historical sense makes the past a burden for us. Today our culture may be far more ignorant of the past than previous generations have been, but Nietzsche of course lived at a time when formal education was structured around the memorization of ancient texts and, in his view, the dry recitation of history as cumulative knowledge. Remembrance of all the great actions of one's historical forebears, of the great cultures that have come before, may make one feel impoverished in comparison or regard one's own present moment as insignificant. Too much respect for the past, Nietzsche argues, makes us graveyard attendants of past actors of history rather than actors in the now. What he calls the "historical sense," in too great a quantity, diminishes our energy, vitality, and above all imagination of what is possible by outweighing our temporal present and diminishing our capacity for presence in the sense of contributive attention to it. Since the past may carry with it the authority of tradition and habit, Nietzsche advises his readers to develop a healthy sense of forgetting. We ought to regard the present and its possibilities with a fresh, unburdened perspective, and only as such may we find courage to act.

While the past is held in suspicion, so too is any future life. The present for Nietzsche is to be savored in all its vital ephemerality. Nietzsche rejected philosophies or religions that sought eternal truths, insofar as they valued the permanent and unchanging ideal over the shifting and temporary present. This had the effect, Nietzsche thought, of diminishing the importance of "this" life for an imagined eternity in a future hereafter. Rejecting the notion of an afterlife along with such ideal truths, Nietzsche implores us to savor the now. He writes: "But even if the future leaves us nothing to hope for, the wonderful fact of our existing at this present moment of time gives us the greatest encouragement to live after our own rule and measure."

Nietzsche's idea of the "eternal return" also intensifies the importance of the present. In *The Gay Science* and *Thus Spoke Zarathustra*, Nietzsche presents the idea of the eternal return or recurrence, a repetition of one's life exactly as one has lived it, over and over again. As a kind of thought experiment, the idea allows us to test our present actions against the idea of their future repetition. When we regard our immediate experience, a choice we must make, the life that we are living now, it may look different to us if we ponder having to undertake the same again and again. The ultimate confirmation of a life, Nietzsche suggests, would be to rejoice at the knowledge that it would be repeated over and over indefinitely, just as it is and has been.

This does not necessarily mean that one must aim for perfection or for a life free of suffering or risk. For Nietzsche also praises risk-taking, courage, and noble failure over meekness, passivity, or inactivity. He advises the attitude of *amor fati*, or "love of fate," and that we should lead our lives with deliberate and vigorous choice. He asks us to appreciate "the inexplicable fact that we live precisely today and yet had the infinity of time in which to come into being, that we possess nothing but this brief today in which to show why and to what purpose we have come into being at precisely this moment." Seeing the significance of this moment, he continues, "We shall have to approach existence with a certain boldness and willingness to take risks: especially since in both the worst and the best instances we are bound to lose it." Nietzsche asks us to live in our moment such that we would not regret it were we to have to live it over and over again. How might we live the present differently if we thought we could never escape the repetition of our actions?

If for Nietzsche the present is maximized by imagining the possibility of its return, for Heidegger it is best lived when we recognize that it happens only once. The present is a moment Dasein gathers to itself from out of the future and the past. For as we recall, Dasein's authenticity is won by reckoning with finitude. While Heidegger defines Dasein as "being-possible" and thus always directed toward the future, he also describes a moment of authentic self-reckoning that casts the present in a privileged light.

In a "moment of vision," Heidegger argues, Dasein may realize the future but definite possibility of its death, a possibility that is certain but unpredictable as to when and how. Dasein is in such a moment seized, as it were, by the certain but indeterminate extremity of the future. In such reckoning Dasein awakens to the singularity of our existence in the here and now. In light of our future impossibility—the certain future possibility of our not (no longer) being—we are to embrace the present as genuinely our own.

For Heidegger, however, the authentic experience of existential time is not only futurally directed but circular. In being-toward-death, or projecting the possibility of the ultimate future impossibility that is its own death, Dasein is thrown back upon the present as its very own present. But in this authentic self-reckoning, Dasein also looks back upon its past in a new light. Dasein retrieves or "repeats" the past in an authentic mode, recognizing it as the condition of possibility for a singular present. The future is too then projected on the basis of this singular present and authentically retrieved past.

Sartre does not express such concern for involving the past—however authentically it may be understood—in our conception of the living present. Echoing Nietzsche's suspicion of the past, Sartre draws rather severe conclusions from the obvious fact that the past no longer exists. Sartre conceives of the past as literally nothing. Thus even our own personal past—where we come from, what has happened to us, the choices we have made in the past—offers no genuine indication of who we really are in the moment now. For Sartre, the past and future, as non-existent, are existentially irrelevant, except insofar as our projects that provide meaning for our lives in the present must be elaborated over time.

Sartre illustrates this point in *Nausea*. The protagonist Roquentin looks back over his life, his memories and adventures.

Having met the "self-taught man" in the library, Roquentin agrees to show him some photographs from his travels, many of which involved international intrigue, danger, and close escapes in exotic locations. The self-taught man is eager to learn from Roquentin's experiences, for he has himself had no real-life adventures. But as Roquentin looks over his photographs, he realizes that these are not identical with, or even genuine manifestations of, his original experiences. He realizes the real experiences have crumbled away "like dead leaves" when his memory grasps hold of them. The problem is not that his memory is faulty; it is that a memory itself is only a faded copy of a former present experience that itself no longer clings to being. Roquentin thus has an epiphany about time and existence: "The real nature of the present revealed itself: it was what exists, all that was not present did not exist."

Yet Sartre recognizes that if, in rejecting the past, we have only the present, we must also give this present a meaning. Anny's failed attempts at perfect moments or flawless curations of the present show that this cannot be won on an aesthetic basis alone. If this meaning cannot be authentically derived from our past experiences, it must be won from our present projects. Any substantial project requires effort and direction toward a future yet to be shaped. While this will entail an unfolding over time, and thus a continuity between past and present, any authentic project must continually, in the present, affirm and be affirmed by our freedom.

Roquentin comes to this realization somewhat symbolically in Sartre's novel. When he comes to see clearly the non-existence of the past, he abandons his project of the historical biography he had been writing. Attempting to capture the story of the Marquis de Rollebon, the eighteenth-century diplomat, paramour, and spy, was a futile project, since, he discovers, the past cannot be resurrected in any convincing way, or even known with any certainty at all. After struggling to verify anything about the life of this long-gone figure—the available evidence leading to discrepant conclusions—Roquentin resolves instead to write a novel. This would mean to create a fictional world that does not yet and never will exist, characters for which there are no determining prescriptions, and events that could never be derived from knowledge of the past. The fictional world will exist only as the imagined projection of the reader, and only for that present moment in which the reader is reading. At least in this sense, imaginative literature assumes an advantage over history.

Of course, the form our lives in the present take tends to be shaped by commitments we have made in the past, by our past accomplishments as well as errors. Is it merely in deference to the past that we continue to honor our promises or stick to our projects in the present? Sartre of course recognizes that our present projects—even those which are at the time genuinely innovative rather than habitual—will inevitably become past commitments with the passage of time. Eventually Sartre must abandon the severity of his ontological dismissal of the past as mere nothingness, and proposes the idea of a primary or fundamental project by which one can shape one's life. Such a project inevitably involves affirmation not only of the present but of past moments of initiation and development, and intentional movement toward its continuation. The freedom of the absolute present thus must be complicated somewhat by the conditions set by the past and the possibilities they open up for the future.

Beauvoir attends to these complications in *The Ethics of Ambiguity*. She suggests, like Sartre, that we are, in any given present moment, free to choose. Yet Beauvoir explores the problem that every choice we make in exercise of our freedom sets up a new situation that contextualizes and potentially limits its further exercise. Without such continuity we would not be able to achieve anything of more than momentary value. As Beauvoir puts it, "An existence would be unable to found itself if moment by moment it crumbled into nothingness." This temporal complication of freedom is one aspect of what Beauvoir calls the "ambiguity" of our existential situation.

> If I leave behind an act which I have accomplished, it becomes a thing by falling into the past. It is no longer anything but a stupid and opaque fact. In order to prevent this metamorphosis, I must ceaselessly return to it and justify it in the unity of the project in which I am engaged. Setting up the movement of my transcendence requires that I never let it uselessly fall back upon itself, that I prolong it indefinitely. Thus I cannot genuinely desire an end today without desiring it through my whole existence, insofar as it is the future of this present moment and insofar as it is the surpassed past of days to come.

Acknowledging these ambiguities gives a more complex rendering of freedom. Yet for both Beauvoir and Sartre, it is the present moment that must be privileged in light of the freedom of authentic action. Even a long-term project that unfolds over the course of a lifetime must be freely seized in a new moment and should never obscure our freedom to change course. The past should be engaged in service to the present and future. Again, in Beauvoir's words:

> The creator leans upon anterior creations in order to create the possibility of new creations. His present project embraces the past and places confidence in the freedom to come.

There is an implicit notion of repetition in these existential renderings of the relation between past and present—in Nietzsche's eternal return, Heidegger's notion of an authentic retrieval of the past, and Sartre's and Beauvoir's acknowledgments of the present's continuity with the past. They all reflect the influence of Kierkegaard, who in his book *Repetition* explored possibilities for regarding the present in light of the past or, alternatively, the past in light of the present.

For Kierkegaard, there is authentic and inauthentic repetition. Inauthentic repetition that may take place in the aesthetic stage of life can affect a vain attempt to re-create over and over again an aesthetically satisfying experience one has had in the past. Merely aesthetic repetition makes one but a collector of experiences, where the differences only add variety among the same. Authentic repetition is, however, a continuation of the past not by merely securing the self-same experience or action over and over again. Rather in authentic repetition, the past is made ever anew. Fidelity in marriage, the experience of religious faith, and perhaps genuine friendship may be categorized by authentic repetition. One says yes over and over again, and it is, paradoxically, a new affirmation of the same each time.

Kierkegaardian repetition is echoed in Marcel's notion of creative fidelity. One of the examples of creative fidelity concerns faithfulness to the memory of someone who is no longer present. As Marcel explains it, one aims, in creative fidelity, to retain in the present the intensity or presence of the remembered other. It involves "an inner struggle against interior dissipation" of the importance and presence of the one remembered. This should be not mere idolatry of a past, the construction of an emotional "effigy" of a person. Creative fidelity requires more than merely backward-looking subservience to the past. Rather, it involves an active and constant maintenance in one's own subjective sphere of the other's permanence—a permanence which, however, depends on its constant renewal in the present of the one remembering.

Much like Kierkegaardian authentic repetition, creative fidelity involves the "active perpetuation of presence, the renewal of its benefits—of its virtue which consists in a mysterious incitement to create." It involves both active commitment in the present and being present as a self before the world. Marcel uses the analogy of artistic creation, in which "the world is present to the artist in a certain way—present to his heart and to his mind, present to his very being."

According to Marcel, I can be creatively faithful to the memory of a lost loved one, or of a loved one far away to whom I am bound predominantly in the past. While some forms of deference to the past can turn a memory into a sort of effigy, everything depends upon my attitude of openness. "Even if I cannot see you, if I cannot touch you, I feel that you are with me." In order to maintain a sense of presence, the regard for the lost beloved must be vital and unfixed by past experience. A presence is a reality, depending on myself to be permeable to it: "Creative fidelity consists in maintaining our-selves actively in a permeable state."

Creative fidelity can also be maintained of course to one who remains present but to whom one's initial commitment lies in the past. What is essential, according to Marcel, is that one's own openness and availability render a faithful person vitally present to the world and more specifically to the other. The presence of the other to one's own mind and feeling, in one's own life, is in-wardly realized. To be present to the world or to another person is a form of selfless generosity, the value of which cannot be cal-culated or verified. Such being present means being available and open, willing to appreciate and cherish.

On such a model, to be present in the present moment may concern then not only accomplishing my own projects but open-ness and attentiveness to the world around me, with specific atten-tion to the one to whom I choose to maintain fidelity. There must be respect for the past as it is what makes a present action possible. Yet in order to be fully present to the world and others, our under-standing cannot be closed off by the accumulation of past experi-ence and the categories that arise from it.

If we can retain openness to the present even in light of the past, perhaps we could imagine a healthier form of the historical sense against which Nietzsche warned. We can respect a given historical institution for its past value and for its continuity with people and traditions of the past, for example. But such reverence need not serve as a measure of discrimination against the present which fails to embody it, or against those who, being of the present, fail to live up to the past values we may conjure in our historical imagina-tion. When our understanding remains permeable and revisable,

Marcel thinks, we avoid being captivated by nostalgia. We realize our freedom in light of openness to others and to the new. It is this kind of presence, and not only anxiety about our individual finitude, that may protect against despair of a world we may feel to be without mystery or meaning.

An existential seizing of the day, then, would be more nuanced than a simple embrace of the moment for the sake of a fleeting pleasure or a temporary triumph. Existentialists suggest that the present ought to be affirmed, seized in light of its possibilities, taken up actively in action and commitment, and may also involve being present to the world and being present for others. Camus wrote that any "real generosity toward the future consists in giving all to the present." The present can be regarded as a moment to be achieved, one that will become the future's inheritance.

18 | LOVE IN THE TIME OF EXISTENTIALISM

Love anchors human existence and resonates across our awareness of being and becoming. Falling in love can invest our whole world with a sense of renewed possibility. Delighting in love, we may feel ourselves in moments in harmony with the cosmos itself, while our romantic tribulations may be wrapped up with our highest existential despair. Love may even challenge the sense of our singular being; in those moments we may feel to be fused with the soul of another. If we should aim for an authentic life, a creative becoming, and hope to embrace our freedom, how might this be reflected in our experiences of love? Can love be informed by existential awareness?

We can begin by pointing out how far existentialist thinking diverges from classical philosophical views of love. Philosophy's interest in the subject goes back to Plato, who depicted *eros* as harboring a metaphysical and even religious awakening. In the *Symposium*, Plato has Socrates discussing the topic with a number of interlocutors including Alcibiades, a famously beautiful, if also vain, young man, and likely a real-life love interest of Socrates. At the gathering depicted in the dialogue, participants debated the nature of the relationship between a lover and a beloved.

While Alcibiades emphasizes sexual desire in his description of love, Socrates evokes Diotima's view that love draws upon and evidences the eternity of the soul. Eros, and the admiration of the beloved's beauty, is held to provoke in the lover a memory of a divine origin. At the symposium Aristophanes represents the myth that every human soul was in a previous form of existence rent in two halves by the gods, and in coming to bodily form in earthly life, each soul would have to seek its completion through bonding with another. Eros then expresses a longing for wholeness, the state in which the human soul would be made complete again. The notion of "Platonic" or physically unconsummated love originates with Socrates's suggestion that the soul, while entranced by the beloved's beauty, should keep its vision upon the divine recollection. The fulfillment of bodily desire would, Socrates argues, distract from divine contemplation.

For all the philosophical reverence with which Plato adorns the subject of love, his view will be opposed by every existentialist rendering. In an essay titled "Eros, Platonic and Modern," Simmel points out that Plato treats the experience of love as emblematic of an ideal beauty, to which any of its manifestations would be equivalent. If the beauty of the beloved reminds us of a previous state of the soul, or of our divine origins, such beauty is (merely) ideal. The ideal of love is abstract rather than concrete, universal rather than particular. In such a situation love may be idealized as an index to a beyond, rather than realized in concrete relation to the beloved.

In contrast, a modern view of love concerns the relationship between one individual and another as a "unique, irreplaceable being." The individual, and the relation between two individuals, would anchor the modern experience of love. Existentialists focus on the freedom of these individuals and the ways in which love can exercise or alternatively hamper their freedom. Yet this relation will be rendered in very different ways by different existentialist thinkers.

We can begin with the example of existentialism's most famous couple, for the relationship between Sartre and Beauvoir, and their respective commentaries on love, dominates the prevailing view of existential eros. Sartre and Beauvoir met in 1929 as fellow graduate students in philosophy, both studying for the elite aggregation diploma. Sartre was brilliant and charismatic, but Beauvoir was considered by their professors the superior mind. At age twenty-one, Beauvoir was also the youngest person to have sat the examination, but as a woman she was given second place behind Sartre in their results. Sartre however recognized Beauvoir's prodigious philosophical talent, as she recognized his. The young philosophers embarked on a passionate affair and subsequently maintained an open, life-long relationship, during which, in the name of freedom, they both pursued or enjoyed other lovers.

Sartre himself had proposed the following plan: they would remain together as primary partners, but they would be free to have other romantic entanglements. These other relationships might offer adventure and all-consuming, but momentary, passion. While he regarded theirs as an "essential love," Sartre wanted the freedom to experience love affairs that were "contingent." Above all, to respect the other's freedom, they would agree on total transparency with each other, and tell each other "everything." Despite the boldness exhibited in making such a proposal, Sartre was astonished that Beauvoir accepted. They embarked on a mutual, but non-exclusive, relationship that would last in some form for the rest of their lives.

However appealing or unappealing such an arrangement may seem to readers today, it was in any case exceptional for its time. Beauvoir later wrote of their relationship: "We were two of a kind, and our relationship would endure as long as we did: but it could not make up entirely for the fleeting riches to be had from encounters with different people." While promoting their freedom, the arrangement provoked jealousy and hurt, particularly on Beauvoir's side. For while Beauvoir over time had relatively few, often longer-lasting relationships apart from her primary partner, Sartre was a serial seducer and had countless affairs, and the detrimental effect this had on Beauvoir was sometimes expressed in her writings. Yet the partnership maintained for both of them personal and philosophical collaboration, and a form of loyal friendship, for over half a century.

Beauvoir, for her part, acted as she did in stark revolt against the conventions of her time. As a woman she would have been, and was, stigmatized far more than any male partner would have been—Sartre himself in the arrangement simply exercised a then long-tolerated male prerogative in French culture. Beauvoir was well aware of the oppressive inequality between the sexes, and illuminated its existential parameters in *The Second Sex*. Yet Beauvoir's relationship with Sartre nevertheless offered a companionship of deep intellectual respect. Since they never lived or kept house together, she evaded the domesticity into which she almost inevitably would have fallen in a conventional relationship. Sartre in turn respected and encouraged Beauvoir intellectually and consulted her on everything, including his dalliances. They read almost all of each other's work, lectured and presented and sometimes interviewed together, and remained almost perpetually devoted. Their open relationship was meant to attest to an existential freedom in which each lover would never hinder the beloved's becoming, and it became emblematic of an existential model for romantic relations.

Yet the long-received view of the relationship between Beauvoir and Sartre does not tell the whole story. Neither Beauvoir nor Sartre entirely escaped the conventional determinants of romantic love. Perhaps unsurprisingly, their intimate physical relations did not survive throughout their tumultuous "contingent" affairs, for although they continued to see each other nearly every day for the rest of their lives, they ended intimacy with one another after the war. Sartre eventually proposed marriage to a lover (not Beauvoir). Beauvoir herself later cohabitated for years with a lover (not Sartre, but the filmmaker Claude Lanzmann), to whom she referred in private letters as her "husband." In some moments, their largely unconventional lives chimed with those of more conventional people. It does not follow that in these moments they were less authentic than when they were breaking boundaries. The key to authenticity in their philosophies was open-eyed and transparent choice, recognition of freedom to choose, and responsibility for the values one's actions generate, and their relationship seems to have manifested such qualities.

Yet the vision of romantic love Sartre offers in his philosophical writings is not encouraging of the mutual freedom his "essential" love with Beauvoir was meant to ensure. One might assume that an existential love would involve a mutual invitation for two selves together to maximize the meaning of existence, to merge two freedoms in bidirectional care. Perhaps in some ways Beauvoir and Sartre achieved this. Yet philosophically Sartre describes love, or at least erotic love, as a seductive contest, a conflict of subjectivities in which each is a threat to the other's freedom. Since for Sartre the primary mode of being-for-others is modeled on the master-slave dialectic, love too is understood as a contest of objectifying gazes. Sartre's descriptions of love mention no tenderness or genuine intimacy, no concern for the other's welfare, focusing instead on the affirmation the lover might win for himself at the expense of the other's subjectivity. For in yielding such affirmation, the other is held to sacrifice their own freedom as the prize to the conquering subject.

Sartre was adamant in his writings on the subject that monogamy in love was contrary to freedom. He argued that feelings of romantic love were inevitably doomed to die out and a new object of the erotic contest would always be necessary. But it seems that Sartre engaged in one form of love with Beauvoir—a form of love that gradually became the romantic friendship he failed to theorize in his philosophy—and another form of erotic love with respect to the objects of his many seductions. It was the latter which became the paradigm for his theoretical model of love.

We can look beyond Sartre and Beauvoir of course for further existential elaborations on the subject. Given the centrality of love in human happiness and indeed in our sense of life's meaning, it is not surprising that other existentialist thinkers attended to the subject of love. In "The Seducer's Diary" section of *Either/Or* we find of course Kierkegaard's famous exploration of seduction, in the young man's pursuit of love at the aesthetic stage of life. The young man wishes to collect interesting experiences and his seductions may callously disregard their effects on the objects of his erotic interest. But the young man's experimental seductions are held to be inherently unfulfilling by Judge Wilhelm, who advocates for precisely the marital form of love to which Kierkegaard himself could not commit. In so small agony over his decision, Kierkegaard broke off his engagement to Regina Olsen, for he was unable to commit to a bourgeois life to the neglect of his own life of writing, with its endless philosophizing and its advocacy of inwardness. Kafka similarly broke off multiple engagements with Felice Bauer, determined as he was to dedicate his life to writing, though he too agonized over the conflict and embedded coded references to his former fiancée within his stories. Nietzsche proposed twice, unsuccessfully, to Lou Andreas-Salomé, whose unconventionality, for her time, would rival that of Beauvoir. Nietzsche's ill health would eventually preclude any serious efforts at further romantic ventures. Rilke left behind his wife, Clara, and their infant daughter to pursue poetic greatness—at one time traveling to Russia with Andreas-Salomé, the same woman Nietzsche had courted—though Rilke remained a good friend to Clara and convincingly urged respect for women. Camus, on the other hand, was notoriously unfaithful to both of his successive wives and caused them much despair.

What existentialist thinkers have to say about love is as diverse as their biographies, and one could counter the above examples of unfaithful or uncommitted love with other, very different cases. Jaspers, author of *Existenz* long before the French existentialists made any serious use of that term, stood by his Jewish wife under the Nazi reign in Germany, during which he was dismissed from his professorship and forbidden to publish. Marcel wrote of family life, including marriage and parenthood, with metaphysical and existential reverence. These counterexamples are not to be taken as existential models for imitation by readers any more than the relationship of Sartre and Beauvoir should be. Yet they illuminate the variety of loves lived and written about in light of existential thinking.

In "Phenomenological Notes on Being in a Situation," Marcel writes of commitment in marriage as not possessing the other, but as freely giving oneself to the other. Such generosity is not conceived, as in Sartre's account, as a sacrifice of one's free subjectivity. Rather, giving oneself to another is freedom's ultimate expression. We can also recall Marcel's notion of creative fidelity, or a persistent commitment of giving oneself to another. To be creatively faithful in a love relationship is not merely to avoid unfaithfulness or betrayal but also to maintain one's presence and openness for the other.

Even Nietzsche, whose notorious comments on women can suggest a rather negative view of relations between the sexes, may be considered in a more nuanced way than his reputation invites. As a philosophical provocateur Nietzsche wrote outrageous things about many groups of people, including women. But he also sometimes contradicted these same comments with other statements— never shying from experimental thinking and, since his thinking was always progressing, from the risk of self-contradiction. As a Grecophile, Nietzsche admired the idea of friendship between males as a privileged form of association, yet he also held some women in high esteem. He lobbied for women's admission to the university and had intellectual friendships with women, such as

Andreas-Salomé, whom he not only loved romantically but engaged in illuminating discussion. Along with Andreas-Salomé and Rée, he had for a time hoped to create an artistic and philosophical commune in Italy, which would be devoted to, among other things, noble friendship among intellectual and artistic creators. Nietzsche advised against erotic bonds based merely upon infatuation or physical attraction and advocated genuine companionship of souls. He surmised that a successful marriage—which he himself would never enjoy—could only be grounded in a great friendship.

Existentialism's focus on the individual self need not preclude fulfilling and even reverent forms of bonding with others. In *Letters to a Young Poet* Rilke described romantic lovers as two solitudes who "protect and border and greet each other" in a relationship of mutual care. Recognizing that one's own subjectivity is ever-in-progress and becoming, one may in love recognize the same process of becoming and need for existential fulfillment for and on behalf of the other. True love in an existential sense would need to be ever-open to the other's becoming, and involve recognition on the part of each individual of their responsibility to the love that is their common creation.

Like other existentialist thinkers, Beauvoir diverged from the Platonic idealization of love, thinking that "the union of two souls is impossible." Yet her own philosophical articulations on the subject of love differed considerably from those of Sartre. While Beauvoir recognized the possibility of domination and subordination in love relationships, she also held out the prospect of authentic love. Such a love is compatible with and furthers mutual freedom, if it is "founded on the mutual recognition of two liberties." One's freedom need not be defended against the other, but may be exercised in respect for the freedom of self and other. Individuality must be respected in such a love relation, and differences not denied but maintained.

Such mutuality within difference, at least in the case of heterosexual love, will be difficult to achieve, she wrote in *The Second Sex*, in a society that maintains inequality between the sexes. If women are expected to abandon themselves to a relationship while men maintain their individuality, misunderstanding as well as suffering will arise. Authentic love must be embraced by both parties who each neither subordinate the other nor allow themselves to be subordinated. Beauvoir's campaign for sexual equality does not abandon the prospect of erotic love between the sexes but reimagines what such an experience would be like for both subjects.

Of course, every choice leads to a situation that obstructs some further choices. Rather than commitment in love, one may instead aim for a greater freedom from ties and approach love primarily with the spirit of adventure. However if one chooses commitment in love, Marcel would add, exclusivity should be undertaken not merely as a sacrifice of other opportunities, but as an opportunity of its own. Commitment of course may be experienced as a burden that drags the fixed past incompatibly into a living present. Authentic commitment, however, would be engaged as a living project to be ever-renewed in free and generous acts of self-giving. In a relationship of such mutual giving to the other, to love is to breathe life into something larger than each individual, a situation which however does not leave the self behind but manifests free and creative choice.

19 | EXISTENTIAL SUFFERING, HAPPINESS, AND HOPE

Existentialist thinkers recognize the human condition as wrought with difficulty. They offer no one-size-fits-all answer to the problem of suffering, but they all dignify suffering philosophically by analyzing such experiences as anxiety, anguish, forlornness, dread, and despair. While this has led to the stereotype of existentialism as a gloomy or moodily self-indulgent philosophy, some existential thinkers also propose joyful responses to our human condition. They suggest that the possibility of anxiety is linked to that of happiness in any substantial sense, the prospect of despair to the possibility of hope.

The most prominent form of suffering treated in existential accounts is perhaps the concept of anxiety. Kierkegaard devoted a whole book to that notion, *The Concept of Anxiety,* while despair is a persistent theme in *Concluding Unscientific Postscript.* In *Fear and Trembling,* Kierkegaard chose Abraham as emblematic of a singular religious trial. We recall that Abraham—who at an advanced age had long awaited the birth of his son Isaac—was then ordered by God to kill his beloved son. How Abraham interpreted this command leads to a discussion of the paradox involved in faith, and the overarching mood in Kierkegaard's illustration is one of extreme uncertainty. In fear and trembling one must choose and take responsibility for the choice.

Yet Kierkegaard also suggests that we may feel anxious not only in moments of extreme duress or identifiably fearful situations but also in thinking about our own freedom and the freedom that choice entails. While some may face the future with equanimity and confidence, for others facing choices provokes anxiety, since whatever we do we will shape the present and future in ways we cannot predict with any certainty. We may feel anxious recognizing the extension of responsibility beyond our knowledge, knowing for certain only that each possibility we choose forecloses others, and that we are responsible for the consequences. It may be very difficult to change a given state of affairs for a new but uncertain future. If we do so, we may despair knowing that we are responsible for the impact of our choices on others.

Dread is another paradigmatically existential emotion. While we are always aware of our finitude at some level, occasionally we may become aware of this with an uncanny clarity. Thinking about the fact that we will someday no longer exist can lead to a feeling of dread. Dread may come with a sense of our smallness in the universe. Dread can arise in any situation, whether fighting our way home through a rush-hour crowd or graced with a view of the starry sky, suddenly aware that while the stars are billions of years old, our lives are extremely brief. Whether or not we believe in God, we may feel forlorn in the absence of any feeling of a divine presence to us, any answer to our need or prayer.

Heidegger followed Kierkegaard in considering anxiety and dread, recognizing in *Being and Time* that when we think about the inevitable fact of our death, we may feel frightened of exposure to the "nothing." Sartre peppered his discussion of an existential ethics with commentary on anguish, forlornness, and despair—all of them arising as consequences of human freedom and the existentialist irrelevance of any rules for action given in advance. Camus analyzed the suffering of Sisyphus, condemned to roll his boulder again and again up the mountain, in fruitless toil. Many of Kafka's protagonists suffer catastrophe, and it seems an implicit question to his readers exactly why and wherefore the suffering, whether under the auspices of the protagonist's own agency or in helpless submission to an obscure power.

Of course, sadness and distress need not issue from a dramatic confrontation, from fear of death or a godless universe, or in grappling with questions of obvious existential import. Most suffering seems to arise in circumstances of everyday life. We may experience illness or pain or poverty or insecurity or the loss of loved ones or rejection or failure or loneliness. Suffering can be mundane. You may be there in a particular café or bookshop or on the train with no one to talk to, and while sometimes you may enjoy the experience, today the solitude feels lonely. You may feel yourself to have little in common with the people with whom you work or go to school or live. Perhaps you would like to attend a party but don't want to go alone. You may regret making a particular mistake. You may worry about aging parents or your child's welfare. Perhaps you have everything you need and much of what you want, and yet you still feel frustrated, unsettled, or disaffected. One is disappointed in particular circumstances or hurt by particular people. One feels a lack of satisfaction at a particular job, in the drudgery of unrelenting but meaningless tasks. One feels unappreciated or overlooked or the victim of prejudice. The particulars are specific to each one of us and constitute our own personal theater of suffering which plays out beneath the elevated talk of philosophers. Yet there is existential relevance to all of these situations and their attending emotions.

Existentialism counters a philosophical tradition that for the most part ignored the difficulties of life as it is actually lived. Marcel charges philosophers with valuing ideals above real human experience. This, he argues, has led to a willed ignorance of suffering:

> Because they ignore the person, offering it up to I know not what ideal truth, to what principle of pure inwardness, they are unable to grasp those tragic factors of human existence. . . . [T]hey banish them, together with illness and everything akin to it, to I know not what disreputable suburb of thought.

Suffering may have been neglected by traditional thinkers as the merely particular details of life, irrelevant to the search for universal truths. Personal pain may be dismissed along with the bodily and emotional entanglements in the world from which the rational mind has been abstracted.

Rather than focusing on suffering, classical ethical theories tend to stress the ideal state of life. Aristotle defined happiness—or perhaps better, to translate the ancient Greek term *eudaimonia,* flourishing—as activity of the soul in accordance with virtue. Aristotle acknowledged that happiness in this sense may require some basic conditions, like health, some material comfort, and companionship. But by identifying happiness chiefly with virtue, as Aristotle does in his *Nicomachean*

Ethics, he illuminates the individual's own role in how they fare. Aristotle offers some guidance on how to achieve this—virtue, for a human being, is associated with rationality and its activity. Virtue is exercised as aiming for the right end or goal, and acting toward that end in the right way. Aristotle outlines a number of individual virtues which, as means between extremes, add up to an individual whose qualities include being reasonable, contemplative, courageous, temperate, and magnanimous. These must be enacted in practice, with the right goals in mind as the "ends" or purposes of action.

Existentialists may praise Aristotle's focus on action in shaping self and life. How does one become virtuous, and thus happy? By acting as a virtuous person would—and of course we can recall that the meaning of the ancient Greek word *ethos* is, among other things, habit. We become as we habitually act. We can see this view reflected in Sartre's claim that "the coward makes himself cowardly, the hero makes himself heroic; and that there is always a possibility for the coward to give up cowardice and for the hero to stop being a hero." Sartre recognizes that our personalities may have particular characteristics that tend toward certain feelings and forms of action rather than others. Yet he thinks that we are responsible too for our personalities as they result from our habitual actions. While Sartre's position echoes Aristotle's view of habit, Sartre acknowledges that the modern self is aware of its own freedom, and the freedom of consciousness can be a burden. What if, despite expressing all the Aristotelian virtues and enjoying the basic necessities of life, one experiences anxiety, forlornness, or despair? What if in the context of such experiences virtue seems impossible to manifest?

The Stoics, as mentioned earlier in this book, aimed to diminish the significance of suffering and even eradicate suffering itself by arguing that we can overcome pain simply through an exercise of will. We can, in our minds, take up a liberating perspective on whatever discomfort or injury we face. Seneca argued that "pain is slight if opinion has added nothing to it. . . . [I]n thinking it slight, you will make it slight." This attribution of interpretive power to subjectivity of course resonates with some aspects of existential philosophy. The perspective one takes on any negative object or event is crucial. Yet anxiety about choices, dread of death, or forlornness in the absence of divine care, may not be so easily adjusted by an exertion of the mind. The Stoic view would deny the potential inescapability of existential suffering.

Existential suffering, as Camus might describe it, is a pained response to the ill-fit between ourselves and a world that defies or evades our need for security and meaning. The experience of such suffering would be regarded by existentialist thinkers not as evidence of our personal insufficiency, of our lack of virtue or self-control, but only of our uniquely human being and our possibly excessive self-awareness. Of course, any existentialist would acknowledge that we are sometimes weak or unvirtuous, that we make mistakes or wallow in unnecessary malaise and thus bring suffering upon ourselves. But even our failure to thrive is worthy of thinking about philosophically.

Not the first, but perhaps the most radical philosophical acceptance of suffering arises with Schopenhauer, in whom Nietzsche at the outset of his philosophical career was enamored. In his own treatise "On the Sufferings of the World" Schopenhauer points to predecessors who have considered human pain, including Buddhists, Empedocles, Pythagoras, Cicero, and Christian theologians. In sharp contrast to Stoic indifference, however, Schopenhauer goes so far as to identify suffering as the very purpose of existence:

> Unless *suffering* is the direct and immediate object of life, our existence must entirely fail of its aim. It is absurd to look upon the enormous amount of pain that abounds everywhere in the world, and originates in needs and necessities inseparable from life itself, as serving no purpose at all and the result of mere chance.

Schopenhauer adds that even a life spared from pain, worry, labor, and trouble will have to cope with the reality that everything good in our existence will be snatched away by time. The passage of time, Schopenhauer argues, only contributes to the general "torment of existence."

If this pessimism seems severe, Schopenhauer also gives a positive role for suffering in his view of the world and of the self as becoming. We develop ourselves, and add to our pleasures, by overcoming adversity, loss, and need. Suffering thus has its place in a human life as that from which we must continually strive to recover, and that which makes our triumphs and good fortunes all the more appreciable to us. Schopenhauer also recognized that suffering serves to bond us to our fellow human beings. Suffering allows us to feel sympathy and solidarity for others, thus creating a sense of human community.

It should be said that none of the existentialist thinkers were philosophizing at a time when the underlying physiology of depression, anxiety, and other mood disorders was understood in any adequate medical or biological sense. Physiological causes for mental suffering are better understood today and suffering for many people may be mitigated by medical treatment or therapy. We recall that some existentialists—including Merleau-Ponty and Marcel—view the body and mind as inseparable. Existential despair may be rooted in our physical and mental health, just as the anxiety so many existentialists have studied may have physiological sources.

Yet an existentialist thinker would be wary of regarding all dysphoria in exclusively biological terms, to be combated with pharmacological interventions alone, and they would point to the conditions of modern life that may promote many familiar forms of mental suffering. The demands of modern life toward maximum efficiency, productivity, competitiveness, social conformity, and mobility—demands which may be compounded by economic factors, communication technology, and social media—may promote depression, anxiety, or other forms of mental suffering in our lives. Many human beings may live in conditions of isolation, financial insecurity, social oppression, or environmental toxicity that are incompatible with human flourishing. Suffering in this context should be addressed not only as a problem for the isolated individual, but also as a cultural and existential situation. When seeking solutions to concrete problems, an existentialist would keep in mind our human need for a meaningful life, our awareness of the lack of any guaranteed meanings, and our need to contribute freely to the values a life expresses.

We recall that Rilke began his *Duino Elegies* with a cry for help to the angels. It is a call that goes unanswered. His speaker depicts those same angels as terrifying. Rilke offers in the *Elegies* an image of existential forlornness. In the *Elegies* we are told that human beings always look at the world as if they are departing from it rather than open to it. We feel always apart from the center of being. Rilke invites his readers to consider the existential ramifications of human self-awareness and finds in our alienation from being a source of sorrow. Yet despite these elevated themes, Rilke also appreciated that sorrow is known in ordinary lived experience. The *Elegies* evoke more concrete grounds for suffering, for example, with reference to the medieval poet Gaspara Stampa and her experience of unrequited love, recorded in hundreds of sonnets she wrote to her beloved. Rilke evokes, too, the sorrow of a mother mourning the death of her son in war—a sadly common theme in the First World War a few years after which the *Elegies* were completed. His *Sonnets to Orpheus* are dedicated to the memory of a young dancer, a daughter of Rilke's friends, who died of leukemia while still practically a girl. In his *Letters to a Young Poet*, too, Rilke responds to the young poet's confession of vulnerability to everyday sadness.

Rather than something to be wholly eradicated, Rilke considers sadness an index to what lies beyond our mastered realms of self and its familiar world. The elder poet advises his addressee not to attempt to overcome sadness, to try to conquer it as an enemy. This may be futile. Rather Rilke suggests that he might find a way to appreciate the experience of sadness for its own sake. Rilke writes:

> If only it were possible for us to see farther than our knowledge reaches, and even a little beyond the outworks of our presentiment, perhaps we would bear our sadnesses with greater trust than we have in our joys. For they are the moments when something new has entered us, something unknown;

our feelings grow mute in shy embarrassment, everything in us withdraws, a silence arises, and the new experience, which no one knows, stands in the midst of it all and says nothing.

In sadness, Rilke thinks, something reaches us from beyond ourselves. This something may be negative and yet it may be something which potentially sustains us. In sharp contrast to the Stoic advice to overcome suffering by adopting an attitude of indifference, Rilke offers a reassuring image of sadness as an intrinsic and natural part of life. He thus tells the young poet:

So you mustn't be frightened . . . if a sadness rises in front of you, larger than any you have ever seen; if an anxiety, like light and cloud-shadows, moves over your hands and over everything you do. You must realize that something is happening to you, that life has not forgotten you, that it holds you in its hand and will not let you fall.

I think what Rilke might mean here is that, rather than attempting to conquer ill feeling, one can recognize something vital in every experience and feeling, even difficult ones. Were we to feel no pain or suffering at all ever, we would not be wholly alive, we would not carve out room within ourselves that allows us to be most touched by being. Even pain is evidence "that life has not forgotten you," but affects you, means something to you. As Rilke sees it, we become sad or forlorn only because existence matters to us, whether that be our own existence or that of those we love. Such valuing of life is in itself motivation to press forward in living.

That existence is shot through with possibility, and never fixed, may offer some existential consolation to those beset by sorrow. The present will not rest, as all is becoming, and what is to come may be good or bad for us, we do not know. Camus advises that we can, like Sisyphus, be happy even in conditions of absurdity. This is because life itself, by virtue of our continuing to live it no matter what the conditions, is given value.

It is perhaps commonplace to suggest, as some existentialists do, that we can feel joy, and the pleasurable vitality of our freedom, only at the cost of possible suffering. We can be happy only insofar as we value our being and that of others, and this valuation arises in a context that is inherently unfixed, full of possibility, and thus uncertain. Because of this, Marcel links difficult existential emotions with the possibility of hope. He argues that "the truth is that there can strictly speaking be no hope except when the temptation to despair exists." Marcel suggests that even if "the structure of the world we live in permits—and may even seem to counsel—absolute despair, yet it is only such a world that can give rise to an unconquerable hope."

Marcel acknowledges the sense of betrayal and despair that may arise from having no security for our well-being, from having no guarantees in reality for the value of our own being. Yet just as Camus finds happiness in the absurd, Marcel advocates hope in the face of such insecurity. Hope arises from a sense that being is more encompassing than I can understand. As Marcel describes it:

> Hope consists in asserting that there is at the heart of being, beyond all data, beyond all inventories and all calculations, a mysterious principle which is in connivance with me, which

cannot but will that which I will, if what I will deserves to be willed and is, in fact, willed by the whole of my being.

Hope, in other words, is a felt sense of the non-isolation of a deserving wish. Whatever I hope for, if it deserves to be wished for, cannot be an isolated phenomenon even in an apparently indifferent world. It is in Marcel's concrete examples that we might see more clearly how hope links us to an existential awareness.

Marcel describes, for example, the possibility of being hopeful in the face of serious illness. On the one hand, we may face dreadful statistics, while on the other, we know that these indications of the facts are not fully encompassing of the possible. Such hope may be especially significant when it relates to another person one holds dear. Marcel writes:

> To hope against hope that a person whom I love will recover from a disease which is said to be incurable is to say: It is impossible that I should be alone in willing this cure; it is impossible that reality in its inward depth should be hostile or so much as indifferent to what I assert is in itself a good.

Hope is the sense that beyond experience, beyond probability, beyond statistics, "reality is on my side in willing it to be so." It does not matter that, in the majority of cases, my hope may be disappointed, and may in the end turn out to appear an illusion. As Marcel conceives it, existential hope suspends that kind of calculation. Hope emerges with the recognition that, despite factual probabilities, all is not yet determined within the vital mystery of being.

Of course hope in and of itself may not offer for many people any compelling strategy for coping with adversity. Must one not, as Dylan Thomas put it, "rage against the dying of the light"? Beauvoir counsels that one must learn to look reality "straight in the face" and not submit to illusions. But as Marcel conceives it, existential hope does not encourage passivity or mere fantasizing in order to escape from the pressures of reality. Existential hope involves living and acting to the fullest of one's capacity. Marcel writes:

> Hope is not a kind of listless waiting; it underpins action or runs before it . . . the prolongation into the unknown of an activity which is central—that is to say, rooted in being.

Yet hope involves a willingness to remain related to the unknown and to what is other. Existential hope is a refusal to mistrust reality, a refusal grounded in our involvement with being. Such a position taken toward existence cannot be fathomed objectively, but, Marcel thinks, it can be lived as a subjective truth.

While in hope we do not succumb to the despair that looms as an alternative, we also do not deny the suffering of one before us or of ourselves. Hope simply acknowledges the positive aspect of possibility that pertains when we do not know all of the answers with certainty. Recognizing suffering in light of hope can also encourage sympathy with others who share our human condition. To look at others as fellow-sufferers, Schopenhauer wrote, "reminds us of that which is after all the most necessary thing in life—the tolerance, patience, regard, and love of neighbour, of which everyone stands in need, and which, therefore, every man owes to his fellow."

Reading existentialism, or existentially themed literature, cannot banish the sources of suffering, or conquer even those that appear to arise solely from and within ourselves. Yet existentialism lifts such experiences out of private obscurity. It makes them cause for philosophical reflection, communication, and concern, and lets one know one is not alone in suffering, however indeterminate or specific it may be. Existentialism offers a philosophical vocabulary, and at times a metaphysical justification, for such experiences so central to our lives, refusing to relegate them to some lesser level of life remote from higher cognition. Existentialism associates suffering with the most important metaphysical questions—truth, being, the meaning of life—perhaps even at some risk of indulging our vulnerabilities or validating our human foibles.

20 | LIFE AS A WORK OF ART
THE EXISTENTIAL NEED FOR CREATIVITY

In the preceding chapters of this book we have seen that existentialists express wildly diverging views about many topics. Yet in one way or another they all invite the human individual to live life with creativity. In order to embrace our lives as our very own, to shake free from inherited expectations, the pressures of the crowd, or mere habit, we may need to exercise invention. Only creatively can we envision new paths or interpret familiar aspects of life in new ways, as existentialist philosophy tends to invite. Existentialist thinking encourages living life as a work of art. Creativity may be required to become who we are, as Nietzsche wrote, or who we may want to be.

Artistic experience can offer a number of analogies for existential creativity. Just as artists cannot hope to make original works of art merely by following a prescribed set of rules or by copying the works of others, existential selves must seek new meanings in some freedom from the impositions of tradition. Whether we embrace or depart from an inherited way of life, it must be freely chosen in order to be lived in a state of authenticity. Just as looking at the world from an artistic point of view allows the artist to see things otherwise than habit or convention would dictate, the existentialist would take up a situation from an individual perspective. While artists create new objects, images, or experiences, existential selves make decisions and commitments and engage projects that generate what is for them new values and ways of being.

It is not surprising then that art has been important to all of the thinkers associated with existentialism we have discussed in this book. To begin with, in his philosophical writings Kierkegaard included many studies of literary works, from the plays of Sophocles and Shakespeare to novels and stories by Goethe and Hans Christian Andersen. Kierkegaard described Mozart as an artist in touch with the eternal, and in *Either/Or*, Kierkegaard devoted an essay to the opera *Don Giovanni* along with the literary iterations of the legend. Kierkegaard's own style of writing and thinking is experimentally artistic, even kaleidoscopically so. There is conceptual as well as linguistic creativity in Kierkegaard's philosophy, which often blends philosophical essay with fictional prose, evokes vividly imagined scenes, invents characters, and playfully illustrates his otherwise lofty conceptual contemplations.

Of course as discussed earlier in this book Kierkegaard was critical of the merely aesthetic stage of life. That would involve a life fed by aesthetic or sensuous experiences only for the pleasures they would bring the self. The aesthete would cultivate what is "interesting" for the sake of distraction, indulge endlessly in entertainment or momentary stimulation. We can assume that Kierkegaard would not celebrate art that primarily indulges in the artist's own self-promotion, or any originality that aims primarily for shock value. He would undoubtedly look askance at aspects of the contemporary art market oriented around materialist consumption. With these qualifications in mind we can say nevertheless that

Kierkegaard's understanding of the stages of life, particularly the qualitative leap to the religious stage, invokes a radical sense of both possibility and uncertainty that is evocative of artistic creation.

For beyond what Kierkegaard's own philosophy may sanction, it may be possible to imagine an artist who, like the knight of faith, risks all for a higher purpose or idea, one that evades common understanding or logic, in commitment to a project that offers no guarantee of success. In faith, as Kierkegaard conceived it, one does not leave the world of the aesthetic or ethical forever behind, but regains them from a higher plane of existence. Analogously artistic experience, whether beautiful or sublime, abstract or defamiliarizing, need not transport us wholly beyond everyday life, but may allow us to look at everyday life from a new perspective. Through art we may achieve a deeper and more illuminating vision of the world.

Heidegger devoted much of his later thinking to interpreting poetry and art. He regarded all art as a form of poetry and described the latter as nothing less than the "revealing" and "founding of truth." In interpreting van Gogh's paintings of peasant shoes, for instance, Heidegger claimed that the artist revealed the world of the one who wore them. The ancient Greek temple established a "world" for the human experience of the divine. The interpretation of such artworks occasioned Heidegger's own philosophical reformulation of the idea of truth itself. Heidegger argued that, however necessary pragmatic and scientific thinking may be for human life, their orientations toward beings objectify them in calculating ways. In contrast, artistic and poetic thinking enables the revealing of beings apart from their pragmatic value and not merely as objects of knowledge or manipulation. Such thinking,

Heidegger argued, thus reveals the special existential calling of the human being.

As noted previously in this book, Heidegger argued that overcoming the technological enframing of the earth demanded not only philosophical and pragmatic thinking but poetic thinking. In order to achieve a new means of dwelling upon the earth, Heidegger thought, modern humanity must become both more receptive and more generous to the being of nature. With his idea of "poetic dwelling" Heidegger did not of course mean we must write or read poetry itself in order to learn to live differently. Rather he meant that a poetic form of thinking, or a thinking that learns from the stance of "listening" poetry often endows, could cultivate a receptive and generous comportment toward and in the midst of being.

Sartre and Beauvoir also embraced the idea that art can reveal reality, but they emphasized the social dimension of this revelation. In addition to his own literary fiction, Sartre wrote extensively about literature and art, and praised writers who hold up a "mirror" to reality, particularly the reality of social oppression— thus removing any excuse of ignorance of how things really are. Beauvoir, in "What Can Literature Do?," argued for the special existential merit of literary fiction. For literature can allow us to reveal how the world may look from the perspective of others.

Both Sartre and Beauvoir held the artist in esteem for creating anew without deference to predetermined rules or models. We recall that in Sartre's *Nausea*, the protagonist Roquentin gives up his research in order to write a novel. This is inspired by his hearing a jazz song played on the phonograph in the café. The song itself is less important perhaps than the fact that it stands for the vitality of innovative art. Jazz encourages improvisation and free variation and thus expresses the intrinsic contingency of life. Creating one's values, or one's self-defining projects, is much like jazz in this sense: there are no rules for its improvisation. The music, while sometimes expressing a feeling of urgent necessity, must emerge out of freedom.

Camus explicitly related art to the existential situation of humanity. The artist, Camus thought, acknowledges and responds to the inherent uncertainty of existence. The artist does so, however, not by locking down an answer to existence, or by fixing a point of view, but through diverse explorations and an open-ended practice of freedom. The creation of art promotes freedom at the same time it attests to our reality. Camus writes:

> Of all the schools of patience and lucidity, creation is the most effective. It is also the staggering evidence of man's sole dignity: the dogged revolt against his condition, perseverance in an effort considered sterile. . . . But perhaps the great work of art has less importance in itself than in the ordeal it demands of a man and the opportunity it provides him of overcoming his phantoms and approaching a little closer to his naked reality.

In this passage Camus implicitly values art not merely for art's sake or even for the sake of the artist's personal self-expression but for art's exercise of human liberty and its link to truth. Like Heidegger, Sartre, and Beauvoir, Camus associates art not with illusion or mere fantasy, but with a clear and unadorned revelation of the reality of existence.

Yet the idea that art can be revelatory of existence does not of course mean that art must be realistic in its representational style. In a series of radio lectures collected as *The World of Perception*, Merleau-Ponty argued that even the distortions of Cubist painting, such as in the works of Picasso, could be phenomenologically illuminating because they "led us back to a vision of the things themselves." The obvious distortions of perception in some abstract art can reveal something about the way we perceive in ordinary experience. Similarly Merleau-Ponty appreciated the "unfamiliar gaze" on the ordinary we find in Kafka's fiction. The presentation of a human being transformed into an insect in *The Metamorphosis*, however grotesque, can enable a "healthy" defamiliarization because it makes us think in a new way about what can go wrong in a human life and what a good life ought to entail. In an essay called "Indirect Language and the Voices of Silence" Merleau-Ponty wrote that it is often "in the name of a truer relation between things that their ordinary ties are broken." Sometimes art can reveal our human reality all the more through its fantastical transformations, far beyond anything we might find in our ordinary world.

Yet while art can reveal reality, Camus recognized the inherently rebellious nature of art and creativity—that it can demand a transformation of reality, or of any given configuration of it. In a century dominated by totalitarian regimes, Camus understood art as working contrary to absolutist ideologies. To be creative in such a context can be a risky enterprise. Camus writes:

> To create today is to create dangerously. . . . The question, for all those who cannot live without art and what it signifies, is

merely to find out how, among the police forces of so many ideologies . . . the strange liberty of creation is possible.

The value of art is not so much in the objects it produces or the messages that it communicates but in maintaining our relationship to possibility. That we can create, Camus suggests, is itself an exercise of and testament to freedom.

In his study of tragedy, Nietzsche famously argued that life is justified only as a work of art. He argued that life's inevitable suffering, its intrinsic instability and unpredictability, are best expressed in an artform such as tragedy. Yet tragedy also allows us to cope with these aspects of existence. In tragic art, Nietzsche writes,

> We are to recognise that all that comes into being must be ready for a sorrowful end; we are forced to look into the terrors of the individual existence—yet we are not to become rigid with fear: a metaphysical comfort tears us momentarily from the bustle of transforming figures.

Tragedy, of course, by definition portrays intense suffering and makes art of disaster. But as an artform, tragedy elevates suffering, shaping it into an image through which we can perceive the vitality and intensity of our existence. We need art, Nietzsche thought, to be able to cope with the truth.

Of course, many artists and writers transformed real-worldly sufferings of life into creative works. They may not have agreed with Nietzsche that art was required to justify existence. For a life can be intrinsically valued, as Camus argued, simply by the fact of one's continuation of it, particularly in the midst of hardship. Yet the creation of artworks under extreme duress seems to testify both to the value of life and to the existential need for living creatively.

A few examples may suffice to suggest the existential value of creativity. Miklós Radnóti was a Hungarian poet who perished in the Holocaust, writing throughout his terrible ordeal. In a concentration camp he wrote on salvaged scraps of paper—keeping to his formal meter almost to the end—and he wrote even on the death march along which he would be murdered. His poetry could not save him from the bullets that would kill him, but by continuing to write, Radnóti maintained his humanity in the face of imprisonment, hunger, and violence. Music-making was commanded by the SS in concentration camps, with forced singing and official orchestras. Yet prisoners also composed their own music in secret, on bits of wood and tissue and packaging, and these works took on a wholly different significance. Oliver Messiaen wrote his famous *Quartet for the End of Time* as a prisoner of war in Görlitz. With other inmates performing on broken instruments, he premiered the work in the winter of 1941 before hundreds of freezing prisoners. Other writers transformed oppression into works of great art. Oscar Wilde wrote "The Ballad of Reading Gaol" while in exile, having been condemned to two years' hard labor for his homosexuality. Richard Wright, James Baldwin, and Ralph Ellison are among those writers who turned experiences of racist violence and demeaning prejudice into exquisite, if difficult, works of literary fiction, some of which would be avidly read by existential philosophers.

These examples suggest a connection between art and a distinctly human existence, prompting the question whether there is something salutary in the liberty of creative making. Camus described artistic creativity as the double task of exposing the difficulties of existence and promoting its intrinsic value. While he thought that in art "it is essential to condemn what must be condemned," art is also an affirmative act. While revealing and criticizing injustice, the artist should also "praise at length what still deserves to be praised." His own life as a literary artist was dedicated to this project:

> After all, that is why I am an artist, because even the work that negates still affirms something and does homage to the wretched and magnificent life that is ours.

Camus argues that even when faced with "cruel truths" we can, in defiance of such cruelties, affirm life as a matter for rejoicing.

Nietzsche understood that tragic art does not necessitate a gloomy view of life. The capacity to transform sufferings into art may elevate even the most painful experiences by restoring subjectivity into the equation. We recall Nietzsche's view that the ancient Greeks excelled at tragedy precisely because they were so vital, so capable of life. They could look into the most difficult experiences and create from out of them works of art. The beauty of tragedy expresses life's value even in the face of catastrophe. Tragic art is thus, according to Nietzsche, paradoxically affirmative. The fullness of life embraces the whole range of possibility from joy to despair, and in tragedy we may recognize that they are sometimes inseparable.

Beyond the making of art, what might we say about existential creativity in the project of life? Nietzsche did not only praise great artworks. He also thought of the task of becoming oneself as an artistic process. To become oneself, to come into one's own, requires stepping out of ordinary, accumulated habits, and exercising freedom. To become ourselves authentically demands courage to face the disapproval or rejection of others. Nietzsche recognized that even "to give 'style to one's character'" is "a rare and great art."

In what ways might the creativity of art instruct creative living in general? Art seeks new vision. Its creative impulse pushes thinking outside the boundaries of what we already understand and expect. Art is generative, taking hold of whatever is there before one and transforming it deliberately, reflectively, in light of possibility, a transformation that requires effort and commitment. In making art, one may learn from the past, but in order to avoid merely copying it, one has to push further and beyond. One explores uncharted territory, pressing beyond the certain or probable, never wholly knowing what the end result might be. While art is inherently communicative, it often proceedes without the immediate recognition or understanding of others.

Such creativity can be exercised not only in making but in living. It demands creativity in the first place to recognize and to remain open to our own possibilities, possibilities for being in and relating to the world. This may require finding sources of creative inspiration to help wrest ourselves from accumulated habits of thinking and feeling. Existentialism invites us to consider the reality within and before us in new ways, to recognize how by our projects and commitments and relations to others we contribute to creating what is meaningful to us and for us. As existential beings we see the world as inviting our participation, and recognize our freedom to take this up.

To live one's life as a work of art, then, means recognizing our being as becoming, invigorating our lives with a sense of possibility, making free choices even in defiance of accumulated habit or expectation. To live creatively does not necessitate the frenetic production of novelty, or a narcissistic overinvestment in self-expression. It can involve cultivating a more patient or generous revealing of the world, an adjustment of attunement to others, critical self-reflection as well as newly inspired affirmations of one's own being. To live creatively means to recognize and attend to one's choices, finding in them meaning-creating projects—ones which, however, may find no justification outside themselves and the life of the existential subject they manifest. It may involve finding new ways to be receptive and present to the world, whether in rebellion against its injustices or in deference to its hidden splendors.

Revealing and creation are interrelated, particularly in the case of becoming oneself. For in this case we create that which we attentively reveal, as we develop a project or an understanding of life. Rilke suggests this to his young poet interlocutor:

> Allow your judgments their own silent, undisturbed development, which, like all progress, must come from deep within and cannot be forced or hastened. Everything is gestation and then birthing. To let each impression and each embryo of a feeling come to completion, entirely in itself, in the dark, in the unsayable, the unconscious, beyond the reach of one's own understanding, and with deep humility and patience to wait for the hour when a new clarity is born: this alone is what it means to live as an artist: in understanding as in creating.

Rilke's own poetry, of course, attests to attention to the world, listening, and developing an original point of view. But Rilke is also the poet whose speaker declared, "You must change your life," and he was well aware of the dangers to comfort and convention such action may entail.

The best poetry and art are rarely only about expressing the self, but rather bring to realization a unique perspective on the world. While we often associate creativity with the solitary genius, with inventiveness of the individual mind and spontaneous innovation, Marcel writes of the "deep rootedness in being" of true creativity. Echoing the phenomenological notion of art as revealing the world, Marcel argues that creativity is not merely self-centered or, as Marcel puts it, "self-hypnotic," but devoted to discovery. Living one's life as a work of art does not have to be motivated by self-oriented interests but can be devoted to revealing, in an individual way, the world one after all shares with others.

Marcel reminds us too that creativity as a form of life does not have to produce art objects but may instead cultivate ways of being and communicating. Creativity may be expressed in our being-with-others through love, friendship, and admiration. Creativity, in other words, can be generous. As Marcel suggests:

> A really alive person is not merely someone who has a taste for life, but somebody who spreads that taste, showering it, as it were, around him; and a person who is really alive in this way has, quite apart from any tangible achievements of his, something essentially creative about him.

Creative communication may involve the making of some form of art, but it can also be manifested in countless other ways in concrete social experience. This may involve attentive listening and response, enabling others to take up a new perspective on their difficulties and to realize their freedom of choice. It may involve curating shared experiences of everyday creativity. It may involve inventing new solutions to problems that face others or even humanity as a whole.

Creativity can be expressed through what Camus considered creative rebellion, elaborated through the practices of striving against oppression and toward freedom. Camus supported political action against suffering. But he warned against the dangers of ideology, of absolute solutions that ended up sacrificing freedom in the process of liberation. For Camus, the goal of living, like that of art, is "to increase the sum of freedom and responsibility" in every human being. As Camus sees it, the artist is one whose "passion is freedom." Just as we acknowledge, in our own freedom, the freedom of others, we may approach others as those whose potential for creativity is a part of their being, and perhaps essential to their flourishing.

Since we are not gods, we cannot create from out of nothing. We may be haunted by anxiety over our future non-being, but our freedom is never experienced in a vacuum. We are always part and parcel of a world. Recognizing our subjectivity as transcendence illuminates the distance to cross from here to a projected elsewhere, from whatever is there before us, as it is, to something further or otherwise. We move from the immediate present to an as-yet-unknown future. Yet the very situatedness of our freedom, which all existentialists recognize, makes it possible to live life creatively. In another recent work I studied the phenomenon of creativity as what I called "situated transcendence." By this I meant that creativity and the imagination it manifests emerge from our interaction and engagement with what is there before us. Living life creatively means engaging with our situation, fully participating to shape and transform it. Such transformation sometimes requires letting go of some of our habituated fixations and finding new ways to live and to create. Living life as a work of art means, from an existentialist point of view, accepting in full freedom our being-possible, and creatively bringing our choices to fruition in whatever ways we can.

BIBLIOGRAPHY

PRIMARY SOURCES

Aristotle, *Nicomachean Ethics*, Third Edition, trans. Terence Irwin (Indianapolis, IN: Hackett, 2019).

Augustine, *Confessions*, trans. Henry Chadwick (Oxford: Oxford University Press, 2008).

Baldwin, James, *The Fire Next Time* (New York: Dell, 1963).

Baudelaire, Charles, *The Painter of Modern Life and Other Essays*, ed. and trans. Jonathan Mayne (London: Phaidon Press, 1964).

Beauvoir, Simone, *Adieux: Farewell to Sartre*, trans. Patrick O'Brian (New York: Pantheon Books, 1985).

Beauvoir, Simone, *All Men Are Mortal*, trans. Leonard M. Friedman (New York: W.W. Norton, 1992).

Beauvoir, Simone, *The Ethics of Ambiguity*, trans. Bernard Frechtman (New York: Citadel Press, 1976).

Beauvoir, Simone, *Memoirs of a Dutiful Daughter*, trans. Hazel Rowley (New York: Harper Perennial, 2005).

Beauvoir, Simone, *The Second Sex*, trans. Constance Borde and Sheila Malovany-Chevallier (New York: Vintage Books, 2011).

Beauvoir, Simone, *She Came to Stay*, trans. Yvonne Moyse and Roger Senhouse (London: Fontana, 1984).

Beauvoir, Simone, "What Can Literature Do?" in *"The Useless Mouths" and Other Literary Writings*, ed. Margaret A. Simons and Marybeth Timmerman (Urbana: University of Illinois Press, 2011), 197–209.

Beauvoir, Simone, *When Things of the Spirit Come First: Five Early Tales*, trans. Patrick O'Brien (New York: Pantheon Books, 1984).

Camus, Albert, *Create Dangerously*, trans. Justin O'Brien (London: Penguin Random House, 2018).

Camus, Albert, *The Fall,* trans. Justin O'Brien (New York: Vintage, 1991).

Camus, Albert, *The Myth of Sisyphus and Other Essays*, trans. Justin O'Brien (New York: Vintage, 1991).

Camus, Albert, *The Plague*, ed. Tony Judt, trans. Robin Buss (New York: Penguin, 2013).

Camus, Albert, *Resistance, Rebellion, and Death*, trans. Justin O'Brien (New York: Alfred A. Knopf, 1960).

Camus, Albert, *The Stranger*, trans. Matthew Ward (New York: Vintage, 1988).

Daoud, Kamel, *The Mersault Investigation*, trans. John Cullen (New York: Other Press, 2015).

Descartes, René, *Meditations on First Philosophy*, trans. and ed. John Cottingham (Cambridge: Cambridge University Press, 1986).

De Unamuno, Miguel, *Selected Works of Miguel de Unamuno*, Volume 3: *Our Lord Don Quixote*, ed. Anthony Kerrigan (Princeton, NJ: Princeton University Press, 1968).

De Unamuno, Miguel, *Selected Works of Miguel de Unamuno*, Volume 4: *The Tragic Sense of Life in Men and Nations* (Princeton, NJ: Princeton University Press, 1973).

Dostoevsky, Fyodor, *The Brothers Karamazov*, trans. Richard Pevear and Larissa Volokhonsky (New York: Farrar, Straus and Giroux, 1990).

Dostoevsky, Fyodor, *Crime and Punishment*, trans. Richard Pevear and Larissa Volokhonsky (New York: Vintage, 1993).

Dostoevsky, Fyodor, *Notes from Underground*, trans. Richard Pevear and Larissa Volokhonsky (New York: Vintage, 1994).

Du Bois, W. E. B., "The Comet," in *Darkwater: Voices from within the Veil* (New York: Washington Square Press, 2004), 195–210.

Du Bois, W. E. B., *The Souls of Black Folk*, in *Writings* (New York: Literary Classics, 1986), 357–547.

Eliot, T. S., *Collected Poems* (London: Faber & Faber, 2002).

Ellison, Ralph, interviewed by Richard Kostelanetz, "An Interview with Ralph Ellison," *Iowa Review* 19, no. 3 (Fall 1989).

Ellison, Ralph, *Invisible Man* (New York: Vintage, 1995).

Epictetus, *The Discourses of Epictetus*, revised trans. Robin Hard (London: Everyman, 1995).

Fanon, Frantz, *Black Skin, White Masks*, trans. Richard Philcox (New York: Grove, 2008).

Flaubert, Gustav, *Sentimental Education*, trans. Robert Baldick, revised Geoffrey Wall (London: Penguin, 2004).

Frost, Robert, *The Poetry of Robert Frost: The Collected Poems, Complete and Unabridged* (New York: Henry Holt, 1975).

Goethe, Johann Wolfgang von, *The Sorrows of Young Werther*, trans. Catherine Hutter (New York: New American Library, 1962).

Hegel, G. F. W., *Early Theological Writings*, trans. T. M. Knox (Chicago: University of Chicago Press, 1948).

Hegel, G. F. W., *Phenomenology of Spirit*, trans. A. V. Miller (Oxford: Oxford University Press, 1977).

Heidegger, Martin, *Basic Problems of Phenomenology*, trans. Alfred Hofstadter (Indianapolis: Indiana University Press, 1988).

Heidegger, Martin, *Being and Time*, trans. John Macquarrie and Edward Robinson (New York: Harper & Row, 1962).

Heidegger, Martin, *The Concept of Time*, trans. Will McNeill (Oxford: Blackwell, 1992).

Heidegger, Martin, *Phenomenology of Religious Life*, trans. Matthias Fritsch and Jennifer Anna Gosetti-Ferencei (Bloomington: Indiana University Press, 2004).

Heidegger, Martin, *Poetry, Language, and Thought*, trans. Alfred Hofstadter (New York: Harper & Row, 1971).

Heidegger, Martin, "The Question Concerning Technology," in *The Question Concerning Technology and Other Essays,* trans. William Lovitt (New York: Harper & Row, 1977).

Hölderlin, Friedrich, *Hyperion or The Hermit in Greece*, trans. Willard R. Trask (New York: Frederick Ungar, 1965).

Hölderlin, Friedrich, *Poems and Fragments*, trans. Michael Hamburger (Manchester: Carcanet Press, 2004).

Hurston, Zora Neale, *Their Eyes Were Watching God* (New York: HarperCollins, 2006).

Husserl, Edmund, *Cartesian Meditations*, trans. Dorion Cairns (Dordrecht: Springer, 1973).

Husserl, Edmund, *The Crisis of the European Sciences and Transcendental Phenomenology: An Introduction to Phenomenological Philosophy*, trans. David Carr (Evanston, IL: Northwestern University Press, 1970).

Husserl, Edmund, *Ideas I: Ideas Pertaining to Phenomenology and to a Phenomenological Philosophy*, trans. Daniel O. Dalstrom (Indianapolis: Hackett, 2014).

Ionesco, Eugene, *Rhinoceros and Other Plays* (New York: Grove Press, 1960).

Jaspers, Karl, *Existenzphilosophie* (Berlin and Leipzig: Walter de Gruyter, 1938).

Jaspers, Karl, *The Philosophy of Existence*, trans. Richard F. Grabau (Philadelphia: University of Pennsylvania Press, 1971).

Jaspers, Karl, *Reason and Existence*, trans. William Earle (New York: Noonday Press, 1955).

Kafka, Franz, *The Complete Stories*, trans. Willa Muir and Edwin Muir (New York: Everyman's Library, 1993).

Kafka, Franz, *The Trial*, trans. Mike Mitchell (Oxford: Oxford University Press, 2009).

Kant, Immanuel, "An Answer to the Question: 'What Is Enlightenment?," in *Political Writings*, ed. H. S. Reiss, second edition (Cambridge: Cambridge University Press, 1991), 54–60.

Kant, Immanuel, *Critique of Judgment*, trans. Paul Guyer, ed. Paul Guyer and Eric Matthews (Cambridge: Cambridge University Press, 2000).

Kant, Immanuel, *Critique of Practical Reason*, trans. Mary Gregor (Cambridge: Cambridge University Press, 2015).

Kant, Immanuel, *Critique of Pure Reason*, trans. and ed. Paul Guyer and Allen W. Wood (Cambridge: Cambridge University Press, 1998).

Kant, Immanuel, *Groundwork for a Metaphysics of Morals*, revised edition., ed. Mary Gregor and Jens Timmermann (Cambridge: Cambridge University Press, 2012).

Kerouac, Jack, *On the Road*, 25th anniversary edition (New York: Penguin Books, 1985).

Kierkegaard, Søren, *The Concept of Anxiety: A Simple Psychologically Orienting Deliberation on the Dogmatic Issue of Hereditary Sin,* ed. and trans. by Reidar Thomte with Albert B. Anderson (Princeton, NJ: Princeton University Press, 1980).

Kierkegaard, Søren, *The Concept of Irony, with Continual Reference to Socrates,* trans. and ed. Howard V. Hong and Edna H. Hong (Princeton, NJ Princeton University Press, 1992.

Kierkegaard, Søren, *Concluding Unscientific Postscript to Philosophical Fragments,* ed. and trans. Howard V. Hong and Edna H. Hong (Princeton, NJ: Princeton University Press, 1992).

Kierkegaard, Søren, *Either/Or, Part I,* ed. and trans. Howard V. Hong and Edna H. Hong (Princeton, NJ: Princeton University Press, 1988).

Kierkegaard, Søren, *Either/Or, Part II,* ed. and trans. Howard V. Hong and Edna H. Hong (Princeton, NJ: Princeton University Press, 1988).

Kierkegaard, Søren, *Fear and Trembling,* ed. and trans. Howard V. Hong and Edna H. Hong (Princeton, NJ: Princeton University Press, 1983).

Kierkegaard, Søren, *The Present Age and Two Minor Ethico-Religious Treatises,* trans. Alexander Dru and Walter Lowrie (London: Oxford University Press, 1949).

Kierkegaard, *Repetition: A Venture in Experimental Psychology, by Constantin Constantius,* trans. and ed. Howard V. Hong and Edna H. Hong (Princeton, NJ: Princeton University Press, 1983).

Kierkegaard, Søren, *The Sickness unto Death: A Christian Psychological Exposition for Upbuilding and Awakening,* ed. and trans. Howard V. Hong and Edna H. Hong (Princeton, NJ: Princeton University Press, 1980).

Kierkegaard, Søren, *Stages on Life's Way,* trans. and ed. Howard V. Hong and Edna H. Hong (Princeton: Princeton University Press, 1988).

Kierkegaard, Søren, *Works of Love,* trans. and ed. Howard V. Hong and Edna H. Hong (Princeton, NJ: Princeton University Press, 2013).

King, Martin Luther, Jr., "Pilgrimage to Nonviolence," in *Stride toward Freedom: The Montgomery Story* (Boston: Beacon Press, 1958), 77–95.

Levinas, Emmanuel, *On Escape,* trans. Bettina Bergo (Stanford, CA: Stanford University Press, 2003).

Levinas, Emmanuel, *Otherwise Than Being, or Beyond Essence*, trans. Alphonso Lingus (Dordrecht: Kluwer Academic, 1991).

Levinas, Emmanuel, *Totality and Infinity* (Pittsburgh: Duquesne University Press, 1969).

Marcel, Gabriel, *Being and Having: An Existentialist Diary* (New York: Harper & Row, 1965).

Marcel, Gabriel, *Man against Mass Society*, trans. G. S. Fraser (South Bend, IN: St. Augustine's Press, 2008).

Marcel, Gabriel, "Phenomenological Notes on Being in a Situation," in *Creative Fidelity* (New York: Noonday, 1969).

Marcel, Gabriel, *The Philosophy of Existentialism* (New York: Citadel Press, 1968).

Melville, Herman, *Moby-Dick, or The Whale*, A Norton Critical Edition, Second Edition, ed. Hershel Parker and Harrison Hayford (New York and London: W.W. Norton & Company, 2001).

Merleau-Ponty, Maurice, *The Merleau-Ponty Aesthetics Reader*, ed. and trans. Galen Johnson and Michael B. Smith (Evanston, IL: Northwestern University Press, 1993).

Merleau-Ponty, Maurice, *Phenomenology of Perception* (London: Routledge, 2002).

Montaigne, Michel de, *The Complete Essays*, trans. M. A. Screech (London: Penguin, 2003).

Nietzsche, Friedrich, *Beyond Good and Evil*, trans. Judith Norman (Cambridge: Cambridge University Press, 2001).

Nietzsche, Friedrich, *The Birth of Tragedy and Other Writings*, trans. Ronald Speirs (Cambridge: Cambridge University Press, 1999).

Nietzsche, Friedrich, *Ecce Homo: How to Become What You Are*, trans. Duncan Large (Oxford: Oxford University Press, 2007).

Nietzsche, Friedrich, *The Gay Science*, ed. Bernard Williams, trans. Josefine Nauckhoff and Adrian Del Caro (Cambridge: Cambridge University Press, 2001).

Nietzsche, Friedrich, *On the Genealogy of Morals*, trans. Douglas Smith (Oxford: Oxford University Press, 1996).

Nietzsche, Friedrich, "Schopenhauer as Educator," in *Untimely Meditations*, trans. Daniel Breazeale (Cambridge: Cambridge University Press, 1997).

Nietzsche, Friedrich, "On Truth and Lies in an Extramoral Sense," in *Philosophy and Truth: Selections from Nietzsche's Notebooks of the Early 1870s*, ed. and trans. Daniel Breazeale (New York: Prometheus Books, 1990).

Nietzsche, Friedrich, "On the Uses and Disadvantages of History for Life," in *Philosophy and Truth: Selections from Nietzsche's Notebooks of the Early 1870s*, ed. and trans. Daniel Breazeale (New York: Prometheus Books, 1990).

Nietzsche, Friedrich, *Thus Spoke Zarathustra*, trans. Adrian Del Caro (Cambridge: Cambridge University Press, 2006).

Novalis [Friedrich von Hardenberg], *Heinrich von Ofterdingen, Schriften, Die Werke Friedrich von Hardenbergs, Band 1* (Stuttgart, 1960).

Novalis [Friedrich von Hardenberg], *Philosophical Writings*, trans. and ed. Margaret Mohony Stoljar (Albany: State University of New York Press, 1997).

Plato, *Five Dialogues: Euthyphro, Apology, Crito, Meno, Phaedo,* trans. G. M. A. Grube, rev. John M. Cooper (Indianapolis, IN: Hackett, 2002).

Plato, *The Republic*, trans. G. M. A. Grube, ed. C. D. C. Reeve (Indianapolis, IN: Hackett, 1992).

Rilke, Rainer Maria, *Duino Elegies,* bilingual ed., trans. Edward Snow (New York: North Point Press, 2001).

Rilke, Rainer Maria, *Letters to a Young Poet*, trans. M. D. Herter Norton (New York: W.W. Norton, 1954, reissued 2004).

Rilke, Rainer Maria, *New Poems,* bilingual ed., trans. Edward Snow (New York: North Point Press, 2001).

Rilke, Rainer Maria, *The Notebooks of Malte Laurids Brigge*, trans. Robert Vilain (Oxford: Oxford University Press, 2016).

Rilke, Rainer Maria, *Sonnets to Orpheus*, bilingual ed., trans. M. D. Herter Norton (New York: W.W. Norton, 2006).

Sartre, Jean-Paul, *Being and Nothingness: An Essay on Phenomenological Ontology*, trans. Hazel E. Barnes (New York: Philosophical Library, 1956).

Sartre, Jean-Paul, "Existentialism," in *Existentialism Is a Humanism*, trans. Carol Macomber (New Haven, CT: Yale University Press, 2007).

Sartre, Jean-Paul, "The Itinerary of a Thought," in *Jean-Paul Sartre: Between Existentialism and Marxism*, trans. John Matthews (New York: Morrow, 1974), 33–64.

Sartre, Jean-Paul, *Nausea*, trans. Lloyd Alexander (Norfolk, CT: New Directions, 1949).

Sartre, Jean-Paul, *No Exit (Huis clos), a Play in One Act, and The Flies (Les Mouches), a Play in Three Acts* (New York: Knopf, 1947).

Sartre, Jean-Paul, *Notebooks for an Ethics*, trans. David Pellauer (Chicago: University of Chicago Press, 1992).

Sartre, Jean-Paul, *The Transcendence of the Ego: An Existentialist Theory of Consciousness*, ed. and trans. Forrest Williams and Robert Kirkpatrick (New York: Noonday Press, 1957).

Sartre, Jean-Paul, *What Is Literature?*, trans. Bernard Frechtman (New York: Philosophical Library, 1949).

Schopenhauer, Arthur, *The World as Will and Representation,* vol. I, trans. E. F. J. Payne (New York: Dover, 1969).

Schopenhauer, Arthur, *The World as Will and Representation,* vol. II, trans. E. F. J. Payne (New York: Dover, 1969).

Shakespeare, William, *Hamlet,* ed. G. R. Hibbard (Oxford: Oxford University Press, 2008).

Simmel, Georg, *The Conflict in Modern Culture and Other Essays*, trans. K. Peter Etzkorn (New York: Teachers College Press, 1968).

Simmel, Georg, "Eros Platonic and Modern," in *Georg Simmel on Individuality and Social Forms,* ed. Donald N. Levine (Chicago: University of Chicago Press, 1972), 235–247.

Simmel, Georg, *The Metropolis and Mental Life: The Sociology of Georg Simmel* (New York: Free Press, 1976).

Simmel, Georg, *The Philosophy of Money*, ed. David Frisby, trans. Thomas B. Bottomore and David Frisby (New York: Taylor & Francis, 2004).

Whitman, Walt, *Leaves of Grass* (New York: Modern Library, 1950).

Wittgenstein, Ludwig, *Philosophical Investigations*, 4th ed., trans. G. E. M. Anscombe, P. M. S. Hacker, and Joachim Schulte (Oxford: Wiley-Blackwell, 2009).

Woolf, Virginia, *The Voyage Out*, ed. Jane Wheare (New York: Penguin, 1992).

Wright, Richard, "The Man Who Lived Underground," in *Eight Men* (New York: Pyramid, 1969), 22–74.

Wright, Richard, *Native Son* (New York: Harper Perennial 2005).

Wright, Richard, *The Outsider* (New York: Harper Perennial, 2008).

SECONDARY SOURCES

Aho, Kevin, *Existentialism: An Introduction* (Cambridge: Polity Press, 2014).

Allison, David B., *Reading the New Nietzsche* (Lanham, MD: Rowman and Littlefield, 2001).

Anderson, R. Lanier, "What Is a Nietzschean Self?," in *Nietzsche, Naturalism, and Normativity*, ed. Christopher Janaway and Simon Robertson (Oxford: Oxford University Press, 2012), 202–235.

Anderson, Thomas C., *Sartre's Two Ethics: From Authenticity to Integral Humanity* (Peru, IL: Open Court, 1993).

Aquila, Richard E., "Two Problems of Being and Nonbeing in Sartre's Being and Nothingness," *Philosophy and Phenomenological Research* 38, no. 2 (December 1977), 167–186.

Armstrong, Aurelia, "The Passions, Power, and Practical Philosophy: Spinoza and Nietzsche Contra the Stoics," *Journal of Nietzsche Studies* 44, no. 1, Special Issue: Nietzsche and the Affects (Spring 2013), 6–24.

Beiser, Frederick C., *The Romantic Imperative: The Concept of Early German Romanticism* (Cambridge, MA: Harvard University Press, 2006).

Bergoffen, Debra, "Existentialism and Ethics," in *The Bloomsbury Companion to Existentialism*, ed. Felicity Joseph, Jack Reynolds, and Ashley Woodward (London: Bloomsbury, 2014), 98–116.

Bertram, Ernst, *Nietzsche: Attempt at a Mythology*, trans. Robert E. Norton (Urbana: University of Illinois Press, 2009).

Blue, Daniel, *The Making of Friedrich Nietzsche: The Quest for Identity, 1844–1869* (Cambridge: Cambridge University Press, 2016).

Bourgeois, Patrick Lyall, "Dostoevsky and Existentialism: An Experiment in Hermeneutics," *Journal of Thought* 15, no. 2 (Summer 1980), 29–37.

Bourgeois, Patrick L., "Ricoeur and Marcel: An Alternative to Postmodern Deconstruction," *Journal of French and Francophone Philosophy* 7, no. 1–2 (March 1995), 164–175.

Busch, Thomas W., *Circulating Being: From Embodiment to Incorporation: Essays in Late Existentialism* (New York: Fordham University Press, 1999).

Busch, Thomas W., "Sartre on Surpassing the Given," *Philosophy Today* 35, no.1 (Spring 1991), 26–31.

Caputo, John D., *How to Read Kierkegaard* (London: Granta Books, 2007).

Cole, Ina, "Monsieur Plume: An Existential Anti-Hero," *Art Times* (Summer 2016), 9.

Corrigan, Yuri, *Dostoevsky and the Riddle of the Self* (Evanston, IL: Northwestern University Press, 2017).

Cotkin, George, *Existential America* (Baltimore: Johns Hopkins University Press, 2003).

Cotkin, George, "Ralph Ellison, Existentialism, and the Blues," *Letterature d'America* 15, no. 60 (January 1, 1995), 33–52.

Daigle, Christine, "The Ethics of Authenticity," in *Reading Sartre: On Phenomenology and Existentialism,* ed. Jonathan Webber (New York: Routledge, 2011), 1–14.

Daigle, Christine, "Sartre and Nietzsche," *Sartre Studies International* 10, no. 2 (2004), 195–210.

Danto, Arthur, *Jean-Paul Sartre* (New York: Viking Press, 1975).

Davis, Colin, "Existentialism and Literature," in *The Bloomsbury Companion to Existentialism*, ed. Felicity Joseph, Jack Reynolds, and Ashley Woodward (London: Bloomsbury, 2014), 138–154.

Del Caro, Adrian, *Grounding the Nietzsche Rhetoric of Earth* (Berlin: Walter de Gruyter, 2004).

Del Caro, Adrian, "Nietzsche and Romanticism: Goethe, Hölderlin, and Wagner," in *The Oxford Handbook of Nietzsche,* ed. John Richardson and Ken Gemes (Oxford: Oxford University Press, 2013).

Doleza, Luna, "Shame, Vulnerability and Belonging: Reconsidering Sartre's Account of Shame," *Human Studies* 40, no. 3 (September 2017), 421–438.

Doniger, Wendy, *The Implied Spider: Politics and Theology in Myth* (New York: Columbia University Press, 2011).

Fabre, Michel, "Richard Wright and the French Existentialists," *MELUS* 5, no. 2 (Summer 1978), 29–35.

Flynn, Thomas R., *Existentialism: A Very Short Introduction* (Oxford: Oxford University Press, 2006).

Flynn, Thomas R., *Sartre: A Philosophical Biography* (Cambridge: Cambridge University Press, 2019).

Flynn, Thomas R., "Toward the Concrete," *Journal of Speculative Philosophy* 26, no. 2 (2012), 247–267.

Flynn, Thomas R., "Toward the Concrete: Marcel as Existentialist," *American Catholic Philosophical Quarterly* 80, no. 3 (2006), 355–367.

Fraser, Giles, "How Ludwig Wittgenstein Helped Me Get Over My Teenage Angst," *The Guardian*, August 19, 2013.

Gadamer, Hans-Georg, "Rainer Maria Rilke's Interpretation of Existence," in *Literature and Philosophy in Dialogue: Essays in German Literary Theory* (Albany: State University of New York Press, 1994), 139–152.

Gendreau, Bernard, "Gabriel Marcel's Personalist Ontological Approach to Technology," *Personalist Forum* 15, no. 2 (Fall 1999), 229–246.

Giles, James, "From Inwardness to Emptiness: Kierkegaard and Yogācāra Buddhism," *British Journal for the History of Philosophy* 9, no. 2 (2001), 311–340.

Gines, Kathryn T., "'The Man Who Lived Underground': Jean-Paul Sartre and the Philosophical Legacy of Richard Wright," *Sartre Studies International* 17, no. 2 (2011), 42–59.

Gines, Kathryn T., "Simone Beauvoir and the Race/Gender Analogy in *The Second Sex* Revisited," in *A Companion to Simone Beauvoir*, ed. Laura Hengehold and Nancy Bauer (Oxford: Wiley-Blackwell, 2017).

Gordon, Lewis R., ed., *Existence in Black: An Anthology of Black Existential Philosophy* (New York: Routledge, 1997).

Gordon, Lewis R., *Existentia Africana: Understanding Africana Existential Thought* (New York: Routledge, 2000).

Gosetti-Ferencei, Jennifer Anna, "Death and Authenticity: Reflections on Heidegger, Rilke, Blanchot," *Existenz* 9, no. 1 (Spring 2014), 53–62.

Gosetti-Ferencei, Jennifer Anna, *The Ecstatic Quotidian: Phenomenological Sightings in Modern Art and Literature* (University Park: Pennsylvania State University Press, 2007).

Gosetti-Ferencei, Jennifer Anna, *Heidegger, Hölderlin, and the Subject of Poetic Language: Toward a New Poetics of Dasein* (New York: Fordham University Press, 2004).

Gosetti-Ferencei, Jennifer Anna, "Imaginative Ecologies in Rilke's Sonnets to Orpheus," in *Rilke's Sonnets to Orpheus: Philosophical and Critical Perspectives*, ed. Hannah Eldridge and Luke Fischer (Oxford: Oxford University Press, 2019).

Gosetti-Ferencei, Jennifer Anna, *The Life of Imagination: Revealing and Making the World* (New York: Columbia University Press, 2018).

Gosetti-Ferencei, Jennifer Anna, "Nietzsche and Cognitive Ecology," in *Anti-Idealism: Re-Interpreting a German Discourse*, ed. Juliana Albuquerque and Gert Hofmann (Berlin: Walter de Gruyter, 2019).

Gosetti-Ferencei, Jennifer Anna, "Tragedy and Truth in Heidegger and Jaspers," *International Philosophical Quarterly* 42, no. 3, issue 167 (September 2002), 301–314.

Gounard, J. F., "Richard Wright's 'The Man Who Lived Underground': A Literary Analysis," *Journal of Black Studies* 8, no. 3 (March 1978), 381–386.

Grimsley, Ronald, "Kierkegaard and Descartes," *Journal of the History of Philosophy* 4, no. 1 (January 1966), 31–34.

Gupta, Anoop, *Kierkegaard's Romantic Legacy: Two Theories of the Self* (Ottawa: University of Ottawa Press, 2005).

Haar, Michel, *The Song of the Earth: Heidegger and the Grounds of the History of Being*, trans. Reginald Lilly (Bloomington: Indiana University Press, 1993).

Huntington, Patricia, "Heidegger's Reading of Kierkegaard Revisited," in *Kierkegaard in Post/Modernity*, ed. Martin J. Matustik and Merold Westphal (Bloomington: Indiana University Press, 1995).

Jackson, Lawrence P., *Chester B. Himes: A Biography* (New York: Norton, 2017).

Janaway, Christopher, "Schopenhauer as Nietzsche's Educator," in Christopher Janaway, ed., *Willing and Nothingness: Schopenhauer as Nietzsche's Educator* (Oxford: Oxford University Press, 1998), 13–36.

Jephcott, E. F. M., *Proust and Rilke: The Literature of Expanded Consciousness* (New York: Barnes & Noble Books, 1972).

Joseph, Felicity, Jack Reynolds, and Ashley Woodward, eds., *The Bloomsbury Companion to Existentialism* (London: Bloomsbury, 2014).

Judaken, Jonathan, "Introduction," in *Situating Existentialism: Key Texts in Context,* ed. Jonathan Judaken and Robert Bernasconi (New York: Columbia University Press, 2012), 1–36.

Kaufmann, Walter, *Nietzsche: Philosopher, Psychologist, Antichrist*, 4th ed. (Princeton, NJ: Princeton University Press, 1975).

Kearney, Richard, "Kierkegaard on Hamlet," in *The New Kierkegaard*, ed. Elsebet Jegstrup (Bloomington: Indiana University Press, 2004).

Kearney, Richard, *Poetics of Imagining: Modern to Post-Modern* (New York: Fordham University Press, 1998).

Kirmmse, Bruce H., "Out with It': The Modern Breakthrough, Kierkegaard, and Denmark," in *The Cambridge Companion to Kierkegaard*, ed. Alastair Hannay and Gordon D. Marino (Cambridge: Cambridge University Press, 1998).

Kobayashi, Chinatsu, "Heidegger, Japanese Aesthetics, and the Idea of a 'Dialogue' between East and West," in *Migrating Texts and Traditions*, ed. William Sweet (Ottawa: Ottawa University Press, 2012), 121–153.

Linsenbard, Gail, "Sartre's Criticisms of Kant's Moral Philosophy," *Sartre Studies International* 13, no. 2 (2007), 65–85.

Lyon, Laurence Gill, "Related Images in Malte Laurids Brigge and La Nauseé," *Comparative Literature* 30 (1978), 53–71.

Marino, Gordon, ed., *The Basic Writings of Existentialism* (New York: Modern Library, 2004).

Marx, Werner, *Heidegger and the Tradition*, trans. Theodore Kisiel and Murray Greene (Evanston, IL: Northwestern University Press, 1971).

Menand, Louis, "The Hammer and the Nail: Richard Wright's Modern Condition," *New Yorker*, July 20, 1992.

Mendieta, Eduardo, "Existentialisms in the Hispanic and Latin American Worlds: El Quixote and Its Existential Children," in *Situating Existentialism: Key Texts in Context,* ed. Jonathan Judaken and Robert Bernasconi (New York: Columbia University Press, 2012), 180–209.

Moi, Toril, *Simone Beauvoir: The Making of an Intellectual Woman* (Oxford: Oxford University Press, 2009).

Moi, Toril, "Simone Beauvoir's 'L'Invitée': An Existentialist Melodrama," *Paragraph* 14, no. 2 (July 1991), 151–169.

Moi, Toril, "What Can Literature Do? Simone Beauvoir as a Literary Theorist," *PLMA* 124, no. 1 (January 2009), 189–198.

Murdoch, Iris, *Existentialists and Mystics* (New York: Allen Lane, 1997).

Murdoch, Iris, *Sartre, Romantic Rationalist* (New Haven, CT: Yale University Press, 1953).

Natanson, Maurice, "The Strangeness in the Strangeness: Phenomenology and the Mundane," in *Edmund Husserl and the Phenomenological Tradition*, ed. Robert Sokolowski (Washington, DC: Catholic University of America Press, 1988).

Norman, Judith, "Nietzsche and Early Romanticism," *Journal of the History of Ideas* 63, no. 3 (July 2002), 501–519.

Nussbaum, Martha, "Pity and Mercy: Nietzsche's Stoicism," in *Nietzsche, Genealogy, Morality: Essays on Nietzsche's "On the Genealogy of Morals,"* ed. Richard Schacht (Berkeley: University of California Press, 1994), 139–167.

Parkes, Graham, "Staying Loyal to the Earth: Nietzsche as Ecological Thinker," in *Nietzsche's Futures*, ed. John Lippit (New York: St. Martin's Press, 1999), 167–188.

Pattison, George, "The Bonfire of the Genres: Kierkegaard's Literary Kaleidoscope," in *Kierkegaard, Literature, and the Arts*, ed. Eric Ziolkowski (Evanston, IL Northwestern University Press, 2018), 39–53.

Pattison, George, "Existentialism and Religion," in *The Bloomsbury Companion to Existentialism*, ed. Felicity Joseph, Jack Reynolds, and Ashley Woodward (London: Bloomsbury, 2014), 117–137.

Pattison, George, *Kierkegaard, Religion, and the Nineteenth-Century Crisis of Culture* (Cambridge: Cambridge University Press, 2002).

Pattison, George, "Kierkegaard and Copenhagen," in *The Oxford Handbook of Kierkegaard*, ed. John Lippitt and George Pattison (Oxford: Oxford University Press, 2013), 44.

Pattison, George, *The Philosophy of Kierkegaard* (Montreal: McGill-Queen's University Press, 2005).

Pettersen, Tove, "Love—According to Simone Beauvoir," in *A Companion to Simone de Beauvoir*, ed. Laura Hengehold and Nancy Bauer (Oxford: Wiley-Blackwell, 2017), 160–173.

Pippin, Robert B., *Modernism as a Philosophical Problem*, 2nd ed. (Oxford: Blackwell, 1999).

Pöggeler, Otto, *Martin Heidegger's Path of Thinking*, trans. Daniel Margurshak and Sigmund Barber (Atlantic Highlands, NJ: Humanities Press International, 1987).

Pyyhtinen, Olli, "Ambiguous Individuality: Georg Simmel on the 'Who' and the 'What' of the Individual," *Human Studies* 31, no. 3 (September 2008), 279–298.

Robertson, Ritchie, "Modernism and the Self, 1890–1924," in *German Philosophy and Literature 1700–1900*, ed. Nicholas Saul (Cambridge: Cambridge University Press, 2002).

Rockmore, Tom, *Heidegger and French Philosophy: Humanism, Antihumanism, and Being* (Abingdon: Routledge, 1995).

Rockmore, Tom, "Jaspers and Heidegger: Philosophy and Politics," in *Heidegger and Jaspers*, ed. Alan M. Olson (Philadelphia: Temple University Press, 1994).

Salm, Peter, "Werther and the Sensibility of Estrangement," *German Quarterly* 46, no. 1 (January 1973), 47–55.

Sanchez, Carlos Alberto, *Contingency and Commitment: Mexican Existentialism and the Place of Philosophy* (Albany: State University of New York Press, 2016).

Schrag, Calvin O., "The Kierkegaard Effect in the Shaping of the Contours of Modernity," in *Kierkegaard in Post/Modernity*, ed. Martin J. Matustik and Merold Westphal (Bloomington: Indiana University Press, 1995).

Shapiro, Gary, *Nietzsche's Earth: Great Events, Great Politics* (Chicago: University of Chicago Press, 2016).

Shatz, Adam, "Writing Absurdity," *London Review of Books* 40, no. 8 (April 26, 2018), 10–15.

Simons, Margaret A., "Existentialism: A Beauvoirean Lineage," *Existentialism, Journal of Speculative Philosophy* 26, no. 2, Special Issue with SPEP (2012), 261–267.

Strawson, Galen, "The Phenomenology and Ontology of the Self," in *Exploring the Self: Philosophical and Psychopathological Perspectives on Experience,* ed. Dan Zahavi (Amsterdam: John Benjamins, 2000), 39–54.

Strawson, Galen, *Things That Bother Me* (New York: New York Review of Books, 2018).

Szwed, John, *So What: The Life of Miles Davis* (New York: Simon & Schuster, 2004).

Taylor, Charles, *The Ethics of Authenticity* (Cambridge, MA: Harvard University Press, 2018).

Taylor, Charles, *Sources of the Self: The Making of Modern Identity* (Cambridge, MA: Harvard University Press, 1992).

Tillich, Paul, "Heidegger and Jaspers," in *Heidegger and Jaspers*, ed. Alan M. Olson (Philadelphia: Temple University Press, 1994).

Versénsi, Laszlo, *Socratic Humanism* (New Haven, CT: Yale University Press, 1963).

Webber, Jonathan, *The Existentialism of Jean-Paul Sartre* (Abingdon: Routledge, 2009).

Webber, Jonathan, ed., *Reading Sartre: On Phenomenology and Existentialism* (Abingdon: Routledge, 2011).

Westphal, Merold, *Becoming a Self: Reading of Kierkegaard's Concluding Unscientific Postscript* (West Lafayette, IN: Purdue University Press, 1996).

Westphal, Merold, *Kierkegaard's Critique of Reason and Society* (University Park: Pennsylvania State University Press, 2006).

White, Holly, "Practicing Camus: The Art of Engagement," *CrossCurrents* 55, no. 4 (Winter 2006), 554–563.

Widmer, Kingsley, "The Existential Darkness: Richard Wright's 'The Outsider,'" *Wisconsin Studies in Contemporary Literature* 1, no. 3 (Autumn 1960), 13–21.

Wilkerson, William, "Beauvoir and Merleau-Ponty on Freedom and Authenticity," in *A Companion to Simone Beauvoir*, ed. Laura Hengehold and Nancy Bauer (Oxford: Wiley-Blackwell, 2017), 224–235.

Young, Julian, *Friedrich Nietzsche: A Philosophical Biography* (Cambridge: Cambridge University Press, 2010).

Young, Julian, *Nietzsche's Philosophy of Art* (Cambridge: Cambridge University Press, 1992).

Zahavi, Dan, ed. *Exploring the Self: Philosophical and Psychopathological Perspectives on Experience* (Amsterdam: John Benjamins, 2000).

Zahavi, Dan, "Shame and the Exposed Self," in *Reading Sartre: On Phenomenology and Existentialism*, ed. Jonathan Webber (Routledge: Abingdon, 2011).

Zimmerman, Michael E., "Nietzsche and Ecology: A Critical Inquiry," in *Reading Nietzsche at the Margins*, ed. Steven V. Hicks and Alan Rosenberg (West Lafayette, IN: Purdue University Press, 2008), 165–186.

INDEX